14399

The Art of Literary Research

FOURTH EDITION

The Art
of Literary
Research

RICHARD D. ALTICK
AND
JOHN J. FENSTERMAKER

Fourth Edition

W. W. NORTON & COMPANY

New York   London

The text of this book is composed in Garamond with the display
set in Optima. Manufacturing by The Haddon Craftsmen, Inc.
Book design by Suzanne Bennett

Library of Congress Cataloging-in-Publication Data
Altick, Richard Daniel, 1915–
    The art of literary research / Richard D. Altick and
John J. Fenstermaker.—4th ed.
      p. cm.
    Includes bibliographical references and index.
    1. English literature—Research—Methodology.
    2. American literature—Research—Methodology.
    3. Literature—Research—Methodology.
    4. Criticism—Authorship.   I. Fenstermaker, John J.
II. Title.
PR56.A68   1992
807'.2—dc20   91-36247

ISBN 0-393-96240-7

W. W. Norton & Company, Inc., 500 Fifth Avenue,
New York, N.Y. 10110
W. W. Norton & Company Ltd., 10 Coptic Street,
London WC1A 1PU

6 7 8 9 0

Contents

EIGHT *The Scholar's Life*   247

       For Further Reading   259

       Exercises   281

       Index   333

Preface to the Fourth Edition

With this newly revised edition, *The Art of Literary Research,* which for three decades has served as a vade mecum for readers interested in the whys, whats, and hows of literary investigation, fully enters the computer age. Its chief innovation in both the text and the exercises is its consideration of the various ways in which word processors and data-storage-and-retrieval equipment have virtually revolutionized certain procedures of "traditional" literary scholarship. At the same time, however, our stress on the irreducible element of brain work that lies at the heart of productive research remains undiminished.

We have also sought to align historically oriented literary scholarship with the latest trends in theory and criticism, showing how they work in tandem rather than as adversaries in the ceaseless effort to throw new light on texts. Recent developments in the theory of textual editing and broadened conceptions of the purposes of source study and the tracing of an author's reputation and influence, which have lent new life and importance to those familiar aspects of literary genetics, receive due attention.

Some portions of the book have been extensively rewritten.

Many fresh examples in the text and exercises have been drawn from recent scholarship, and the documentary footnotes and the For Further Reading list contain references to numerous pertinent books and articles published in the past ten years. So, more than ever, readers can be assured that they are surveying the busy scene of literary scholarship as it exists today.

R. D. A.
J. J. F.

In no other subject [but literature] is the pupil brought more immediately and continuously into contact with original sources, the actual material of his study. In no other subject is he so able and so bound to make his own selection of the material he wishes to discuss, or able so confidently to check the statements of authorities against the documents on which they are based. No other study involves him so necessarily in ancillary disciplines. Most important of all, no other study touches his own life at so many points and more illuminates the world of his own daily experience. I see no reason why we should be afraid to confess that our subject is highly delightful to study and to teach at any and every level.

—Helen Gardner, "The Academic Study of English Literature," *Critical Quarterly* 1 (1959): iii

A love of precision joined to aspirations toward general ideas; respect for historical facts, and warm appreciation of beautiful writings; minuteness in research, and breadth of view; finesse in analysis; strictness in criticism; penetration in aesthetic judgments; lastly, exacting loyalty toward oneself, toward facts, toward the ideas and the men studied,—these are a few of the valuable qualities that, thoroughly understood and thoroughly carried out, literary studies tend to develop.

—André Morize, *Problems and Methods of Literary History* (Boston, 1922) viii

Genuine scholarship is one of the highest successes which our race can achieve. No one is more triumphant than the man who chooses a worthy subject and masters all its facts and the leading facts of the subjects neighbouring.

—E. M. Forster, *Aspects of the Novel* (New York, 1927) 22

Life is a continuous process of finding the holes and plugging them and making as few new ones as possible.

> —Sir William Haley, then editor-in-chief of the *Encyclopaedia Britannica,* quoted in the *New York Times,* March 10, 1968

Over all [the scholar's work] should rule a searching intelligence, asking that fundamental question of the sceptic: just what do you mean by that? And if that question is asked with a real desire to know and understand, if the imagination is centred upon people—dead people once alive—and sympathy and judgment are controlled by scholarship and by a mind of quality, the work can be done. All the deficiencies of knowledge and writer notwithstanding, the historian can rest assured that he can fulfill his ambition to know and tell about the past. His can never be the last word, an ambition in any case bred out of vanity, but he can establish new footholds in the territory of truth.

> —G. R. Elton, *The Practice of History* (New York, 1967) 141

Le spectacle de la recherche est rarement ennuyeux. C'est le tout fait qui répand la glace et l'ennui.

> —Marc Bloch, French historian, quoted in Iris Origo, *Images and Shadows: Part of a Life* (New York, 1970) 184

It is an article of my faith that scholarship and criticism should be fun for the practitioner. Else why forgo the rewards of indolence?

> —S. Schoenbaum, *Shakespeare and Others* (Washington, D.C., 1985) 9

ABBREVIATIONS OF TITLES USED IN THIS BOOK

AL   *American Literature*
BL   British Library
BNYPL   *Bulletin of the New York Public Library*
ELN   *English Language Notes*
JEGP   *Journal of English and Germanic Philology*
MLN   *Modern Language Notes*
MLQ   *Modern Language Quarterly*
MLR   *Modern Language Review*
MP   *Modern Philology*
NCBEL   *New Cambridge Bibliography of English Literature*
NUC   *National Union Catalog*
OCLC   Online Computer Library Center
PBSA   *Papers of the Bibliographical Society of America*
PMLA   *PMLA: Publications of the Modern Language Association of America**
PQ   *Philological Quarterly*
RES   *Review of English Studies*
SB   *Studies in Bibliography*
SEL   *Studies in English Literature*
TLS   [London] *Times Literary Supplement*
UTQ   *University of Toronto Quarterly*
VS   *Victorian Studies*

Except in one or two respects, notably the omission of the publisher's name in citations of books, the *form* of documentation throughout has been made to agree with that urged by the

---

*The initials are the official title.

MLA Style Manual. However, rigid consistency in the distribution of references between text and footnotes and in the fullness of citations in the text has not been sought, in order that the various alternatives available to the scholarly writer might be illustrated. Conciseness, clarity, and convenience are more to be desired than absolute standardization of practice.

The Art of Literary Research

FOURTH EDITION

CHAPTER ONE

Vocation

> . . . *the governing context of all literary investigations must ultimately be an historical one. Literature is a human product, a humane art. It cannot be carried on (created), understood (studied), or appreciated (experienced) outside of its definitive human context. The general science governing that human context is socio-historical.*
> —Jerome J. McGann, *The Beauty of Inflections* (Oxford, 1985)

Underlying the following chapters is the simple premise that the literary scholar and the critic are engaged in a common pursuit, so that the findings of one are indispensable to the work of the other. Some professional students of literature prefer to regard themselves primarily as critics, some as scholars; but the dichotomy between the two is far more apparent than real, and every good student of literature is constantly combining the two roles, often without knowing it. The difference is mainly one of emphasis. The critic's business is primarily with the literary work itself—with its structure, style, and content of ideas. Scholars, on the other hand, are more concerned with the facts attending its genesis and subsequent history. Believing that every work of art must be seen from without as well as from within, they seek to illuminate it from every conceivable angle, to make it as intelligible as possi-

1

ble by the uncovering and application of data residing outside itself. The ultimate beneficiary of their fact-gathering is criticism. While facts have a certain charm in themselves, as every history-minded person knows, the scholar values them in direct proportion to the help they afford—at once or in prospect—in illuminating specific pieces of literature and the interaction of many works that constitutes what is called literary history.

Neither criticism nor scholarship occupies an exclusive territory; the center of interest as well as the raison d'être for both is the literary work itself. The inseparability of the two disciplines has been well stated by the late scholar-critic George Whalley:

> No true scholar can lack critical acumen; and the scholar's eye is rather like the poet's—not, to be sure, "in a fine frenzy rolling," but at least looking for something as yet unknown which it knows it will find, with perceptions heightened and modified by the act of looking. For knowing is qualitative and is profoundly affected by the reason for wanting to know. Again, it is clear that no critic can afford *not* to be a scholar—even a scholar in a pretty impressive degree—if his work is to go much beyond delicate impressionism, penumbral rhetoric, or marginal schematism. Without scholarship every synoptic view will be cursory, every attempt at a synthesis a wind-egg; without scholarship the criticism of a poem may easily become a free fantasia on a non-existent theme.[1]

These pages will be devoted for the most part to that portion of the common enterprise that conventionally (however arbitrarily and with due respect for textual scholarship) is supposed to be the research scholar's province: the quest for truth in places outside the literary work. Apart from brief discussions of the methods of establishing a sound text and of dealing with disputed authorship, this book will not touch on questions that presumably can be decided by a close analysis of the author's

---

[1]"Scholarship and Criticism," *UTQ* 29 (1959): 40–41.

words alone. But it will continually try to show how vital external data are to the accurate and adequate understanding of a text.

Here is a *Hamlet,* here is a lyric by Shelley, here is a *Great Expectations.* Each is intelligible in itself, and any attentive reader can derive immense pleasure from it. But almost every literary work is attended by a host of outside circumstances that, once we expose and explore them, suffuse it with additional meaning.

It is the product of an individual human being's imagination and intellect; therefore, we must know all we can about the author. Sainte-Beuve's critical axiom *tel arbre, tel fruit* ("like the tree, like the fruit") is a bland oversimplification, to be sure, but the fact remains that behind the book is a man or woman whose character and experience cannot be overlooked in any effort to establish what the book really says. The quality of the imagination, the genetic and psychological factors that shaped a writer's personality and determined the atmosphere of his or her inner being, the experiences, large and small, that fed the store from which such an artist in words drew the substance of art: all these must be sought, examined, and weighed if we are to comprehend the meaning of a text.

Moreover, no one writes in a vacuum. Whatever private influences are involved, authors, whether conformists or rebels, are the products of time and place, their mental set fatefully determined by the social and cultural environment. To understand a book, we must also understand the manifold socially derived attitudes—the morality, the myths, the assumptions, the biases—that it reflects or embraces. And because, in the overwhelming majority of instances, it was written not for its author's private self alone but for a specific contemporary audience and only incidentally for us ("posterity"), we must try to find out precisely how the mingled ideas of that earlier world affected the book's shape and content. Most especially is it necessary to reconstruct the standards of taste, of literary intention, and of craftsmanship that then prevailed.

Again, a book has both antecedents and a history of its own. Not only can its content be related to more or less immediate models or sources of inspiration; it may belong to a tradition that stretches back for centuries or even millennia and can be traced in the literature of half a dozen countries. "No poet, no artist of any sort," wrote T. S. Eliot in his seminal essay on "Tradition and the Individual Talent," "has his complete meaning alone. His significance, his appreciation is the appreciation of his relation to the dead poets and artists. You cannot value him alone; you must set him, for contrast and comparison, among the dead." But at the same time, he must be set among the poets and artists who were to come. His book has cast its shadow across later ages, perhaps inspiring new fashions and traditions, and in any event affecting other writers and suggesting the form and manner of other works. To read *Gulliver's Travels* or *Erewhon* with ideal perception, we have to know how they fit into the perennial quest for a happier society, either through satire or through the vision of Utopia; and that means ranging from Plato's *Republic,* Juvenal's satires, and medieval Celtic imprecations to *Candide, News from Nowhere,* and *1984.*

Literary research, then, is devoted, for one thing, to the enlightenment of criticism—which may or may not take advantage of the proffered information. It seeks to illuminate the work of art as it really is, and—the difference may be considerable—as it was to its first audience; equally, it tries to see the writer as he really was, his cultural heritage and the people for whom he wrote as they really were. But while this is unquestionably its major purpose, it has at least one other important function. Literary history constitutes one of the strands of which the history of civilization itself is woven. Like its sister disciplines of musicology and art history, it finds its material in the vast array of records we have inherited of the imaginative side of human experience—in its case, the representation in language of that experience. Literature preserves for us, for example, the poignance of the medieval aspiration toward Heaven though held down by mortal chains; the excitement of the Renaissance awareness of the splendors that environ Western mankind in the here and now; the cool and candid re-estimate of the world and the human self that the eighteenth century made under the auspices of revolutionary science and skeptical philosophy; and the spiritual chiaroscuro of wasteland and earthly paradise, the bewildering series of shocks and recoveries, to which modern society has been subjected in the past two centuries. Literature, then, is an eloquent artistic document, infinitely varied, of mankind's journey: the autobiography of the race's soul. And whatever the practical "uses" of history may be, one of the marks of a civilized person is an absorbed interest in the emotional and intellectual adventures of earlier generations. Looked upon solely as a branch of cultural history, the reconstruction and interpretation of our literary past has its own dignity.

Finally, there are the unmeasurable but intensely real personal satisfactions that literary research affords men and women of a certain temperament: the sheer joy of finding out things that have previously been unknown and thus of increasing, if but by a few grains, the aggregate of human knowledge. One of us has sought to describe the sources and qualities of this pleasure in earlier books, and they will occasionally appear again in the following chapters. The genuine scholar is impelled by a deeply ingrained curiosity, an undeniable urge to learn as well as to teach. "And *gladly* wolde he lerne."

Dramatic discoveries do not occur as often now as they did earlier in the century, when a steadily enlarging body of scholars first studied great hoards of rare books and manuscripts, in both institutional and private ownership, which had hitherto been inaccessible to inquirers or were simply unknown. Still, significant finds do occur from time to time. In 1988–89, the unearthing of the remains of London's Globe and Rose playhouses, at a moment when historians of the drama were hungry for new information on the structure of Elizabethan theaters and minutiae of the ways in which Shakespeare's plays were first performed, provided an apt symbol of the continuing excitement and promise of literary research, another kind of archeology.

Two notable discoveries in English Renaissance studies involved, as it happened, faculty members at the same institution, the University of Toronto. Almost a century ago, a remarkable series of events had brought to light the previously forgotten poems of the seventeenth-century mystic Thomas Traherne. In 1981, history repeated itself. A graduate student brought to the attention of Elliot Rose, a Toronto professor of history, a seventeenth-century manuscript whose provenance was obscure (it had come into the possession of its Canadian owner some years earlier). Its title was *"Commentaries* of Heaven wherein the Mysteries of Felicite are opened: and *All Things Discovered* to be Objects of Happiness" [etc.]. "I thought," Rose recounted, " 'Another unsuspected religious genius, like Traherne.' I never imagined it *was* Traherne. But it is." The handwriting matched that of the poet, and the themes, the language, and even a reference to one of his favorite books supported the identification. Thus an important prose item was added to the poet's canon.[2]

The other Canadian episode concerned Sir Philip Sidney. One aspect of his brief career as a poet that has long engaged scholars has been the breadth of reading, particularly among the classics, that is reflected in his works. An important key to the question (which pertains to many other authors as well: see below, pp. 116–18) is the size and contents of Sidney's library. From various fragmentary records, it had long been known that the books at Penshurst, the seat of the Sidney family, were dispersed on several occasions in the eighteenth and nineteenth centuries, but no one knew how many or what their titles were. In 1985, a professor at Victoria College, University of Toronto, was working among the Sidney papers, transferred from Penshurst to the Kent County Archives Office in Maidstone by the then head of the family, Lord De L'Isle. There, amidst many

[2]For the whole story, see Rose's article in *Times Literary Supplement*, March 16, 1982: 324. The word *canon* will appear frequently in these pages, in both of its senses: the totality of a given author's known works (as here) and the list of authors and works in a nation's literary heritage— always unstable, but more so at certain times than at others—that are deemed most significant and the most deserving of sustained, intensive study. In the latter sense, the current term "revision of the canon" simply refers to the normal, ongoing process that is otherwise called "changes in literary taste."

other documents relating to life at Penshurst over the centuries, she found the all-important key: a suede-bound 228-page volume dating from the seventeenth century that listed the books the Sidneys owned from the late years of the preceding century, some forty-five hundred volumes in all. Now, for the first time, Sidney students are able to compensate for the dispersal of the library and concentrate on the books the poet is known to have had available to him before his early death in 1586, many of them acquired on his European tour fourteen years earlier.[3]

Private collections of rare books and manuscripts, containing items hitherto unknown or inaccessible to scholars, are perhaps less numerous than they used to be. But those that remain often contain surprises. Virtually no one apart from a few members of the antiquarian book trade had ever heard of Miss Doris Louise Benz, a shoe-leather manufacturer's heiress, who amassed a large collection of rarities in her home in Lynn, Massachusetts. When it was sold after her death in 1984, it proved to contain one of the largest and most valuable sets of books in literary history, the forty-one interleaved volumes of Sir Walter Scott's Waverley novels in their original editions, in which the ailing and debt-ridden novelist entered all the revisions and additions he intended for the "Magnum Opus" edition that was to appear in 1829–33. Until 1929, when it came to the United States, the set had been passed down through a succession of British publishers, but its existence, too, was known to only a few people, and no one had ever looked into it, let alone made it the basis of serious study. When it finally surfaced in a New York auction house in 1985, it was bought by the National Library of Scotland.[4]

---

[3]See Germaine Warkentin, "Ins and Outs of the Sidney Family Library," *TLS*, December 6, 1985: 1394, 1411.

[4]The full story is told in the chapter titled "The Exile and Return of the 'Magnum Opus': Episodes in the Life of a Literary Wanderer" in Iain Gordon Brown's *Scott's Interleaved Waverley Novels* . . . (Aberdeen, 1987), a splendidly illustrated publication of the National Library of Scotland. Like many such narratives of rescue from oblivion, this one has an extra twist. When the books were taken to the auction house, several

Not too long ago Charles W. Mignon, a professor at the University of Nebraska, upon being informed that there was "some old book" at Ernie Long's bookstore in Lincoln that might prove interesting, dropped into the shop for a browsing session and found, in a batch of books awaiting assessment, a hitherto unidentified manuscript of thirty-six sermons written in the seventeenth century. These were no ordinary sermons, because they were from the pen of the Colonial New England poet Edward Taylor, whose devotional poems themselves had come to light as recently as 1936. This manuscript had been owned by one of the poet's descendants, whose great-grandmother had brought it to Nebraska from North Carolina in 1877. A second-hand bookstore in Lincoln, Nebraska, "right next to Marie's Oasis bar and—on the other side—Dirty Dick's Pawn Shop and not too far from the Adult Bookstore and Cinema X," is not the most likely nor even the most suitable place for the long-lost sermons of a Colonial poet and divine to resurface. But, as Mignon says, "Rising up out of this scum I think would somehow have pleased Taylor."[5]

An obviously undeterminable amount of material bearing upon literary history and biography remains in private hands, not only in Britain and America but wherever a writer's descendants or the purchasers or inheritors of his manuscripts may have settled. In the 1760s, Bishop Thomas Percy, an early student of English literature from Chaucer to Dryden and the

---

volumes were missing. "In due course," we are told, "the missing volumes turned up in circumstances still unsatisfactorily explained: the books mysteriously appeared in the spring of 1985 in a room in the Benz house which had already been searched."

[5]Literary items of value continue to turn up at equally unlikely places. An edition of Donne's poems (1633), unknown even to the poet's great bibliographer, Sir Geoffrey Keynes, found its way to the United States Air Force Academy in Colorado. It was in a collection of rare books received from Colonel Richard Gimbel, a bibliophile as well as a pioneer aviation enthusiast, who bought it because he was interested in all aspects of flight, angelic as well as terrestrial: "At the round earths imagin'd corners, blow / Your trumpets, Angells. . . ."

editor of the first collection of old ballads (*Reliques of Ancient English Poetry,* 1765), wrote in at least two copies he owned of Langbaine's *An Account of the English Dramatic Poets* that a number of manuscript plays by one Cosmo Manuche, who was writing in the 1650s, were in the library of the earl of Northampton at Castle Ashby. A century and a half later, in 1907, Sir Sidney Lee, gathering material for an article on Manuche in the *Dictionary of National Biography,* came upon Percy's list of those plays in the copy of Langbaine that had been acquired by the British Museum. Inquiries established that the manuscript of one Manuche play was indeed at Castle Ashby, but access to it was not to be had. The possible presence of others prompted Alfred Harbage, when he was writing his *Caroline Drama* (1936) and again when preparing the first edition of his *Annals of English Drama* (1940), to send letters of inquiry to Castle Ashby. They went unanswered.

There matters rested until 1977, when another American scholar, William P. Williams, was editing Manuche's play *The Banished Shepherdess* from the manuscript copy owned by the Huntington Library in California. Another copy of this play was among those that, Percy had recorded, "usually lie on ye shelf over the Door" in the library at Castle Ashby. Now an editor of a literary text must take account of all manuscript copies of the text that he can locate; and so Williams, though he had no expectation of succeeding where Harbage and others had failed, wrote to the ninety-two-year-old marquess of Northampton. After an interval during which one reply was lost in the mail, the marquess's son, the Earl Compton, reported to Williams that, quite by accident, he had found the manuscript of *The Banished Shepherdess* at the back of a drawer in an old desk.

Williams flew at once to England and, welcomed by Lord Compton and his household staff, was given the rediscovered manuscript to inspect prior to taking it away to be microfilmed. "After I had examined the manuscript for about thirty minutes," says Williams, "Lord Compton came back to see how I was getting on, and after a few minutes of conversation I framed the crucial question. 'Have you,' I asked, 'found any other manuscripts along with this one?' He replied that he had found these other 'things'—indicating a pile of manuscript volumes—in the same drawer. 'Why, would they be of interest to you?' I indicated that they would, and we began to work through the pile." One by one, each of the plays in Percy's list turned up in these volumes, some of which also contained plays that were *not* in the list. During that September afternoon in the heart of the Northamptonshire hunt country, no fewer than seventeen old plays came to light. The next year, the entire collection was bought by the British Library.[6]

One more instance: A century ago, in 1884, a London auction catalogue listed a copy of the 1617 folio of Edmund Spenser's works that was said to contain copious annotations by its owner, Ben Jonson. Nothing had been heard of it before that date, and after the sale, it disappeared into the library of an unknown collector. The standard edition (Herford-Simpson) and the latest bibliography (David McPherson's in *SP*, 1974) noted its brief appearance, but no one knew of its present whereabouts if, indeed, it still existed. But what a treasure it might be if found—intimate evidence of the impact Spenser's poetry had on his fellow poet! Modern students of both writers understandably regarded its resurfacing as a consummation devoutly to be wished, but a near-impossible dream.

Many scholars make a practice of keeping major antiquarian booksellers aware of their interests, in case something pertinent to their specialties might turn up on the market. James Riddell, of California State University at Dominguez Hills, is one such scholar, a Jonson specialist. In the summer of 1986, a rare-book expert with the London firm of Maggs Brothers mentioned to him that he knew of a book that fitted the description in the century-old auction catalogue, and Riddell expressed his desire to see the volume and, if possible, obtain it for a research library like the Huntington (see below, pp. 194–95). But before ar-

[6]We are grateful to Professor Williams for providing this narrative. For details of his discovery, see his article "The Castle Ashby Manuscripts: A Description of the Volumes in Bishop Percy's List," *The Library* 6th series 2 (1980): 391–412.

rangements could be made, the book was sold to another private collector and again vanished. While it was still in Maggs's possession, however, a microfilm had been made of its contents and this was sent to California, where it was transcribed by Riddell and his collaborator, Stanley Stewart of the University of California at Riverside, a specialist in Spenser. (Subsequently they were given access to the book itself by its purchaser, J. Paul Getty, Jr.) The value of the volume has exceeded their fondest expectations. It contains, according to Stewart, "literally hundreds of markings"—brackets, pointing fingers, underlinings—and "scores of annotations, many of them lengthy. It is much more heavily annotated, for instance, than Jonson's copy of Puttenham." While probably nobody would claim that the volume is as important as the two copies of Shakespeare, one at Harvard and the other at the Keats House in Hampstead, that the enraptured Keats copiously marked as he read, its unique contents will enrich Renaissance scholars' understanding of both Jonson and Spenser.[7]

As has been said, such headline news events, as they are in the scholarly world, probably occur less often than they once did. But the total body of literary knowledge continues to expand through less heralded finds and the increased accessibility of vital materials. The latest edition of Byron (McGann's, 1980–) contains no fewer than eighty-five pieces previously uncollected, over half of which, in fact, had never even been printed. Again, the depth, breadth, and labyrinthine complexity of Coleridge's thought are only now beginning to be fully appreciated, thanks to the great Princeton/Bollingen edition, which has brought long-sought order out of the appalling chaos of his notebooks, his lectures, and the teeming marginalia he wrote in his and other people's books (the printed edition of the marginalia alone runs to 2,086 pages printed in two colors of type). The lectures have proved particularly challenging to their edi-

[7] We are indebted here to Professor Stewart. The first fruit of the find is the article by these collaborators, "Jonson Reads 'The Ruines of Time,' " *SP* 87 (1990): 427–55.

tor, because Coleridge never wrote them out and their texts had
to be assembled from his notebooks, auditors' notes, newspaper reports, and other miscellaneous and scattered sources.

Moreover, ongoing revisions of the literary canon are extending the traditional boundaries of scholarly and critical interest.
The burgeoning of women's studies and black studies has directed attention to numerous authors whose works have in-
vited, until now, only cursory interest if indeed they were
known at all. A good example, out of many that could be cited,
is the dramatist and novelist Aphra Behn (1640–89), England's
first professional woman author. Until the last few years, she
was lucky if she could claim a mere paragraph in histories of
English fiction or drama; today, she and her works are the
subject of a 557-page volume, Mary Ann O'Donnell's *Aphra
Behn: An Annotated Bibliography of Primary and Secondary
Sources* (1986), an impressive testimony to the recent boom in
Behn studies. Until recently, Mary Shelley's *Frankenstein,* although so popular that it is said never to have been out of print
since it was published in 1818, was regarded simply as a thriller;
now it has been upgraded into a veritable classic, examined in
scores of books and articles that deal with it either as a work by
a previously underestimated woman author or as a landmark in
the history of popular literature. Bram Stoker's equally popular
Dracula likewise had been dismissed as of no consequence in
literary history, but by 1985 it was taken seriously enough for its
manuscript, in the Rosenbach Foundation Library and Museum
in Philadelphia, to be retrieved and made the subject of a critical
article (David Seed's "The Narrative Method of *Dracula," Nineteenth-Century Fiction* 40 [1985]).

As a consequence of this recent dramatic expansion of the
scope of literary interest, it is certain that, given a fair degree of
imagination, originality of approach, solidity of learning, and
the wish and the will to see works of literary art and their
creators from new perspectives, everyone called to the profession will discover amply rewarding projects.

In America during the past half century or so, most literary
research has been done by academic people, and publishing

the results of research has provided the traditional boost up the professional ladder. Unfortunately, the notorious cliché "publish or perish" still describes the attitude of many college and university administrators charged with deciding the fate of young untenured faculty members. The validity of such a criterion for promotion and tenure remains, as it has been for many years, a hotly debated issue. A three-word slogan, of course, grotesquely oversimplifies what is, in truth, a complicated academic situation and an equally complicated relationship between published scholarship and the purposes of higher education. Any external pressure to write scholarly books and articles is pernicious not only because it may well divert a career from its natural course, thus causing a good deal of personal unhappiness, but because scholarship performed under duress is seldom very good scholarship. Indeed, it is to the "publish or perish" mentality that we can attribute the present bloated condition of the annual bibliographies and the appearance, in the proliferating journals, of a lamentable amount of incompetent, pretentious, or trivial writing that should have been intercepted somewhere between the typewriter or personal computer and the press.[8] Furthermore, and perhaps worst of all, this mentality falsifies the whole rationale of scholarship, placing it on a crass mercenary basis whereas, if it deserves to be supported in a humanistic society, its practice must be motivated by altruism.

Among the wisest words ever uttered on this much-vexed topic are those of the late Morris Bishop, the Cornell specialist in French literature and writer of light verse and detective stories:

> . . . I am not against research. I practice it, I honor it, I love it. But a taste for literary research is something special. It is not the same thing as delight in reading, or delight in introducing others to the pleasures of reading or the pleasures of writing. We do well to encourage literary research. We do ill

[8]The *MLA International Bibliography* for 1960 included 13,000 entries from approximately 1,000 periodicals; in 1990, 3,146 serials and journals produced over 50,000 citations.

to impose it as a requirement for promotion and status in the
teaching profession. Literary research is a privilege, deserving
of no reward except the writer's joy in his article, his book,
his public utterance of his precious thought.[9]

It may well be that, as Dr. Johnson held, "no man but a
blockhead ever wrote, except for money"; if so, the history of
literary scholarship at its best is populated with amiable block-
heads. Scholars may value the creature comforts as highly as do
people in any other line of work, but it is their itch to know
more, not primarily the prospect of enlarged salary checks, that
draws them to the library after their classes are met, their papers
graded, their committee meetings attended.[10]

[9]*PMLA* 80 (1965): A–6. Similar sentiments were expressed a decade later
by William D. Schaefer, executive director of the Modern Language Association of America, 1971–78: ". . . during that critical period of the 1960's
our record was flawless in that, as a profession, we managed to do everything wrong and nothing right. . . . The stupidest thing we did, and this was
not forgivable because its implications were and are so ugly, was to
perpetuate a rewards system based on publication. . . . What should have
been a natural and healthy act, sharing ideas with colleagues through
print, became unnatural, sick. What should have remained student papers
or notes for undergraduate lectures became 'articles' in which, in emula-
tion of the sciences, we more often than not pretended to 'solve' literature
rather than to interpret, understand, and appreciate it" (*Profession 78*
[1978]: 2).

[10]Of course, not all scholars are on academic payrolls, and the very fact that
a few business and professional men do literary research in their spare
time is the best possible evidence of the pleasure scholarship affords
people who have nothing else to gain from it. They are scholars for the
same reason that T. S. Eliot, a publisher, Wallace Stevens, an insurance
executive, and William Carlos Williams, a pediatrician, were poets. Sir
Geoffrey Keynes, the editor and bibliographer of Donne, Browne, and
William Blake, was a distinguished Harley Street surgeon; Sir Edmund
Chambers and John Dover Wilson, two of the greatest twentieth-century
students of the Elizabethan drama, were officials in the Board of Education; a third, R. B. McKerrow, was a member of a publishing firm, as was
Michael Sadleir, the leading specialist in the bibliography of Victorian

Among the readers of this book there probably are under-graduates contemplating careers as students and teachers of literature, and graduate students, some of whom may be wondering, as we all do now and then, whether they have chosen the right profession. A bit of self-examination therefore is in order. What are the chief qualities of mind and temperament that go to make up a successful and happy scholar?

The thought occurs that the ideally equipped literary scholar should have come to his or her profession after serving a practical apprenticeship in one or the other of two occupations: law and journalism. The practice of law requires a thorough command of the principles of evidence, a knowledge of how to make one's efficient way through the accumulated "literature" on a subject (in legal terms, the statutes and decisions applying to a given case), and a devotion both to accuracy and to detail. It was perhaps no accident that James Boswell himself, who often would "run half over London, in order to fix a date correctly," was a lawyer by profession. Journalism, more specifically the work of the investigative reporter, also calls for resourcefulness—knowing where to go for one's information and how to obtain it, the ability to recognize and follow up leads, and tenacity in pursuit of the facts. Both professions, moreover, require organizational skill, the ability to put facts together in a pattern that is clear and, if controversy is involved, persuasive.

Ideal researchers must love literature for its own sake, that is to say, as an art. They must be insatiable readers, and the earlier they have acquired that passion, the better. The kind of work

---

fiction and the author of the standard bio-bibliographical study of Trollope. William St. Clair, author of a recent first-rate biography of William Godwin and his relations with the Shelley circle, is a senior official of the British Treasury. The New York publisher Robert Giroux is a respected Shakespeare scholar. His book *The Book Known as Q: A Consideration of Shakespeare's Sonnets*—a notoriously treacherous subject—was well received when it appeared in 1981. The late George Spater, who wrote a magisterial two-volume life of William Cobbett, the early nineteenth-century English political journalist, was president of American Airlines.

involved in meaningful literary study requires the peculiar impetus and intellectual sympathies that only devotion to an art, and a desire to share it with others, can provide. In her presidential address at the Modern Language Association's annual convention in 1980, Helen Vendler took her text from the end of Wordsworth's *Prelude:* "What we have loved, / Others will love, and we will teach them how." That same dedication infuses one's activity as a professional scholar. As Vendler said: "as scholars, we . . . love, beyond philology and composition and literature, the worth of scholarship, by which we mean accurate evidence on literary matters. We are engaged in teaching others—our more advanced students—how to love what we love in the discipline of scholarship: how to prize the exact edition over the inadequate one; how to value concision and clarity over obscurity and evasiveness; how to appreciate a new critical vocabulary when it brings energy or insight into our world" (*PMLA* 96 [1981]: 346).

In the second place, researchers must have a vivid sense of history: the ability to cast themselves back into another age. They must be able to adjust their intellectual sights and imaginative responses to the systems of thought and the social and cultural atmosphere that prevailed in fourteenth-century England or early twentieth-century America. They must be able to think as people thought when Newton was educating them in the laws of physics, and to fantasize as people fantasized when Byron was spinning out his Oriental romances. Otherwise, they cannot comprehend the current attitudes or artistic assumptions that guided an author as he or she set pen to paper. At the same time, scholars must retain their footing in the twentieth century for the sake of the indispensable perspective the historian needs. Their sense of the past, then, must be a double vision— intimate and penetrating (in no way confined to the externalities of an age, as that of historical novelists and popular biographers too often is) and yet detached.

Once there was an illusion, nourished by the plodding methodicalness of German philology, that literary research was an exact science. Unlike the natural sciences, however, literary research tolerates to a degree the subjective impression, as is inevitable in a discipline that deals with the human consciousness and the art it produces. But as assemblers and assayers of historical facts, literary scholars need to be as rigorous in their method as scientists. And indeed, a background in science is almost as good preparation for literary research as is one in law or newspaper work, because some of the same qualities are required: intellectual curiosity, shrewdness, precision, imagination—the lively inventiveness that constantly suggests new hypotheses, new strategies, new sources of information, and, when all the data are in, makes possible their accurate interpretation and evaluation. A source overlooked, a wrong date, a carelessly transcribed document, a confusion of persons with similar names, an unsupported assumption silently converted into a certainty—these lapses on the part of a literary researcher are as much a violation of the scientific spirit as any analogous error committed in the laboratory.

Once in a while the substance, as well as the spirit, of such extra-literary training gives the scholar an advantage. The British scientist Desmond King-Hele, with his special knowledge of meteorology, was particularly well equipped to interpret such poems as the "Ode to the West Wind" and "The Cloud" (*Shelley: His Thought and Work,* 1960). Some years ago a lawyer, reviewing a book on *The Keats Inheritance,* drew upon his professional knowledge to correct the author's misunderstanding. The latter had found what he took to be evidence of a family quarrel in the hostile tone pervading the principal document of a lawsuit involving the inheritance that the poet's grandfather left to the four Keats children. The reviewer pointed out that the phraseology was deliberately made hostile, as a conventional means of ensuring that the court would adjudicate on all issues. In the lack of any evidence to the contrary, he asserted, the suit seems to have been wholly amicable and designed simply to clarify the ambiguities of the will to the satisfaction of all concerned.[11]

Scholarship involves a great amount of detail work, in which

[11]John Rutherford in *Keats-Shelley Journal* 15 (1966): 17–21.

no margin of error is allowed and over which the analytic intellect must constantly preside. It is no occupation for the impatient or the careless; nor is it one for the easily fatigued. Scholars must not only be capable of hard, often totally fruitless work—they must actually relish it. "The test of a vocation," the aphorist-essayist Logan Pearsall Smith once wrote, "is the love of the drudgery it involves." The researcher pays for every exult-ant discovery with a hundred hours of monotonous, eye-sear-ing labor. Even despite technological advances in information storage and retrieval, there are numerous bibliographies to be searched, item by item if the indexing is undependable; calen-dars of manuscripts, book auction records, lists of dissertations, long files of periodicals to be plowed through; boxfuls of fragile and half-illegible holograph letters to be examined in quest of a single clue; volumes upon volumes of dull reminiscences to be scanned for the appearance of a single name. Weariness of the flesh and congestion of the brain are inescapable occupa-tional diseases. Yet they are not a high price to pay for the satisfactions people of a certain temperamental and intellectual constitution derive from research.

Uniting all these qualities, and imparting coherence and meaning to the facts collected, must be a creative imagination. Without it the scholar is "lost," as Wordsworth put it, "in a gloom of uninspired research." Human limitations being what they are, the profession has always had its share of members resembling Scott's Dr. Dryasdust and George Eliot's Mr. Casau-bon. Their earnest labors have often furnished the foundation on which more imaginative workers have built, but they have been fact-grubbers, not scholars—pack-rats, not beavers. True scholars, while conceding the apparent triviality of many of the individual fragments of data they gather, always look forward toward an eventual synthesis. They are constantly seeking the final substance that will precipitate from the cloudy solution of facts a crystal of significant truth. And from those crystals they or their grateful colleagues or successors will in time assemble the new masterpieces of literary history—the monumental overviews that radically revise our knowledge of the literary past.

Here, for example, is the famous manuscript of Malory's *Le Morte d'Arthur,* discovered at Winchester College, England, in 1934. Its great immediate importance lay in the fact that its text plainly was much closer to what Malory had written than was that of the edition Caxton printed in 1485. The theory at which scholars arrived was that the Winchester and Caxton versions each came from separate older versions, and that these older versions were both descended in turn from a single ancestor, which derived, ultimately, from Malory's own manuscript. But when a rare-book expert on the staff of the British Library, which acquired the Winchester manuscript in 1976, noticed unexplained blots and smudges on many leaves, she subjected the manuscript to minute physical examination, including the use of mirrors, a binocular microscope, infra-red light, and photography, and finally a day-long visit to the forensic science laboratory at Scotland Yard. The smudges turned out to be "offsets" of printer's ink from types known to have been used by Caxton during the period when he printed *Le Morte d'Arthur,* the result, presumably, of the manuscript having been brought into repeated contact with freshly printed (and therefore still damp) pages from the press. The inescapable conclusion was that the manuscript had been in Caxton's printing house as early as 1483 and as late as 1489. Was it, then, the actual copy from which the printed text was set? Since it does not bear the usual marks of printer's copy, the supposition is that for printing purposes it was itself copied into another manuscript, which was edited to bring Malory's Midland language and spelling into conformity with the London English of the day. But no solid evidence identifies it as having come directly from Malory, and its precise place in the textual history of *Le Morte d'Arthur*—the line of descent from author to printer— has still not been determined.[12]

Here is a list of misspelled words compiled from the manuscripts of Keats's letters: *affod, depeciate, expession, gieved, peach, poof, procue, shot, surpised, sping, thead, thee, witten,*

---

[12]For details of these findings, see Lotte Hellinga and Hilton Kelliher, "The Malory Manuscript," *British Library Journal* 3/2 (Autumn 1977): 91–113.

wost.[13] Mere cases of careless orthography, of interest to the psychologist perhaps, but to no one else? Again, hardly. For Keats's obvious difficulty in writing *r* seems to point to an equal difficulty in pronouncing the sound, which in turn constitutes a valuable clue to his craftsmanship. As he composed, how did he hear—and pronounce—his lines? Seemingly with a minimum of *r*'s (he wrote *folorn* in the "Ode to a Nightingale"). In such a manner the evidence of a poet's manuscripts supplies a sort of vicarious recording of his voice, and we are enabled to reconstruct his melodic and rhythmic intention as he worked over the sound-texture of his verse.

These are more or less random examples of the data and procedures that characterize literary research and of the results that make it something more. For although in this book the words *research* and *scholarship* are used interchangeably, as is the common practice, much that has been said so far implies a distinction between the two that certainly exists, if not in the letter of present usage, at least in the spirit. It is pithily embodied in a proverb that H. L. Mencken attributes to the Japanese: "Learning without wisdom is a load of books on an ass's back." One can be a researcher, full of knowledge, without also being a scholar. Research is the means, scholarship the end; research is an occupation, scholarship is a habit of mind and a way of life. Scholars are more than researchers, for while they may be gifted in the discovery and assessment of facts, they are, besides, persons of broad and luminous learning. They have both the wisdom and the knowledge that enable them to put facts in their place—in two senses. They are never either engulfed or overawed by mere data, because their minds are able to see them in the long perspective of mankind's artistic ambitions and achievements.

Especially memorable among the observations made on this distinction are those of John Livingston Lowes, spoken in 1933 but really dateless:

[13]*The Letters of John Keats,* ed. Hyder E. Rollins (Cambridge, MA, 1958) 1: 17.

Humane scholarship . . . moves and must move within two worlds at once—the world of scientific method and the world, in whatever degree, of creative art. The postulates of the two are radically different. And our exquisitely difficult task is to conform at once to the stipulations of each without infringing on those of the other. The path of least resistance is to follow one and let the other go. Research, which is the primary instrument of science, is felt to be the easier and it is also the more alluring. I too have heard the Sirens sing, and I know whereof I speak. And so we tend to become enamored of the methods, and at times to forget the end; to allow, in a word, the fascination of the means to distract us from the very object for which they are employed. And that end is, in the broadest sense of the word, *interpretation*—the interpretation, in the light of all that our researches can reveal, of the literature which is our professional concern.[14]

[14]"The Modern Language Association and Humane Scholarship," *PMLA* 48 (1933): 1403. The whole article, especially pp. 1403–8, still is well worth reading. How "dateless" Lowes's remarks prove to have been has been demonstrated by two fairly recent MLA presidential addresses—Helen Vendler's, already quoted, and Wayne C. Booth's in 1982 (*PMLA* 98 [1983]: 312–22). Both concentrate on the "central experience" for which the scholarly profession stands—"critical understanding" (Vendler's "love"), the precious quality scholars must first cultivate in themselves, and then propagate in their students. Both eloquent statements of purpose should be read by every newcomer to the profession.

CHAPTER TWO

The Spirit of Scholarship

*And as I would not take the least Iota upon Trust, if possible;
I examin'd the Original Authors I could meet with: . . . I think
a Writer of Facts cannot be too critical: It is Exactness I aim at,
and would not have the least Mistake if possible pass to the
World.*
   —Thomas Prince, *A Chronological History of New-England*
   (Boston, 1736)

However sensitive our esthetic perceptions, there is little use in talking about any topic associated with the circumstances or the result of literary creation if we do not have our facts straight. Criticism conducted in the shadow of error is criticism wasted. Douglas Bush, a great student of Renaissance literature, once quoted an "able critic" who, as he sketched the intellectual background of *Dr. Faustus,* asked: "Had not Harriot seen the satellites of Jupiter, and had not Raleigh come back from Guiana with reports [of a fabulous country]?" "Well," said Bush, "if these questions are not merely rhetorical, the answer is 'No, they hadn't'. Raleigh did not set off for Guiana until two years after Marlowe's death, and there seems to be no evidence that Harriot made any major observations until years later."[1]

A number of years ago F. R. Leavis, in *The Great Tradition,* praised the "sustained maturity of theme and treatment" in Henry James's first novel, *Roderick Hudson* (1876). To support the contention that even in this earliest stage of his career James was capable of a "formidable intellectual edge," Dr. Leavis quoted three long paragraphs from the novel. The only trouble was that he took the passage from the New York edition of 1907, in which *Roderick Hudson,* like the rest of James's work, had been subjected to detailed and extensive revision by the author. "This," said Gordon Ray, an authority on the nineteenth-century novel and for many years president of the John Simon Guggenheim Memorial Foundation, "leaves him [Dr. Leavis] in the position of having proved at length what nobody would think of denying, that James's writing at the age of sixty-four has all the characteristics of maturity."[2]

The scholar's business is in part constructive—to add to the sum of knowledge relating to literature and its makers—and in part constructively destructive—to expose and dispel the mistakes that, as the present chapter will show, fox the pages of the literary record. In the latter pursuit, the scholar wars upon the seemingly invincible legend (cultivated by the poet himself) that Burns was a barely literate plowboy, and seeks to cast in correct historical perspective Ben Jonson's remark, seized upon with glee by the "anti-Stratfordians," that Shakespeare had "small Latin and less Greek." Amassing his biographical facts and studying his texts with patient care, the scholar peels off the labels by which earlier critics simplified the reading of literature—"sensuous" Keats, "waspish" Pope, "ethereal" Shelley, and the rest—and reveals how resistant to facile categorizing are both the artist and his art.

[1]"The New Criticism: Some Old-Fashioned Queries," *PMLA* 64 (1949): supplement, part 2, p. 15.

[2]"The Importance of Original Editions," *Nineteenth-Century English Books* (Urbana, IL, 1952) 22.

1. ERROR: ITS PREVALENCE, PROGRESS, AND PERSISTENCE

Good researchers are, by virtual definition, thoroughgoing skeptics. Though in personal relations they may be benevolent and trusting, professionally they must cultivate a low opinion of the human capacity for truth and accuracy—beginning with themselves. The wellspring of wisdom in research, as elsewhere in life, is self-knowledge. Human beings, it seems, have an inherent tendency to shy away from the exact truth, and even though our profession enjoins upon us the most rigid standards of procedure, in research and writing (and, to carry it to the very end, proofreading as well) none of us, alas, is infallible.

Every practicing scholar, if candid, has a fund of wry stories derived from personal experience. One of the present authors remembers:

In a travel book I wrote some years ago, I had occasion to recall the trip that Charlotte and Anne Brontë suddenly re-solved to take in July, 1848, to reveal their true identities to their London publisher, who knew them only under their masculine pen names of "Currer Bell" and "Acton Bell." These were my words: "After tea, as Charlotte recounted it in a letter, they 'walked through a snow-storm to the station' (yes: in July) and took the night train for Leeds and London." The letter quoted is a long and famous one, dealing as it does with a dramatic episode, indeed a turning point, in the Brontës' lives. It was first printed—accurately, so far as the point at issue is concerned—by Mrs. Gaskell in her biogra-phy of Charlotte (1857). But beginning with Clement Shorter's edition of that book (1900), all writers on the Brontës as well as the editors of their letters, with a single honorable exception, have reprinted or quoted from the let-ter inaccurately. Like most writers who have used it, I was troubled by the July snow in Yorkshire, but, again like them, I failed to take the obvious and simple step of checking the newspapers or the meteorological records to verify that al-most incredible freak of the weather. The fact is that "snow-storm" is a mistranscription, followed since 1900, of "thun-derstorm." As Joan Stevens, the discoverer of the error, has observed, the fictitious snowfall provides "an Instant-Test for scholarly scrupulosity."[3]

Simply because we are made of mortal flesh, we have to reconcile ourselves to a small, irreducible margin of error in our work. But fatalism cannot under any circumstances rationalize carelessness. Granted that perfection is beyond our reach, we must devote every ounce of resolution and care to eliminating all the mistakes we can possibly detect. In the end, our consciences can be at rest. If a slip or two have survived our scrutiny, we can lay the omission to the postlapsarian state of the race to which we belong.

The long, broad stream of history has been contaminated from many sources. When we dip into it in the course of our research, whether we take but a thimbleful or enough to fill a gallon jug, our critical intelligence is the disinfectant that will make the water potable. It is impossible to count all the kinds of bacteria in the water we must perforce drink, nor can we fully catalogue their sources. An error in copying a document; moralistic, political, or personal bias on the part of an early witness; a biographer's striving for artistic effect at the expense of the facts; a slip in the memory of someone recalling an event that happened thirty years earlier; a misprint; a speculation that has been dignified into a "certainty"; an anecdote or an assumption of critics or literary historians that has gone unchallenged so long that it now seems as impregnable as an old-fashioned Gospel truth. . . .

The list is a lengthy one. In these pages, however, we have no intention of providing a systematic treatise on the critical examination of evidence; there are several good books on the subject, the majority written by and for professional historians. Instead of a set of rules, we simply offer a selection of case

[3]"Woozles in Brontëland: A Cautionary Tale," *SB* 24 (1971): 99–108. "Some time after I wrote this confessional paragraph," its author now says, "I learned that snow may indeed fall on the higher elevations of Yorkshire in July. But my point is unaffected: Charlotte Brontë wrote 'thunderstorm,' not 'snow-storm.' "

histories and instances, small and medium-sized, which will suggest the variety of misinformation that lurks in the data we receive from our predecessors. In the end you will have a sense of the spirit of vigilance and skepticism that presides over every good scholar's desk.

Once embedded in literary tradition, erroneous assumptions are hard to dislodge, and when a scholar manages to discredit one, his colleagues have good reason to rejoice. It had long been recognized that Ezra Pound's "The Seafarer," a free translation of the Anglo-Saxon poem, marked a major turning point in his career, but there was also "agreement that this astonishing performance is to a considerable extent the result of schoolboy howlers and naive butchering of the text by a man who had dabbled only superficially in Anglo-Saxon." But research in the huge Pound archive at Yale has revealed that, far from being an ignoramus, Pound had a sustained interest in the old language and literature, even going so far as to write other (unpublished) poetic translations based on the texts he found in Henry Sweet's *Anglo-Saxon Reader.*[4]

The chronicles of literary scholarship are studded with stories that might be entitled "Five Little Half-Truths (or Non-Facts) and How They Grew." Once a mistake is set adrift, it not only harbors its original modicum of untruth but swells and proliferates. The oftener an error is repeated, furthermore, the more persuasive it becomes, and the more hospitably it extends its protective coloration over the additional mistakes that come to be associated with it. As a result, the story becomes increasingly difficult to discredit. The burgeoning of the myth of Christopher Marlowe's death is but one instance out of many.[5]

Books and articles on Robert Louis Stevenson during the 1920s and 1930s contain much discussion of one "Claire," to whom Stevenson often alluded in his letters and poems. Who was she? Certain biographers thought she was an early sweetheart of R. L. S. or, even more excitingly, a prostitute whom the chivalrous young man-about-Edinburgh planned to rescue

[4]See Fred C. Robinson, " 'The Might of the North': Pound's Anglo-Saxon Studies and 'The Seafarer,' " *Yale Review* ns 71 (1981/82): 199–224.

[5]For others, in addition to the few included in the ensuing pages, see For Further Reading, pp. 262–65.

from a brothel. As it progressed, this legend of Stevenson's love acquired quite fancy trimmings. But in *Voyage to Windward* (1951), the journalist J. C. Furnas showed conclusively that "Claire" was simply Stevenson's name for Mrs. Sitwell, a woman some years older than he, who was his intimate confidante.[6]

One compelling reason why a myth persists despite exposure is that it is often so much more picturesque than the prosaic truth; a good anecdote, however doubtful its credentials, appeals to the romanticist in us. Thus a course of investigation sometimes results in a clash within us of two opposed inclinations—the scientist's devotion to austere fact and the artist's sense of the superior beauty that resides in what might have been. Our choice, as scholars, is clear, but our rejection of the palpably untrue or unlikely often is accompanied by a certain regret.

An interesting elementary example of the progress of error is embodied in a passage in Cecil Woodham-Smith's biography of Florence Nightingale (New York, 1951):[7]

> Everything depended on War Office reorganization, and War Office reorganization could be pushed through by Sidney Herbert alone. "One fight more, the last and the best," wrote Miss Nightingale; let him nerve himself to this final task and he should be released.

The context is 1859–60. Yet Browning's "Prospice," from which Nightingale's letter obviously quotes, was not published until May 1864. Unless she was gifted with extraordinary foresight into the future writings of a poet, or unless (which is hardly conceivable) Browning somehow borrowed his phrase from a

[6]Furnas tells the full story of this discovery in his *My Life in Writing: Memoirs of a Maverick* (New York, 1989) 288–90.

[7]P. 239. In the London edition of the preceding year, the passage occurs on p. 353. Here is a good instance of why it is necessary to specify the edition from which one quotes. Although some books issued in England and America have identical pagination because they consist of the same sheets or are printed from the same plates, others are typeset independently or are revised for the transatlantic edition and hence may be paged differently. Moreover, in the case of Woodham-Smith's *Florence Nightingale,* there was a big difference in text between the British and American hardbound editions, the latter being only two-thirds as long.

private letter she wrote to someone else, how can the quotation be reconciled with the date? Let us move a step backward, to Lytton Strachey's profile of Nightingale in *Eminent Victorians* (New York, 1918). On page 185 occur these sentences:

> At any rate, he [Sidney Herbert] could not resist Miss Nightingale. A compromise was arranged. Very reluctantly, he exchanged the turmoil of the House of Commons for the dignity of the House of Lords, and he remained at the War Office. She was delighted. "One fight more, the best and the last," she said.

At least no written document is in question here; Nightingale "said," not "wrote." Still, the difficulty remains: how could she have anticipated Browning, and how did Strachey know she said what she "said"? A second step backward takes us to Strachey's major source, Sir Edward Cook's *Life of Florence Nightingale* (1913). This is what Strachey had seen (1: 403):

> The cause of Army Reform would not be completed, the permanence of the improvements already made would not be secured, unless every department of the War Office was similarly reorganized under a general and coherent scheme. So Miss Nightingale urged her friend forward to "one fight more, the best and the last."

The solution is as simple as the moral to be derived from it. What Cook intended as merely an inlaid phrase, which every reader in 1913 would recognize as being quoted from a famous Browning poem, Strachey converted into words Nightingale allegedly spoke, and Woodham-Smith into words she allegedly wrote. What began as a small artistic effect ended up as a putative quotation from a document that never existed.[8]

[8]Speaking of Florence Nightingale, two articles dealing with her biographers' numerous misdemeanors may be recommended as illustrating the sheer diversity of mistakes that can creep into biographies of a single person: Rosalind Nash, "Florence Nightingale According to Mr. Strachey," *Nineteenth Century and After* 103 (1928): 258–65, and W. H. Greenleaf, "Biography and the 'Amateur' Historian: Mrs. Woodham-Smith's 'Florence Nightingale,'" *VS* 3 (1959): 190–202. Further evidence of Strachey's free handling of facts in his profile of Nightingale is found in Geoffrey Faber, *Jowett: A Portrait with Background* (London, 1957) 308–11.

Although error has an inherent tendency to elaborate itself and to attract collateral untruths, like barnacles on a ship's bottom, sometimes it retains its original form through many repetitions. Such is usually the case with bibliographical "ghosts"—the inspired technical term for books, or particular editions thereof, which, though listed, were never seen by mortal eyes. (This is a spectral field of study—literally a never-never land—which Jacob Blanck once called "psychic bibliography.") The original edition of the *Short-Title Catalogue of Books Printed in England . . . 1475–1640,* an indispensable guide to Renaissance studies, contained hundreds of ghosts, mainly of imperfectly identified editions but also including one created by an accident in setting type for the *STC* itself (see the preface). The editors, A. W. Pollard and G. R. Redgrave, were aware of the haunting when the book appeared, but perfection in an undertaking so vast as the *STC,* especially when done by only two men, was not to be sought for. These bibliographical apparitions have been exorcised in the revised edition. Meanwhile, one ghost the *STC* never contained is that of a certain edition of Chapman's *Bussy d'Ambois.* Here is what the principal authorities, 1812–1900, say about the dates of the various seventeenth-century editions of the play:

	1607	1608	1616	1641	1646	1657
Baker: *Biographia Dramatica* (1812) 2:73:	1607	1608	1616	1641		1657
Watt: *Bibliotheca Britannica* (1824) 1:212:	1607	1608	1613*	1641	1646	
Hazlitt: *Hand-Book* (1867) 82:	1607	1608	1616	1641		1657
[In his *Bibliographical Collections and Notes* (2nd ser., 1882) 90 he added . . .					1646	]
Lowndes: *Bibliographer's Manual* (1869) 1:410:	1607	1608	1616	1641	1646	
Fleay: *A Biographical Chronicle of the English Drama* (1891) 1:50:	1607	1608	1616	1641		1657
Greg: *List of English Plays* (1900) 19, 20:	1607	1608	1616	1641	1646	1657

*This is probably simply a misprint for "1616." At least, it was one ghost that did not prove viable.

Two years after his *List of English Plays* appeared, W. W. Greg pointed out (*List of Masques* cxxiii) that the 1616 edition was probably a mistake of Baker (1812) for 1646, an edition that, significantly, Baker failed to include in his list. George Watson Cole, from whose article on bibliographical ghosts (*PBSA* 13 [1919]: 87–112) we have taken this example, says that neither Baker nor Watt "makes any pretense of locating copies nor even lays claim to having seen a single copy of any of these early editions. . . . Hazlitt . . . appears to have been one of the earliest English bibliographers who attempted to locate copies of the works he describes. Lowndes occasionally gives the location of a copy, as in the Bodleian or British Museum; Fleay makes no such attempt." Greg, on the other hand, systematically lists locations. His failure to find a single copy of the 1616 edition, or in fact any reference to it earlier than Baker's, made him suspect it to be a ghost. And though Greg's subsequent distinguished and influential career as a bibliographer lasted for almost sixty more years, he never did run across a copy of the 1616 edition; it is not listed in his monumental *Bibliography of the English Printed Drama* (1939–59). In such a fashion a misread date, committed to type in 1812, "created" a book that nobody ever saw but that everybody, presumably, believed in until its nonexistence was made reasonably clear ninety years later.

The lesson is really twofold. In the first place, notwithstanding the Bellman's familiar assertion, what is told three times is *not* necessarily true. A rumor, no matter in what various contexts it appears and at what intervals of time, can rise no higher than its source, and a mistake, no matter how often repeated or under whose auspices, remains a mistake. In the second place—but we can do no better than to quote a writer in the *Monthly Review* more than two centuries ago (16 [1757]: 531):

> . . . in proportion as History removes from the first witnesses, it may recede also from truth,—as, by passing thro' the prejudices, or the mistakes of subsequent Compilers, it will be apt to imbibe what tincture they may chance to give it. The *later* Historian's only way, therefore, to prevent the ill effects of that decrease of evidence which the lapse of years necessarily

brings with it, must be, by punctually referring to the spring head from whence the stream of his narration flows; which at once will cut off all appearance of partiality, or misrepresentation. As in law, the rectitude of a person's character is not alone sufficient to establish the truth of a fact, so in history, not merely the Writer's testimony, be our opinion of his veracity ever so great, but collateral evidence also is required, to determine every thing of a questionable nature.

One necessary consequence of this advice is that researchers must be careful to use only the most dependable text of a literary work or a private or public document. Young scholars especially tend to forget that there are good texts and bad, incomplete and/or unreliable editions and definitive ones. We shall have more to say about the crucial importance of reliable texts in the following chapter, but here we should note that the weak link in the chain that connects pre-twentieth-century authors, especially those from Chaucer's time to the end of the eighteenth century, with modern readers is the quality of the editions that have transmitted the texts. Until the gradual professionalization of literary scholarship in the past seventy-five years or so, anybody with some pretensions to literary learning could set up as an editor, often with grievous results. A notoriously unreliable one was the Reverend Alexander B. Grosart (1827–99), "a favorite whipping-boy for modern editors and bibliographers," whose edition of the dramatist Robert Greene's works, one of his numerous editions of Elizabethan and Jacobean authors, "stands before us as a massive Victorian monument to jerry-building. As 'perpetual vicar' of the church of St. George's in Blackburn (Lancs.), he was able to send off his curates (acting in this like the modern American academic's 'research assistants') to undertake transcriptions of texts for which they had neither aptitude nor preparation. Indeed, his claim that his innumerable texts show 'religious fidelity' can only be thought to bring his faith into question."[9]

[9]G. K. Hunter, "Recent Studies in the English Renaissance," *SEL* 23 (1983): 154.

Given the presence of so many well-meaning but unqualified editors in the history of literary texts, the best rule the modern student should adopt is to use the latest scholarly edition, though always with the awareness that even it may well be flawed to a greater or lesser degree. Pope's poems should be cited from the Twickenham edition, Jonson's plays from the Herford-Simpson edition, Spenser's works from the Johns Hopkins Variorum, Swift's prose from Herbert Davis's edition, Burns's poems from Kinsley's, Keats's from Stillinger's, Tennyson's from Ricks's, Arnold's prose from Super's, Hardy's poems from Hynes's, Christina Rossetti's from Crump's. Other noteworthy scholarly editions of authors' collected works, some now complete and others still in progress, include: the Yale Milton (prose), Jonathan Edwards, Thomas More, Samuel Johnson, and Boswell; the Clarendon Marlowe and Bunyan; the California Dryden; the Wesleyan Fielding; the Georgia Smollett; the Cornell Wordsworth and Yeats; and the Cambridge D. H. Lawrence. Authoritative texts of the works of the most important American writers are found in various editions produced under the guidelines of the Center for Editions of American Authors (see below, p. 81). Among these are the Ohio State Hawthorne, the Princeton Thoreau, the Northwestern-Newberry Melville, the Iowa-California Mark Twain, the SUNY/Albany Cooper, the Pennsylvania Dreiser, the Harvard Emerson, and the Twayne Washington Irving.

Likewise, scholars must use the most dependable editions of authors' correspondences. It is axiomatic in the profession that no edition of letters published before the 1920s, at the earliest, can be relied upon. (Nor can some that appeared well after that date: the texts of letters in the superficially impressive nineteen-volume Shakespeare Head Brontë, published in 1932–38, are full of errors.) William Mason's simultaneous mangling and "beautifying" of Thomas Gray's letters (1775) is one of the most notorious examples of editorial malpractice in literary history. Edmund Gosse, editing them again a century later, was a tad more conscientious than Mason, but not enough to inspire confidence in his texts. In the preface to his edition (1884), he wrote, "As far, then, as regards the largest section of Gray's prose writings,—the letters which he addressed to Thomas Wharton [sic],—I am relieved from my responsibility of reference to any previous texts, for I have scrupulously printed these from the originals, which exist, in a thick volume, among the Egerton MSS., in the Manuscript department of the British Museum." What Gosse did not know was that the person he had employed to transcribe the text "direct from the originals" had tired of reading Gray's handwriting and, finding that the letters had been printed by John Mitford in 1816, had taken the far easier course of copying them from the printed versions— which happened to swarm with errors. Hired research assistants, it appears, were no more to be depended upon than Grosart's presumably unpaid curates. For inclusion in his multivolume life of his father-in-law, Sir Walter Scott, John Gibson Lockhart touched up the style of Scott's letters, silently omitting portions (thus changing the meaning of what remained) and cut them apart and recombined them, irrespective of date or recipient, into new letters.[10]

In fact, every scholar who has had occasion to compare the pre-1920 printed texts of a literary figure's private papers with the manuscripts themselves has blood-curdling tales to tell of the liberties their editors took. Sometimes, to be sure, the printed deviations from the original are accidental, the result of the editor's misreading. One of the most charming instances of this occurs in the *Life, Journals, and Correspondence of Samuel Pepys* (1841), where Sir Robert Southwell is represented as saying in a letter to Pepys that he has lost his health "by sitting

[10]On Mason's misdeeds, see Paget Toynbee and Leonard Whibley, *Correspondence of Thomas Gray* (Oxford, 1935) 1: xiv–xv; on Gosse's negligence, see Evan Charteris, *The Life and Letters of Sir Edmund Gosse* (New York, 1931) 188. Lockhart's is described by Davidson Cook, "Lockhart's Treatment of Scott's Letters," *Nineteenth Century and After* 102 (1927): 382–98. Another horror story is the history of the successive editions of Pepys's diary, recounted in the introduction to *The Diary of Samuel Pepys,* ed. Robert Latham and William Matthews (Berkeley, 1970–83) 1: [xviii]–xcvi.

many years at the sack-bottle." Reference to the manuscript reveals that what Southwell really sat at was not the sack-bottle but the "inck-bottle," which is a quite different kind of companion.[11]

The first requisite of a dependable edition of a correspondence, therefore, like that of an edition of a literary work, is scrupulous accuracy, which means going back to the original letter or, if it is not extant or available, the most trustworthy printed text. DeLancey Ferguson's edition of Burns's letters was rightly admired when it appeared in 1931—it cleansed the letters of innumerable expurgations and other corruptions introduced by earlier editors bent upon polishing the earthy Scotsman's image—but Ferguson did not systematically attempt to verify the texts. G. Ross Roy, editor of the new edition (1968), undertook the task of freshly collating every letter, and, he reports, "found that in almost every instance some alteration of Ferguson's text was necessary." Behind the current edition of the essayist William Hazlitt's letters (1978) lies a sad story. When the original editor died, the project was completed by "two supplemental editors" and members of the staff of the New York University Press, who, whatever their competence in other aspects of scholarly publishing, were unversed in scholarly editing. The result, greeted with slashing reviews in the journals, was a volume abounding in errors in the text and apparatus, and seriously incomplete as well. Someone will have to do the job over again; meanwhile, Hazlitt students use the book with great caution.[12]

Year by year, more trustworthy editions of correspondences are joining "standard" editions of literary works on library shelves. The well-informed scholar knows as a matter of course that Pope's letters should be quoted from Sherburn's edition

[11]William Dunn Macray, *Annals of the Bodleian Library Oxford* (2nd ed., Oxford, 1890) 236n.

[12]See Charles E. Robinson, "William Hazlitt to His Publishers, Friends, and Creditors: Twenty-seven New Holograph Letters," *Keats-Shelley Review* 2 (1987): 1–47.

and Horace Walpole's from the magnificent forty-eight-volume Yale edition, the lifework of a wealthy amateur who knew, and followed, all the rules of professional scholarship. Among the Romantic poets, Wordsworth's letters have been edited by Ernest DeSelincourt (but see below), Coleridge's by E. L. Griggs, Byron's by Leslie Marchand, Keats's by Hyder Rollins, Shelley's by Frederick Jones. Among the Victorians, Gordon Haight's edition is standard for George Eliot, Gordon Ray's for Thackeray, Norman Kelvin's for Morris, Cecil Lang's for Swinburne, Richard Purdy and Michael Millgate's for Hardy, and the slowly progressing, encyclopedic Pilgrim edition for Dickens. Outstanding editions of the letters of twentieth-century authors include Dan Laurence's multi-volume Shaw and Nigel Nicolson and Joanne Trautmann's Virginia Woolf. On the American side, one goes to Ralph Rusk for Emerson's letters, Leon Edel for Henry James's, Edwin Haviland Miller for Whitman's, and Robert Elias for Dreiser's. The two biggest projects of the kind, each of which will run to thirty or forty volumes, are the Edinburgh-Duke edition of the letters of Thomas and Jane Carlyle and Philip Kelley and Ronald Hudson's edition of the Brownings' correspondence. The forty-fourth and last volume of the latter is tentatively scheduled to be published in the year 2009.[13]

Even so-called definitive editions of authors' correspondences have proved to be incomplete, unreliable, or both. Ferguson's Burns, as we have seen, had to be done over. While a model of editorial excellence when it first appeared (1935–39), the DeSelincourt edition of Wordsworth's letters called for revision and expansion in the light of newly discovered and newly available manuscripts: the new volumes for the poet's later years contain some six hundred letters not included in the original edition. Grierson's Scott lacks scores if not hundreds of

---

[13]Other writers whose letters have recently been collected in scholarly editions, or are in the process of appearing, include Cowper, Disraeli, Lamb, Tennyson, Yeats, D. H. Lawrence, Conrad, E. M. Forster, Synge, and T. S. Eliot among the British; among the Americans, Hawthorne, Bryant, Whittier, Longfellow, Howells, and Mark Twain.

letters that are known to exist. Bradford Booth's edition of Trollope's letters has been superseded by N. John Hall's much larger one. Ruskin's, gathered in the majestic thirty-nine-volume edition of his complete works, are textually unreliable; in this instance, the deficiency is slowly being made good by separate editions of his correspondence with individuals.

In using the work of an intervening biographer or editor, then, it is best practice for the scholar always to allow for the possibility of error or questionable editorial procedure. Every once in a while, a new edition of a literary work is proclaimed to be "complete" or "definitive" or words to the same laudatory effect, when it is, in fact, nothing of the sort. Emerging from Reading gaol in 1897 after serving a sentence for homosexual practices, Oscar Wilde mailed to his friend Robert Ross a long letter addressed to the man who had got him into his deep trouble, Lord Alfred Douglas. Ross made two typescripts of the letter, approximately half the contents of which he published in 1905 under the title *De Profundis*. Four years later, he gave the original manuscript to the British Museum with the stipulation that it not be examined for fifty years. Before this period expired, Wilde's son, Vyvyan Holland, who owned one of the typescripts, published (1949) what he maintained was "the first complete and accurate version" of the text. But when the London publisher Rupert Hart-Davis, in the course of editing Wilde's letters, compared it with the original, which by that time had become available, he discovered that it contained "several hundred errors," some attributable to misreadings of Wilde's handwriting and the mishearing of a stenographer to whom Ross had dictated while preparing the typescript, others to an effort to "improve" Wilde's grammar. Like William Mason, John Gibson Lockhart, and other easy-going editors, Holland was also guilty of, in Hart-Davis's words, the "inexplicable shifting of passages and whole paragraphs from one part of the letter to another." The text was printed exactly for the first time in Hart-Davis's edition of the letters (1962).

Some literary figures seem to labor under a curse in this respect. Since the 1960s there has been increasing critical interest in the early nineteenth-century rural poet John Clare; editions, selections, biographies, and critical studies have flowed from the press in a steady stream. A scholar had occasion recently to determine the textual reliability of twelve editions (1968–83), and his comparison of their texts with the contemporary transcripts of Clare's poems upon which our knowledge of his work is based revealed that they were replete with error.[14]

The lesson is plain: by accepting on faith, in an article we publish, something we would have discovered was an error had we checked it—a mistaken reading of a line by John Clare, for example—we become an inadvertent accomplice in passing the error one further step down the line. And often the pleasure of exposing an inaccurate statement or a slippery assumption is reward enough for the labor it has cost. In an article on the circulation of newspapers in eighteenth-century England (*RES* 22 [1946]. 29) the respected historian Arthur Aspinall says that "at no time were newspapers beyond the reach of town workers," and he supports his point, or seems to, by saying that "the very slaters had the newspapers brought on to the roofs of the houses on which they were working, that they might read them." The unqualified plural suggests a common practice, so common, indeed, that one can conjure up a vision of all the slaters in London dropping their tools to bury their noses in the paper. But when one turns to the author's source, Montesquieu's fragmentary notes on a visit to London about 1730, he finds that Montesquieu had written: *"Un couvreur se fait apporter la gazette sur les toits pour la lire"* ("A roofer has the newspaper brought to him on the roof so he can read it").[15]

All that the cautious can infer from this statement is that Montesquieu saw one, but not necessarily more than one, slater reading a newspaper. While perhaps other slaters did in fact

---

[14]See Greg Crossan, "John Clare's Poetry: An Examination of the Textual Accuracy of Some Recent Editions," *Studies in Romanticism* 23 (1984): 581–98.

[15]Montesquieu, *Oeuvres Complètes,* ed. Edouard Laboulaye (Paris, 1875–79) 7: 189.

read, up there on the roof, Montesquieu's statement, couched in the singular, is no positive evidence of it. To be sure, a generalization is implied—the single slater, Montesquieu seems to suggest, is typical of many. But is it true, as Aspinall's acceptance and enlargement of it tempts us to believe? A reasonable interpretation of the statement must take into account all the independent evidence that bears on it, for an assertion is good only so long as no evidence substantially contradicts it. In this case, evidence does substantially contradict it, for enough is known about the availability of newspapers in the London of the 1730s and the extent of literacy among the artisan class to cast serious doubt on the historical accuracy of Montesquieu's observation. Furthermore, Aspinall failed to take into account the foreign visitor's characteristic readiness to convert the exceptional into the rule. In evaluating any piece of historical information, especially when it occurs in a primary source, a good working knowledge of human nature is one of the most effective pieces of equipment a scholar can possess. "Man," as George Eliot remarked in *Felix Holt,* "cannot be defined as an evidence-giving animal."

2. EXAMINING THE EVIDENCE

So back to the sources it is, then, if scholars wish to erase the mistakes that are all too likely to have occurred in the process of historical transmission. Back to the documents (or, in practice, to a thoroughly reliable printing thereof, if one exists); back to the people with whom our information began; back to the "collateral evidence" that, according to our sagacious *Monthly* reviewer in 1757, is needed to "determine every thing of a questionable nature." But primary and collateral evidence needs to be weighed every bit as carefully as the statements of intermediate sources. A document's age and unchallenged authenticity are no warrant of the truth of its contents. Again the scholar must bring into play his or her sense of the manifold ways by which people can, whether unconsciously or with full deliberation, distort the facts—or imagine them.

Valuable though authors' autobiographical narratives may be, we can never accept them at their face value. Apart from their frequent unreliability as to specific dates, places, and other historical facts, they often are idealized, embroidered through sheer exuberance of the artistic imagination, colored by compelling motives such as the desire for self-justification (or in Carlyle's case, public expiation—for his inconsiderate treatment of his wife during her lifetime), or simply undependable because of the lapse of time between the events narrated and the moment they were set on paper. Just about every conceivable kind of memorial lapse or embellishment can be illustrated somewhere in the autobiographical writings and oral reminiscences of English and American writers. Coleridge, De Quincey, Whitman, Mark Twain, Shaw, Yeats, Sherwood Anderson, J. M. Barrie, Faulkner, Hemingway, Thomas Wolfe are a constant source of exasperation to their biographers because they recurrently, for whatever reasons, deviated from what is demonstrably the truth in their accounts of their lives. One thinks particularly of Ford Madox Ford, to whom H. G. Wells attributed "a copious carelessness of reminiscence"; of Lillian Hellman, whose elaborate falsehoods were the subject of fierce controversy in her last years and since her death in 1984; and of Frank Harris, a celebrated liar who, energetically assisted by the tendentious and discrepant memoirs of other participants in the events, managed (among other accomplishments) to becloud the history of Oscar Wilde's last years so thoroughly that only with the appearance of Richard Ellmann's biography in 1987 could it be said to be straightened out as far as it lay within a human being's ability to do so.

The scholar's task is no easier when great writers leave behind them several discrepant versions of a single episode. Shelley told the story of his expulsion from Oxford at least five different times, never twice in exactly the same way. Add four more versions from other sources, also disagreeing in certain details, and you have a real puzzle on your hands. Confronted with several variant accounts, one can seldom reconcile the conflicts by counting the number of times each detail occurs and accepting the most frequently recounted one as the truth.

Majority rule is an admirable foundation-stone of democratic politics, but a slippery procedure in scholarship. Instead, one must carefully examine the probability of each detail as well as the circumstances under which each version was uttered (was there any reason why Shelley, on a given occasion, should have altered this detail or that?). And the subject's own versions must then be compared with the testimony of others—testimony that must in itself be delicately evaluated for a possible tincture of fanciful elaboration, slips of memory, personal bias, and so on. In the end, it is not usually possible for a scholar to say with absolute confidence that this, and this alone, is what happened in a given episode; the best one can do is assert that, everything considered, the probabilities favor one set of details more than another.

Consider the famous anecdote told by Boswell, which, he says, he gives "authentically from Johnson's own exact narration":

> I received one morning [said Johnson] a message from poor Goldsmith that he was in great distress, and, as it was not in his power to come to me, begging that I would come to him as soon as possible. I sent him a guinea, and promised to come to him directly. I accordingly went as soon as I was drest, and found that his landlady had arrested him for his rent, at which he was in a violent passion. I perceived that he had already changed my guinea, and had got a bottle of Madeira and a glass before him. I put the cork into the bottle, desired he would be calm, and began to talk to him of the means by which he might be extricated. He then told me that he had a novel ready for the press, which he produced to me. I looked into it, and saw its merit; told the landlady I should soon return, and having gone to a bookseller, sold it for sixty pounds. I brought Goldsmith the money, and he discharged his rent, not without rating his landlady in a high tone for having used him so ill.[16]

[16]*Life of Johnson*, ed. G. Birkbeck Hill, re-ed. L. F. Powell (Oxford, 1934–40) 1: 416.

Thus James Boswell, offering a direct quotation from Johnson. But Mrs. Thrale also printed an account of this charitable transaction. Boswell called it "a specimen of the extreme inaccuracy with which all her anecdotes of Dr. Johnson are related, or rather discoloured and distorted," but the antipathy of one biographer toward another must not be allowed to affect our own judgment:

> I have forgotten the year, but it could scarcely I think be later than 1765–6, that he was called abruptly from our house after dinner, and returning in about three hours, said, he had been with an enraged author, whose landlady pressed him for payment within doors, while the bailiffs beset him without; that he was drinking himself drunk with Madeira to drown care, and fretting over a novel which when finished was to be his whole fortune; but he could not get it done for distraction, nor could he step out of doors to offer it for sale. Mr. Johnson therefore set away the bottle, and went to the bookseller, recommending the performance, and desiring some immediate relief; which when he brought back to the writer, he called the woman of the house directly to partake of punch, and pass their time in merriment.[17]

So much for Mrs. Thrale, offering not a verbatim quotation from Johnson, but the next thing to it. A third version, also attributed to Dr. Johnson himself, was printed by the dramatist Richard Cumberland in 1807:

> I have heard Dr. Johnson relate with infinite humour the circumstance of his rescuing him [Goldsmith] from a ridiculous dilemma by the purchase money of his Vicar of Wakefield, which he sold on his behalf to Dodsley, and, as I think, for the sum of ten pounds only. He had run up a debt with his landlady for board and lodging of some few pounds, and was at his wit's-end how to wipe off the score and keep a roof over his head, except by closing with a very staggering pro-

[17]*Anecdotes of the Late Samuel Johnson* (London, 1786). Quoted here from the "new edition" (London, 1822) 94–95.

posal on her part, and taking his creditor to wife, whose
charms were very far from alluring, whilst her demands were
extremely urgent. In this crisis of his fate he was found by
Johnson in the act of meditating on the melancholy alternative before him. He shewed Johnson his manuscript of The
Vicar of Wakefield, but seemed to be without any plan, or
even hope, of raising money upon the disposal of it; when
Johnson cast his eye upon it, he discovered something that
gave him hope, and immediately took it to Dodsley, who
paid down the price above-mentioned in ready money, and
added an eventual condition upon its future sale. Johnson
described the precautions he took in concealing the amount
of the sum he had in hand, which he prudently administered
to him by a guinea at a time. In the event he paid off the
landlady's score, and redeemed the person of his friend from
her embraces.[18]

In addition to these extended narratives, there are several anecdotes that contain some, but not all, of their components. Johnson's pre-Boswellian biographer, Sir John Hawkins, says simply:

Of the booksellers whom he [Goldsmith] styled his friends,
Mr. Newbery was one. This person had apartments in Canon-
bury-house, where Goldsmith often lay concealed from his
creditors. Under a pressing necessity he there wrote his Vicar
of Wakefield, and for it received of Newbery forty pounds.[19]

Nothing is said of Johnson's intervention. Nor does Johnson
figure in William Cooke's account of the composition of *The
Vicar of Wakefield:*

The doctor [i.e., Goldsmith], soon after his acquaintance with
Newbery, for whom he held "the pen of a ready writer,"

[18]*Memoirs of Richard Cumberland, Written by Himself* (London, 1807) 1:
372–73.
[19]*Life of Samuel Johnson* (2nd ed., London, 1787) 420.

removed to lodgings in Wine Office Court, Fleet-street, where he finished his "Vicar of Wakefield," and on which his friend Newbery advanced him *twenty guineas:* "A sum," says the Doctor, "I was so little used to receive in a *lump,* that I felt myself under the embarrassment of Captain Brazen in the play, "whether I should build a privateer or a play-house with the money."[20]

On the other hand, Goldsmith does not appear in an anecdote, also involving a necessitous author's captivity for nonpayment of just debts, rescue by a comparatively affluent friend, and application to a bottle of wine, which George Steevens, a member of the Johnson circle, alleged Johnson told of himself, referring to his early London years:

> Richardson, the author of Clarissa, was his constant friend on such occasions. "I remember writing to him (said Johnson) from a spunging-house; and was so sure of my deliverance through his kindness and liberality that, before his reply was brought, I knew I could afford to joke with the rascal who had me in custody, and did so, over a pint of adulterated wine, for which, at that instant, I had no money to pay."[21]

In this welter of discrepancies and outright contradictions, where is the truth to be found?

1. *Did the episode happen at all?* Almost certainly, yes; for we have Boswell's word that Johnson described the incident, and Boswell is a remarkably dependable biographer whose testimony has withstood close scrutiny time after time. Mrs. Thrale to some extent corroborates him, though her knowledge can only be second-hand. Independent evidence proves the transaction took place in 1762, and Johnson did not begin to frequent her household until January 1765. She could not, therefore, have been an eyewitness to his departure "after dinner"

[20]*European Magazine* 24 (1793): 92.
[21]*London Magazine* ns 4 (1785): 253.

(note that Johnson, quoted by Boswell, says "one morning") or his return.

2. *How much did Goldsmith—with or without Johnson's aid—collect for "The Vicar of Wakefield," and from whom?* (Boswell: £60, "bookseller" unidentified; Cumberland: £10, from the bookseller Dodsley; Hawkins: £40, from the bookseller John Newbery; Cooke: twenty guineas, from Newbery.) Goldsmith's regular publisher was Newbery. The total amount paid for the novel seems to have been sixty pounds or guineas (the terms were used more or less interchangeably in the period), because an entry in the accounts of the Salisbury printer who brought out the first edition of the *Vicar* says that he bought a one-third share in the work for £21, or twenty guineas. Either Hawkins's figure of £40 or Cooke's of twenty guineas may be reconciled with the total of £60, given by Johnson, if we assume that Johnson garbled the story slightly, and that his true mission was to collect from Newbery the *remainder* of the £60, part of which Goldsmith had already received.

3. *Where was Goldsmith at the time the manuscript was sold?* (Hawkins: Canonbury House [in the then suburb of Islington]; Cooke: Wine Office Court, Fleet Street.) Wine Office Court is where, as attested by Newbery's papers, Goldsmith was living in October 1762. A few months later he moved to Canonbury House, where, as Hawkins says, Newbery also had rooms.

4. *What about Cumberland's version, which is conspicuously different from the others?* Probably sheer embroidery and careless variation on the better attested facts. No other evidence suggests that Dodsley was a party to the transaction, and the landlady whose charms were less than compelling seems so patently a stock character from comic fiction and drama (remember that Cumberland was a playwright) that very likely we are justified in dismissing her with the same alacrity that Goldsmith, according to Cumberland, did.

5. *Might not the story of Richardson's rescuing Johnson have colored the Johnson-Goldsmith anecdote?* Possibly, though the story seems to have come from George Steevens, a very unreliable witness who may well have based it, instead, on the Gold-

smith episode. However, if Steevens can be relied upon and Johnson did celebrate over a bottle of wine, it is conceivable that in telling the Goldsmith anecdote to Boswell, Johnson contributed the Madeira bottle from his own analogous experience. Such accretions, as all of us know who tend to elaborate a story in the telling, almost inevitably accompany the making of anecdotes.[22]

These plentiful discrepancies remind us of the story, famous in the annals of psychology (and told, appropriately, of more than one pioneer psychologist) of a fracas staged in a classroom, and of the wildly different versions of the event that all the student-spectators gave when asked to tell what really happened. Every person views every other person, and every event, through a unique set of mental lenses. Hence, whenever we are dealing with the evidence left by people who participated in or witnessed an event—or by people who knew, or recorded contemporary information about, an author in whom we are interested—we must ask a few simple questions, very much in the manner of an attorney interrogating a witness. What, for one thing, is the person's general reputation and capacity for accuracy? Being proved wrong on other matters does not disqualify a witness, for as Browning was fond of pointing out, a large muddy blob of error may well contain a precious grain of truth. But evidence from such a source must be scrutinized with extra care. Again: Was the witness in a position to know the facts testified to? Can it be demonstrated that he or she was present (and attentive, and sober, and with good eyesight and hearing) and not a hundred miles away that evening? Is it possible that the event was, in fact, reported to the witness by people who were there, and that the story suffered changes in the telling?

One inescapable event in every author's life, as it is in the life of every human being, is its conclusion. This has always been

---

[22]For a closer analysis of this tangle, which has many parallels in literary history, see Temple Scott, *Oliver Goldsmith Bibliographically and Biographically Considered* (New York, 1928) 166–72. Scott's discussion well exemplifies the method of sorting out the various strands of asserted "fact" and, so far as possible, reconciling them.

a potential breeding place of biographical error or myth. Except in cases such as those of Thackeray, who died suddenly in his sleep, the American journalist and satirist Ambrose Bierce, who simply vanished in Mexico in 1913, and the poet Hart Crane, who jumped overboard from a liner off the Florida coast, there have been witnesses to most writers' deaths. Some left first-hand descriptions, brief or elaborate, of the manner of their passing. But for various reasons, including the wishes of the surviving family, the facts often were distorted, prettified, enlarged upon, or otherwise misrepresented in the telling. This was especially true of deathbed scenes in the biographies of Victorian authors, written at a time when the heavily religious and moral climate insisted that their last moments be infused with the odor of piety and, equally, that the unpleasant physical details of fatal illness be suppressed. Moreover, the actual nature of that illness was often misreported, partly out of delicacy and partly because until recent years medical diagnoses were frequently faulty—one reason why in more recent times some literary biographers have submitted the known clinical details of a writer's illness to medical experts for their interpretation.[23]

One of the many species of legends that flourished in Poe lore until Arthur Hobson Quinn's ruthlessly skeptical biography appeared in 1941 was the series of descriptions of Poe's death-bed given to the press by the Baltimore physician who attended him. The authenticated circumstances of the poet's end are sufficiently harrowing, but Dr. J. E. Snodgrass embellished them as he went along. That Poe was "rather the worse for wear" is made certain by the note that summoned Snodgrass to Poe's

[23]For various aspects of the difficulty of separating fact from myth in this phase of biographical scholarship, see, for example, B. R. Jerman, "The Death of Robert Browning," *UTQ* 35 (1965): 47–74, and the same author's "The Death of Tennyson," *Acta Neophilologica* 5 (1972): 31–44; John Maynard, "The Diagnosis of Charlotte Brontë's Final Illness," *Biography* 6 (1983): 68–75; Jack Kolb, "Morte d'Arthur: The Death of Arthur Henry Hallam," *Biography* 9 (1986): 37–58; and Suzanne Ferguson, "The Death of Randall Jarrell: A Problem in Legendary Biography," *Georgia Review* 37 (1983): 866–76.

aid. In a New York temperance paper, in 1856, Snodgrass was more specific: "The muscles of articulation seemed paralyzed to speechlessness, and mere incoherent mutterings," and Poe was afflicted with "deep intoxication." In *Beadle's Monthly* eleven years later, Snodgrass turned the "deep" into "beastly" and maintained (as the Puritan narrators of Christopher Marlowe's demise had done, many years earlier) that as Poe died, he uttered "scarcely intelligible oaths and other forms of imprecation"—which does not quite jibe with the earlier "mere incoherent mutterings." The reason for this intensification of effect, Quinn shows, was that the estimable Snodgrass was a temperance lecturer, who made his account more vivid—and to him, at least, probably no less credible—the oftener he repeated it.[24]

Thanks to Keats's own notes on the advance of his tuberculosis—he was, after all, a medical student—and his friend Joseph Severn's intimate account of his last months, the circumstances of his death are not problematical. But one much-attested-to incident in his life is decidedly so. There is no doubt at all that he met one of his idols, Wordsworth, in a gathering at someone's London house late in December 1817. There is hardly any more doubt that in the course of the evening Keats was prevailed upon to recite his just-completed "Hymn to Pan." Anxious for the older man's approval, all he heard when he finished was Wordsworth's tepid "A very pretty piece of paganism, Mr. Keats." Three men later published accounts of poor Keats's putdown by the lofty Wordsworth—his friends Leigh Hunt, Charles Cowden Clarke, and Joseph Severn—but none of them, as it happened, was present that evening at (they said) the home of still another of Keats's friends, the painter Benjamin Robert Haydon. The only eyewitness report was that of Haydon himself, but curiously (because he kept a voluminous journal) he made no record of the event at the time. Only twenty-eight years later, when he was asked to communicate his memories of Keats to the poet's first biographer, did Haydon write of it—and then he located it at the home of another friend, not his

[24]*Edgar Allan Poe: A Critical Biography* (New York, 1941) 639n.

own! Thus, we are entitled to assume that it occurred, and that Wordsworth had offered Keats only condescending praise. But the evidence—from three people who were not present, and from a fourth who was, but whose memory was necessarily undependable after the passage of almost three decades—reduces the "fact" to the status of converging hearsay and long-term reminiscence, at least as far as the details of the incident are concerned.[25]

If witnesses, unlike the three Keats friends who knew only what they had been told, were clearly in a position to know the facts, there is still the possibility that their testimony was biased. This is one of the pitfalls that biographers must keep alert to as they delve into the lives of English writers who were embroiled in the religious and political controversies of their times. The polemical nature of the documentary sources—pamphlets, newspaper attacks, personal letters, and the rest, vehement in their denunciation of the personal character and deeds of their victims—beclouds the study of Dryden, Defoe, and Fielding as persons. A modern French biographer, for example, asserts that Defoe kept a mistress as well as a tile works at Tilbury, but the only evidence for such a statement, John Robert Moore said, "is that such a charge appeared in *The True-Born Hugonot*, a doggerel poem expressing the attitude of extremists who hated the reformation of manners as much as they hated political freedom and religious toleration" and who therefore sought to smear a fellow-pamphleteer who espoused those causes.[26] The student of Pope, likewise, finds himself floundering in what George Sherburn called a "morass of attack and counter-attack," with the air above him, one might add, filled with flying libels—"a perpetual reciprocation," said Dr. Johnson, who nearly always can be allowed the last word, "of malevolence." Where, in all this furious sniping, can the truth of men and events be discovered? It takes years of patient analysis of per-

[25]All modern biographers of Keats report the episode. See, for example, Walter Jackson Bate's *John Keats* (Cambridge, MA, 1963) 265–67.

[26]*Daniel Defoe: Citizen of the World* (Chicago, 1958) 286.

sonalities and motives, and of the public issues that brought out the worst side of all the people involved, to get anywhere near it.

These instances by no means exhaust the list of reasons why the veracity of contemporary accounts may be questioned. In addition to ideological bias in one respect or another, there are also powerfully personal considerations that color such evidence, either from the outset or introduced subsequently by self-appointed custodians of a writer's fame. After Byron, Shelley, Poe, Joyce, and D. H. Lawrence came scores of men and women who sooner or later recorded their memories of them—and few can be said to have been thoroughly disinterested. The more colorful and complicated the author's personality was, and the more troubled his relationships with other people, the harder it is to distinguish the motivations behind each account of him that survives. The governing prejudices range over the whole spectrum of human partiality, from the vindictive to the adulatory; to filter them out requires not only an expert knowledge of the facts but shrewd insight into human psychology. And, in the midst of complex jealousies and desires for self-justification, the eternal juxtaposition of the whitewash brush and the tar bucket, we never can be sure either of all the relevant facts or of the true motives of people long dead. All we can do is try to see things as clearly as we can, removed as we are from the agitating spell of the writer's presence.

One of the most vexing problems in English literary history is the character and career of Byron, over whose grave an extraordinary warfare raged without intermission for more than 150 years. Byron's life story is, of course, inseparable in its later phase from Shelley's; and inseparable from both is the swashbuckling figure of Edward John Trelawny, whose chief distinction is that he wrote the most detailed description of the burning of Shelley's body on the beach near Pisa. During his long life he wrote ten separate versions of the pyre scene, each differing to some extent from all the rest. The discrepancies of detail are enough to bewilder any seeker after the truth, but troubles multiply with our knowledge that Trelawny's contemporaries regarded him as an indefatigable liar. When he was a member of the Shelley-Byron circle he had already, according to himself, served an exciting life before the mast, jumped ship in Bengal, turned pirate, and embarked on a series of romantic and sometimes melodramatic attachments to women, the first of which was a Haidée-like idyll in the South Seas. Persisting in his adventurous habits, Trelawny subsequently became involved in the Greek War of Independence, and took, as his third wife, the half-sister of the revolutionary leader Odysseus. In 1831, at the age of thirty-nine, he published his autobiography, *Adventures of a Younger Son,* which, if literally true, commemorates one of the most remarkable careers a red-blooded Englishman has ever survived.

As biographers delved ever deeper into the lives of Byron and Shelley, the question persisted and grew more urgent: How far could Trelawny be trusted? Some time ago, two investigators, Leslie Marchand and Lady Anne Hill, examined his narratives afresh. Lady Hill was inspired to check the assertions in *Adventures of a Younger Son* against unimpeachable British Admiralty documents in the Public Record Office. Episode by episode, she sailed in Trelawny's wake, and concluded that "the proportion of truth to fiction in *The Adventures* turns out to be small, no more than one tenth"—the latter fraction representing his astonishingly accurate memories of his pre-nautical childhood. If he was capable of telling the exact truth, why did he spin such outrageous yarns? Lady Hill suggested, in essence, that it was to compensate for his sense of inferiority in the company of well-educated and sophisticated men like Byron and Shelley. His one asset was his career as a sailor, and he not only exploited such excitements as he had had far beyond their worth but actually invented the saga of himself as buccaneer.[27]

The question then arises, did the same incurable bent for romancing about his personal adventures affect his veracity

---

[27]"Trelawny's Family Background and Naval Career," *Keats-Shelley Journal* 5 (1950): 11–32. For an expanded discussion of the *Adventures* and of the life generally of this notorious figure in literary history, see William St. Clair, *Trelawny: The Incurable Romancer* (London, 1977).

when he told of the last days of Byron and Shelley? Marchand, after minutely comparing the multiple versions of the seaside cremation, concluded that those written nearest to the event are the most credible (as such accounts ordinarily are) and the most consistent in detail, one with the others. It is mainly those written from thirty to fifty years later that are suspect—the result of a failing memory, a "lazy disinclination to check anything," and concern for the susceptibilities of the Victorian audience, which resulted in his omitting some of the grisly details he had included in earlier descriptions. The famous volume of Sophocles (or was it Aeschylus?) that Shelley was alleged to have had in his pocket was a late addition (1858) to the story.[28]

The problem of evaluating primary evidence is complicated, of course, when several firsthand witnesses, all presumably of the same dependability, differ among themselves. Those who knew the mature Wordsworth left a remarkable variety of impressions. The favorable reactions added up to the image of a modest poet, receptive to honest criticism, generous to younger men, possessed of wide sympathies and an open mind on political and religious questions. But an equally large body of evidence supports the idea that Wordsworth was egotistic, intolerant of criticism, a religious bigot, and a political renegade. Obviously one version is nearer the truth than the other—but which is it? The source of every statement has to be analyzed in view of the character, reliability, temperamental sympathy, and possible bias of the contributor. Edith Batho, who performed the task in her provocative book *The Later Wordsworth* (1933), concluded that the favorable report of Wordsworth is derived from the testimony of "a heterogeneous assemblage of people . . . all of marked independence of judgment" and therefore trustworthy, while the unattractive image was the product of a closely knit group that included Leigh Hunt, Keats, and Hazlitt. Thus, Batho argued, Wordsworth's reputation as a person has suffered because of the animus of a small but influential coterie

---

[28]"Trelawny on the Death of Shelley," *Keats-Shelley Memorial Bulletin* 4 (1951): 9–34.

operating in the limited period 1818–25. Whether one sub-
scribes to her conclusions—present-day Wordsworthians seem
to concur in the less agreeable estimate of the poet in his later
years—her method, which boils down to an exhaustive inquiry
into Exactly Who Said What, is the right one.

"Exactly Who Said What?"—and, as we have seen, it is
equally important to ask When: soon after the event, or at a long
remove from it? Moreover, as we analyze primary evidence, we
must also consider How and Under What Circumstances. The
very language of a statement sometimes is a clue to its veracity.
An emotional person is unlikely to provide an objective version
of an event or a judicious opinion; and the overwrought terms
in which a piece of evidence is phrased may well cast doubt
upon its dependability except as an index to the witness's state
of mind.

More subtly, there is always the problem posed by the elusive
quality of words. In letters between intimates, only the recipient
has the full key to the special implications and connotations of
the writer's language; the subsequent reader can only infer the
subsurface meaning from whatever else he knows. Swift's letters to Stella are an extreme case of what we are talking about,
but much more common is the irony, the private joke, the
concealed affectionate or knife-twisting phrase—a knowledge
of which may alter the whole residual meaning of a statement.
This sensitivity to tone extends, also, to what has been called
period style. Gordon Ray once pointed out that the high-flying
sentimentality of Victorian correspondence between a man and
a woman may easily be misinterpreted; in that era, as in the
Elizabethan, the plumes of rhetorical smoke did not inevitably
denote the presence of amorous fire, though they may well
have done so in the case of Thackeray and Mrs. Brookfield.[29]
The conventionalities of contemporary discourse, then, must be

---

[29]*Thackeray: The Age of Wisdom* (New York, 1958) 80. For a sensitive
analysis of the nuances of allusion and language in the most famous of all
Victorian correspondences, see Daniel Karlin, *The Courtship of Robert
Browning and Elizabeth Barrett* (New York, 1985).

allowed for when interpreting evidence. Even the different possible stresses in an oral quotation may be taken into account. As Walter Jackson Bate shrewdly observed, Wordsworth's "It is a very nice piece of paganism" "could hardly be considered a crushing blow; and it could have been pronounced in different ways—Wordsworth may have stressed 'very,' or 'pretty,' or both, rather than 'paganism,' " so it is hard to determine just what he intended, or precisely how Keats would have reacted.

A letter, likewise, must be read in the light of its immediate purpose and the relations that existed between writer and recipient. Is the writer affecting self-justification, trying to win sympathy for a cause, to persuade the other person to a certain course of action, to distort the facts? And is the friend one with whom the writer is accustomed to share personal details—or is their relation such that we may suspect a certain reticence, or even a deliberate reshaping of the facts?

We have already alluded to the other force that affects our knowledge of an author's character and of the circumstances surrounding a particular biographical incident—the guardianship of posthumous fame assumed by adoring spouses, children, and other relatives. Throughout her life, Lady Jane Shelley imposed on the world a thoroughly idealized image of her late father-in-law, and Charmian London withheld or manipulated the materials relating to her husband, Jack. After George Eliot's death, John Walter Cross, whom she married after the death of George Henry Lewes, her husband in all respects but legality, wrote a biography that conventionalized her almost beyond a modern scholar's recognition. Hallam Tennyson's heavy two-volume monument to his father (1897) is smothered under the flowery tributes, including a number of rancid blooms of nontruth, that the poet's friends contributed to the memorial atmosphere. The book is notorious for its suppressions. The grim truth about Tennyson's upbringing in a country rectory dominated by an alcoholic and psychotic father was first revealed in 1949, in an excellent biography by his grandson, Sir Charles Tennyson, to whose cooperation and generosity many modern scholars are deeply indebted. (Sir Charles, incidentally, was not an academic himself but a distinguished lawyer and holder of high offices in British government and industry.)

One of the most celebrated cases of a spouse bent on fashioning and guarding a famous author's public persona concerns Thomas Hardy. After he died in 1928, there appeared (1928–30) a two-volume biography that purportedly was the work of his widow, Florence Emily. Many years elapsed before the truth became known: Hardy, who said he was adamantly opposed to writing his autobiography, had written the book himself, to be published after his death without any indication of that fact. His wife assisted him during its composition, but her major intervention occurred after his death, when she made sweeping cuts, alterations, and additions, all in the interests of selectively constituting the Thomas Hardy that she and her advisers desired the public to remember, rather than the person as he actually was.[30]

In our own more "liberal" times, the outside pressures that once enforced evasiveness and reticence upon an author's biographers have diminished almost to the vanishing point. But personal resentments, the jealous defense of turf, and other private motives still flourish, to complicate the problems faced by biographers of writers only recently deceased; the cases of Sylvia Plath and Anne Sexton and the contentious people they left behind are possibly the best known present-day instances.

3. TWO APPLICATIONS OF THE CRITICAL SPIRIT: FIXING DATES AND TESTING AUTHENTICITY

Throughout this chapter, underlying all the diverse illustrations, we have heard one persistent theme: *Be sure of your facts—and if in the slightest doubt, take another look.* (Even

---

[30]Reconstructing the "biography" in the form in which Hardy originally intended it proved to be a formidable undertaking, not least because the main surviving document was a much-revised carbon copy of the typescript that had been made from Hardy's much-revised manuscript. See Michael Millgate's edition of *The Life of Thomas Hardy by Thomas Hardy* (London, 1984) x–xxxv.

if you have no doubt, take another look anyway.) Now, before we turn to the way the critical spirit operates in several broad fields of research, we must look briefly at two problems that are often met in all of those fields, from determination of text to source study. These topics are, to use the formal designations, chronology and critical examination of a document's authenticity.

Nowadays, when most people's historical perspective is unreliable regarding events that happened before their own lifetime, scholars must take particular care to cultivate an acute awareness of time. By very definition, the concern of literary history is with events that occurred in a certain order and are often causally related. Chronology often provides a decisive answer to questions of relationship where other evidence is vague, ambiguous, or simply nonexistent. By applying our sharp time-sense to the documents and received narratives before us, we can often place an event more precisely in the sequence to which it belongs, and even more important, we may thereby prove or disprove a doubtful statement.

For a long time, the accepted story behind "The Triumph of Time," Swinburne's lyric lament over a broken love affair, was that the poet had been in love with Jane Faulkner ("Boo"), the adopted daughter of an eminent London pathologist. According to Edmund Gosse, Swinburne proposed to her "in a manner which seemed to her preposterous and violent. More from nervousness, probably, than from ill-will, she broke out laughing in his face. He was deeply chagrined, and . . . he showed his displeasure, and they parted on the worst of terms." Swinburne went into Northumberland and there poured out his embittered heart in "The Triumph of Time." This is a moving and plausible story, which has but one flaw in it, as John S. Mayfield learned when he found the official record of Jane's birth. She was born on February 4, 1852, and since the year in which she allegedly laughed in Swinburne's face was 1862, the conclusion is fairly obvious. It is not unlikely, to be sure, that a girl of ten *would* have responded thus to a proposal from a man of twenty-five, but it is highly doubtful that Swinburne, whatever his sexual proclivities, would have proposed to a girl of ten in the first place. Thus "Boo" has been discredited as the inspiration of

"The Triumph of Time," and although it is generally agreed that
the poem, along with others from the same period, is the product of a deeply traumatic experience, the girl or woman who
inflicted the damage has not yet been positively identified.[31]

Chronological considerations sometimes may lead us into
deeper waters than we anticipate. When writing his *Crusader in
Crinoline,* Forrest Wilson closely inspected the series of events
preceding and following Harriet Beecher Stowe's publication of
the story of Byron's incest as she had heard it from his widow.
The article that contained the dark narrative appeared in the
Atlantic Monthly for September 1869, and at once the press on
both sides of the ocean denounced Stowe as a vicious scandal-
monger. When, the following year, she published a book on the
subject, *Lady Byron Vindicated,* Stowe declared that she would
never have written her *Atlantic* article had she not been moved
to do so by some aspersions on Lady Byron's character printed
in *Blackwood's Magazine* for July 1869. But by examining the
records of Fields, Osgood, and Company, the *Atlantic's* publishers, Wilson was able to show that Stowe did not tell the
truth, for she had in fact delivered her manuscript to the editor
in late June, before any copy of the July *Blackwood's,* or any
word of its contents, could possibly have arrived in the United
States. Actually, Wilson maintained, her whole purpose in writing the article was to proclaim "the glamorous, stupendous fact
that she . . . had been the bosom friend of Byron's wife and
widow, the sharer of her most intimate secrets."[32]

In addition to chronological problems involving events
whose dates are on record or can be inferred from existing
information, there are those presented by undated or questiona-

[31]Mayfield's article, "Swinburne's Boo," *English Miscellany* [Rome] 4
(1953): 161–77, is a good example of the way a researcher assembles
documentary evidence to piece together the record of an obscure life.
Cecil Y. Lang, "Swinburne's Lost Love," *PMLA* 74 (1959): 123–30, proposes Swinburne's cousin, Mary Gordon, for the place left vacant by
Mayfield's dethronement of the prenubile Boo.

[32]*Crusader in Crinoline: The Life of Harriet Beecher Stowe* (Philadelphia,
1941) 535–51.

bly dated books and manuscripts. For simplicity's sake, take an undated letter by a famous Romantic poet. How can one supply the day, month, and year when it was written? There are several kinds of physical evidence. A postmark, naturally, is a great help, but even assuming (which we have no right to do) that the letter was mailed the day it was written, the practices and accidents of the post office in its earlier days were such that a postmark may have been applied two or three days after the letter was handed in. If the paper's watermark bears the year of manufacture, one can say with confidence that the letter was not written *before* that year, and probably no more than five to eight years later; it is simply a question of how long a supply of such paper would normally have lasted in the warehouse, the stationer's shop, and the purchaser's writing desk. Handwriting is a possible clue: if enough dated specimens are available for comparison, it may be legitimate to say that a given document is in the handwriting the poet is known to have used at age twenty rather than that at age fifty. But handwriting varies so much—a person in a hurry, for instance, may write a quite different hand from that used an hour earlier, when he or she was at leisure—that no conclusions can be reached without expert knowledge and an abundance of documents to examine, and even so, they must remain tentative.[33]

One is on firmer ground in attempting to date a letter from its contents. Allusions to contemporary events can be pinned down by reference to newspapers, diaries, and other firsthand sources for the period. (Large-scale chronological dictionaries

[33]The editors of the Pilgrim edition of Dickens's letters rely heavily, for dating purposes, upon the steady changes in his characteristic embellished signature: see vol. 1: xxiv and the facing plate. The dating of Emily Dickinson's poems is both assisted and complicated by her altering handwriting and the fact that her manuscripts were divided into little packets consisting of various kinds of paper; the problem is to find some kind of rational sequence amidst the variables. See R. W. Franklin, *The Editing of Emily Dickinson: A Reconsideration* (Madison, WI, 1967). In her *Arthur Hugh Clough: The Uncommitted Mind* (Oxford, [1962], 264–66) Lady Katharine Chorley dates certain of the poet's manuscripts by reconstructing the folding of the paper.

or "annals" are often useful also, but their accuracy should be checked against sources close to the event.) Similarly, references to situations and incidents in the writer's personal life, when clarified by other biographical material such as letters and diaries, either those of the writer or of his or her friends, may provide the key to the letter's exact or approximate date. And sometimes it is possible to date a letter by fitting it into the sequence to which it belongs; if it alludes to a statement made in a letter received from a friend of the writer and dated September 18, and if a question it contains is answered by that friend in a letter of October 3, it must have been written some time between September 19 and October 2. Additional evidence, such as knowledge of the respective whereabouts and activities of the correspondents during the period (how long would a letter have taken to pass between them? was one away from home and the mail not forwarded? or ill and unable to write?) and acquaintance with their habits as letter writers (was the one usually dilatory, the other a prompt answerer?), might narrow down the probable date still further.[34]

The same genera of techniques, though of course different species thereof, are used to unknot problems of date presented by books. Incunabula (books printed before 1501) and sixteenth- and seventeenth-century books often bear no dates or places of printing, or if they do, this information may be conveyed in a mysterious fashion. A title page motto GUSTAVUS ADOLPHUS GLORIOSE PUGNANS MORITUR may conceal the fact that the book was printed in 1632 (add up the letters that are also Roman numerals, counting the U's as V's), and an English book purporting to have been issued at "Malborow" actually was printed at Cologne—although "Malborow" means "Marburg"!

---

[34]Individual literary works are sometimes dated, or re-dated, according to the same principles. Constance Drake, "A Topical Dating for 'Locksley Hall Sixty Years After,' " *Victorian Poetry* 10 (1972): 307–20, analyzes a number of topical allusions in Tennyson's late poem to demonstrate that it was written sometime between 1882 and 1884, and not in 1886, as a statement in Hallam Tennyson's *Memoir* of his father has led scholars to assume. For a description of the various kinds of evidence used to date Coleridge's notebooks, see *The Notebooks of Samuel Taylor Coleridge,* ed. Kathleen Coburn (New York, 1957–) 1: xxii–xxvii.

Chronograms, as exemplified by the Gustavus Adolphus motto, and fictitious imprints, usually intended to conceal the origin of obscene, seditious, blasphemous, or otherwise subversive literature, such as the Martin Marprelate tracts, are two of the many riddles the bibliographical sleuth must be prepared to solve in order to ascertain a book's probable date. Others relate to the book's physical characteristics: its paper (watermarks are an important kind of evidence), typography, and ornaments and illustrations. Borderlines, title page devices, elaborate initial letters, and even, in the earliest period of printing, illustrations were kept in stock and used over and over by the same printer. (To complicate matters, one printer might, for one reason or another, have borrowed such devices from another printer because he had run short or needed them for a particular kind of book.) Hence, by minutely examining the degree of wear exhibited by such components in an undated volume and comparing it with that shown in dated specimens, it is possible to establish the approximate year when a book was printed. The progressive wear exhibited by individual pieces of type is now being used to distinguish between early and late states of sheets in copies of the Shakespeare First Folio.

Many of the critical techniques used in determining date are applied to the detection of forgeries. John Carter and Graham Pollard exposed Thomas J. Wise's long career as a manufacturer and seller of spurious rarities by showing that neither the type nor the paper used in his fake "first" and "private" editions had been introduced at the dates given on the various title pages. And in the case of the most famous Wise forgery, Mrs. Browning's *Sonnets from the Portuguese* (allegedly printed at Reading in 1847), one of the most damning bits of evidence was the fact that Mrs. Browning first showed her poems to her husband *in manuscript* in 1849.[35]

---

[35]See that classic of bibliographical detective work, John Carter and Graham Pollard's *An Enquiry into the Nature of Certain Nineteenth Century Pamphlets,* originally published in 1934 and accompanied in its second edition (London, 1983) by an updating volume, *A Sequel to An Enquiry . . . The Forgeries of H. Buxton Forman and T. J. Wise* by Nicolas Barker and John Collins.

Out-and-out forgeries turn up most frequently in connection
with authors who are, or have been, fashionable among collectors and whose holographs have therefore brought unusually
high prices. Burns students are often bothered by unauthentic
letters, and even today a relic of the spate of bogus Shelleyana
that polluted the market in the 1920s occasionally turns up. A
present-day Swiss collector is said to own an impressive assemblage of fake Byron manuscripts.

But these are isolated instances. Scholars encounter forgeries
by no means as often as writers about the adventurous side of
literary research, eager for a touch of melodrama, may imply.
Nevertheless, every investigator must, as a matter of prudent
routine, keep alert to the possibility that a manuscript or book
he is examining was produced with deceptive, if not clearly
criminal, intent. The date may be erroneous; the document's
handwriting may not be that of the putative author; a "new
edition" of a book may contain a text that has been reprinted
without change or, on the other hand, has been silently
abridged. All that glisters is not gold, and as James Sutherland
observed when he was writing about the progress of error in
biographies of the actress Mrs. Centlivre, "the price of . . . truth
appears, indeed, to be eternal vigilance, and eternal skepticism."

CHAPTER THREE

Some Scholarly Occupations

In the preceding chapter, the spirit of scholarship was illus-trated chiefly from one kind of research, the biographical. Now we shall look at several other important branches of literary investigation: the establishment of a dependable text, the determination of authorship, source study, the tracing of reputation and influence, and, finally, at the contiguous fields of history in which the literary student often travels. That these branches are treated seriatim does not imply, however, that literary scholarship is in any way compartmentalized. They are all interdependent and mutually contributory, as fundamentally related as, say, organic, inorganic, and physical chemistry. Like chemists, literary scholars must have a working knowledge of all the basic techniques of their profession, so that they are capable of dealing with whatever unforeseen snags may arise as their investigations proceed. Each of a number of different problems—textual accuracy, disputed authorship, a novelist's indebtedness to a predecessor, or a dramatist's influence on his or her successors—calls for the skillful evaluation and interpretation of evidence. The key to an obscure passage in a poem or to a crucial aspect of an author's thought may lie in an odd corner of intellectual or social history.

In view of the tendency of its several sections, this chapter might just as well be called "Further Applications of the Critical Spirit." For while, like chapter 2, it makes no pretense of offering either a systematic or an exhaustive manual of scholarly procedure, it contains, however informally presented, the essence of such a code. Implicit in the examples and the discussion of problems that are characteristic of one or another of the major scholarly occupations are a few governing principles that will be summarized at the end of this chapter.

1. TEXTUAL STUDY

Nobody yet knows how it happened, but happen it did: in the first American edition of Henry James's *The Ambassadors,* chapters 28 and 29 were reversed. Whether or not James was somehow responsible, we do not know; he supervised the first London edition, published two months earlier in 1903, and there the chapters were in the right order. Whatever its cause, the transposition persisted in all American editions, and not until 1950 was attention called to it. In 1955 the publishers, Harper and Brothers, announced that the forthcoming reprinting of *The Ambassadors* in their Modern Classics series would finally present the chapters in the right order. Hubris is as sure an invitation to disaster in the publishing trade as elsewhere,[1]

---

[1]Further disaster was narrowly averted when this very sentence appeared in the first edition of the present book. A nodding professional indexer wrote a slip reading *"Hubris* (Henry James)," and so it appeared in the galley proofs of the index. Only the vigilance of the proofreading author

and Harpers promptly had a great fall; in the new edition, chapter 29 once again preceded chapter 28. After corporate prayer and fasting, Harpers sent the book back to press in 1957, and, to their relief, the chapters finally came out in the right order. But the next year the firm leased the rights to Doubleday for an Anchor paperback edition. "That edition," they wrote in their house organ in November 1958, "has just been published and with a flourish (how well we recall *our* April, 1955 announcement) the Anchor people have proclaimed to the world that *here* is an edition of the novel with *all chapters in their proper sequence*. And you know what? They aren't."

Subsequently several paperback *Ambassadors* have had the chapters in correct sequence. But it would be a rash prophet who could assure the world that henceforth, without fail, chapter 28 will precede chapter 29.[2]

This example suggests that (as has already been intimated in chapter 2) some errors are, in the strictest sense, incorrigible. They simply refuse to give way to truth. This bibliographical comedy supplied a powerful impetus to the movement for authoritative texts. Although scholars had long been insisting on textual accuracy, the stress upon close reading that resulted from the so-called "new criticism" in the 1940s and 1950s focused interest as never before on the very words the author wrote. More than once in the course of those years, critics were unlucky in their choice of texts from which to quote; the word they celebrated for its aptness or ambiguity or irony or simple wealth of meaning happened not to be the one that the author wrote. The classic case—it has been cited so often as to be a chestnut by now, but no other example makes the point quite so well—was that of F. O. Matthiessen, who lavished much admiration upon what he took to be the inspired incongruity of the "soiled fish" image in Melville's *White-Jacket* (chapter 92).

---

forestalled a fictitious addition to the James canon. This is one way, though admittedly not a common one, by which bibliographical ghosts are made.

[2]For a review of this curious story, see Leon Edel, "The Text of *The Ambassadors*," *Harvard Library Bulletin* 14 (1960): 53–60.

His admiration unfortunately was misplaced. "Soiled" was a printer's error; the word Melville actually had written was "coiled."[3]

If misapprehension about a text is sometimes responsible for errors in interpretation and criticism, it also may result in a mistaken understanding of the history of a book's early reputation. In 1832 Edward Bulwer's novel *Eugene Aram,* a popular success, came under severe critical attack because of the author's sympathy with the murderer-hero and, therefore, his presumptive encouragement of any number of readers to go and do likewise. But modern readers find it hard to understand the basis of this attack, because in the copies of the novel they read, Aram—a historical figure—is not guilty of murder. The answer is that when the novel was to be reissued in 1849, Bulwer-Lytton (as he had then become) considerably revised it. "In the new preface . . . he announced that he had changed his mind about Eugene's guilt: having restudied all the evidence, he had concluded that Eugene Aram was an accomplice in the robbery but no more. In the text . . . Bulwer changed the substance of the criminal's confession, made his attitudes more palatable both before and after the crime, and altered some passages which had been interpreted as showing the author's admiration for the criminal. Aram looked, after all this, a different man indeed."[4] It was this revised text of 1849, with its crucial alteration of viewpoint, that was followed in all subsequent editions, thus giving the reader a totally false impression of the original.

Today we realize that accurate texts, and knowledge of which text of a particular work has a bearing upon a given problem, are indispensable to the progress of literary study. It

---

[3]John W. Nichol, "Melville's ' "Soiled" Fish of the Sea,' " *AL* 21 (1949): 338–39. The author was a graduate student when he discovered this famous example of the untoward results of textual corruption.

[4]Keith Hollingsworth, *The Newgate Novel* (Detroit, 1963) 94. For other examples from the same period of the trouble caused by failure to use the right edition see Ellen Moers, *The Dandy: Brummell to Beerbohm* (London, 1960) 69, 78, 174 (on Bulwer's *Pelham*) and Robert Blake, *Disraeli* (London, 1966) 37–44 (on Disraeli's *Vivian Grey*).

is pointless to try to interpret and evaluate any work of art, whether a poem, a painting, or a sonata, on the basis of an imperfect reproduction, or of a reproduction that does not represent it as a certain critic or audience knew it. Before we presume to judge a work's meaning, its artistic strategy, or the response of its readers from its first appearance down to the present, we must have its *exact* words before us.[5]

Shakespeare offers the most bountiful case in point. The textual history of his plays is incredibly complicated. Half of them appeared in one or more quartos (small-format printings of individual plays) that preceded the first collected ("folio") edition of 1623, and the readings of which differ among themselves as well as from the folio. Moreover, we now know that even among individual copies of the same printing, which one would expect to be identical, there may be hundreds of textual variations. This discovery was made possible by the invention of the Hinman Collating Machine, an ingenious optical device that, by superimposing on a mirror the images of two different copies of a printing, opened at the same page, shows up minute differences of typesetting. And besides the quartos and the four seventeenth-century folios, there have been scores of eighteenth-century and later editions whose editors have constantly introduced their own readings or emendations. During the past seventy years, great effort has gone into straightening out this confusion and establishing as nearly as possible what Shakespeare presumably wrote. Scholars and the ordinary reader alike have profited from this effort; the Shakespeare texts commonly found in the classroom have been scrupulously re-edited and now reflect and incorporate this new knowledge. Such editions include the Arden and Penguin series and rival editions published by the Oxford and Cambridge University Presses. The New Variorum Shakespeare, revived after a long hiatus and

[5]As M. J. C. Hodgart has observed, however ("Misquotation as Recreation," *Essays in Criticism* 3 [1953]: 28–38), inaccurate quotation on the part of both poets and critics sometimes has its own critical significance, representing an attempt at "creative rewriting." But the inadvertent emendations are seldom as good as the authentic originals.

now a major project sponsored by the Modern Language Association, is dedicated to presenting "a complete textual and critical history of each line in [each] play," along with essays on criticism and background subjects.

Although for sheer prolific quantity of error and more or less capricious emendation the Shakespeare canon is probably unmatched in the history of English literature, many other classic texts have suffered the same way, beginning with the original printer's misreading of copy and continuing through subsequent misadventures in the printing house and at the nodding or overingenious editor's desk. Between 1711–12, when the *Spectator* papers were first printed, and 1868, when Henry Morley prepared what remained until recently the best critical edition, some three thousand corruptions worked their way into the text.[6]

In previous editions of this book, it was noted that "except for Jane Austen, no nineteenth-century English novelist can be read in a textually reliable collected edition." This remains true of Scott, but happily it is applying less and less, as the years pass, to the fiction of the great Victorians. The Oxford University Press is leading the way, with authoritative editions of the novels of Dickens, George Eliot, the Brontës, Hardy, and others, under the august imprint of the Clarendon Press. Under another series title (Oxford English Novels), it is also bringing out equally dependable editions of individual novels.[7] An equally desirable edition of Thackeray's novels got underway in 1989 with the issue, under the editorship of Peter L. Shillingsburg, of *Vanity Fair* and *The History of Henry Esmond*.[8] Eventually, the

---

[6]Donald F. Bond, "The Text of the *Spectator*," *SB* 5 (1952/53): 109–28. Bond's critical editions of *The Spectator* and *The Tatler* appeared in 1965 and 1987, respectively. The third periodical in which Steele had a prominent hand, *The Guardian,* was edited by John Calhoun Stephens (Lexington, KY, 1982).

[7]It is also publishing an inexpensive reprint of its Oxford Illustrated Dickens series with a press run of 315,000 volumes. Unfortunately, the text is that of the Charles Dickens Edition of 1867–68, which is known to be seriously corrupt.

[8]See Shillingsburg's article, "The Printing, Proof Reading, and Publishing of

entire canon of major Victorian fiction will be covered in this fashion. Editions like these are, of course, not suitable for ordinary classroom use, and in any event, they are priced too high for individual buyers. But some paperback editions published by commercial houses are well regarded for their textual reliability, notably the many volumes in the Norton Critical Editions series, which embraces a wide range of titles in English, American, and world literature.

American editions of nineteenth- and early twentieth-century British writers are notoriously undependable, since they were often set from uncorrected proofs or advance sheets of the British edition and suffered further indignities at the hands of American editors and printers. Hardy's American admirers, as Carl J. Weber demonstrated with many examples, seldom read exactly what their English contemporaries did; in the Harper edition of *The Return of the Native* that was long current, a whole page was missing, and until recently all of the American editions of *The Woodlanders* reproduced the novel's magazine text, without taking account of the numerous changes Hardy had made in successive London editions.[9]

The list of great literary works that until lately have been, and in many cases still are, read in undependable texts could be extended almost indefinitely. One instance is that of *The Scarlet Letter*. Beginning with the second edition, the type for which was set hastily to meet an unexpected demand and was not proofread by Hawthorne, the text became more and more corrupt, until the "standard" text of 1883 contained many hundreds of variants from the first edition. Only in 1961 did the first-edition text, the only one Hawthorne corrected, become available in a modern printing. David Daiches has pointed out that "in the first one-volume American edition of the collected poems of W. B. Yeats there are at least half a dozen misprints

Thackeray's *Vanity Fair:* The First Edition," *SB* 24 (1981): 118–45, and his textual introduction to the Garland edition, pp. 649–70.

[9]"American Editions of English Authors," *Nineteenth-Century English Books* (Urbana, IL, 1952) 27–50. For more on Hardy's American editions, see the introductions to the Clarendon editions of the various novels.

which completely change the meaning of the passages in which they occur, and in some cases critics have actually analyzed the misprinted poems unaware of the errors, and have justified and even praised the mistaken words. The printing of 'he' as 'she' at the end of the second stanza of 'Crazy Jane on the Day of Judgment' changes the meaning of the whole poem, for the poem is a dialogue and the misprint transfers a key statement to the wrong speaker."

From the very beginning of his career, indeed, Yeats suffered at the hands of editors and compositors. With heavy irony, he wrote to the editor of an Irish periodical that had just printed his "The Protestants' Leap": "I write to correct a mistake. The curious poem in your issue of the 19th inst. was not by me, but by the compositor, who is evidently an imitator of Browning. I congratulate him on the exquisite tact with which he has caught some of the confusion of the master. I take an interest in the matter, having myself a poem of the same name as yet unpublished." But this was but an aspect—the most accidental—of the perplexity that attends a study of Yeats's texts, for he was a ceaseless reviser and his poems, even after publication, were in constant flux.[10]

The best text of *The Great Gatsby* is found in Fitzgerald's posthumous *Three Novels*. Of the seventy-five significant changes between the first edition and the latter text, thirty-eight were suggested by Fitzgerald, the rest being inserted by the publisher without his authorization—and, conversely, a number of other corrections that the novelist proposed were *not* made. Thus even the "best" text does not represent the way Fitzgerald wanted his book to read.[11]

[10]The Daiches quotation is from his *Critical Approaches to Literature* (New York, 1956) 332–33. The most recent review of the textual history of Yeats's poetry, especially as it was transmitted through the faulty "Edition de Luxe" of 1949, is Richard J. Finneran's *Editing Yeats's Poems: A Reconsideration* (London, 1990). Finneran quotes the letter to the Irish editor on p. 125.

[11]Bruce Harkness, "Bibliography and the Novelistic Fallacy," *SB* 12 (1959): 59–73. One major change in *The Great Gatsby* was made with Fitzgerald's

In this unsatisfactory state of affairs, textual scholars, or textual critics as they are sometimes called, have crucial importance. They are the specialists who, reconstructing the history of a literary text from its origin in manuscript to its printed form(s), produce a version on which interpretive critics base their exegeses. This "copy text," as it is usually called, may take either of two forms. It may reproduce, verbatim and in its entirety, a single text that the editor considers to be closest to the author's intention, with variant readings in other editions printed in footnotes. Or it may be an eclectic, synthesized version, made up of what the editor judges to be the most authoritative readings, regardless of where they are found. (The Norton Facsimile of the Shakespeare First Folio is a famous example of the latter, "ideal" text. Each page is a photographic reproduction of the most nearly perfect state of that page—that is, free of corruptions introduced during printing—that can be found in the seventy-nine copies of the Folio owned by the Folger Shakespeare Library in Washington, D.C. See below, pp. 190–91.)

In all literary study there are few more absorbing topics than the hazards an early author's manuscript underwent between the time it was delivered to the printer and the moment the printed and folded sheets of the book were ready for the binder. There was the form of the manuscript itself, fit to baffle any typesetter—illegible handwriting, cryptic interlineations, balloons in the margins, additional matter (inadequately indicated) on the other side of the leaf, abbreviations to be interpreted. There were the manifold accidents of typesetting—reaching into the wrong compartment (or into the right compartment, into which a printer's devil had negligently put the wrong type) and consequently setting a wrong letter; the "memorial" errors

---

reluctant consent, when Maxwell Perkins, the legendary editor at Scribner's, persuaded him to move some of ch. 8 to an earlier place in the novel. For the 1951 edition of *Tender is the Night,* Fitzgerald's longtime friend Malcolm Cowley altered certain sections in accordance with what he said was the author's intention, expressed some years after the novel was first published in 1934 (Fitzgerald died in 1940).

attendant on trying to keep too large a phrase of the copy in mind before taking another look at the manuscript; distractions of every sort, including the many occasions that called for a drink or two (a newly qualified journeyman, completion of a big job, a religious or civic festival). The history of literary texts was deeply affected by what we may call the factor of the trembling hand and the blurred eyesight, as well as by all the other human conditions that conspired to produce an imperfect book: "a harassed author, a testy master printer, a stupid proof-reader, a love-sick compositor, a drunken pressman, a newly articled apprentice."[12] The wonder is not so much that early books contain so many errors, as that, given the conditions under which their type was set, they contain so few. Although many authors supposedly were indifferent to the state in which their well-chosen words finally were set before the public, from the very beginning there were occasional tense scenes in the printing house, such as the one suggested by Thomas Heywood's bitter words:

> The infinite faults escaped in my booke of *Britaines Troy,* by the negligence of the Printer, as the misquotations, mistaking of sillables, misplacing halfe lines, coining of strange and neuer heard of words. These being without number, when I would haue taken a particular account of the *Errata,* the Printer answered me, hee would not publish his own dis-workemanship, but rather let his owne fault lye vpon the necke of the Author . . .[13]

Our knowledge of the way printers worked in the earlier centuries is still far from exhaustive, but it is steadily growing, and as it does, the assumptions on which we base our recon-struction of a book's textual history sometimes have to be re-vised. One such discovery, the implications of which are unusu-ally far-reaching, is that type was not necessarily set in

[12]R. C. Bald, "Evidence and Inference in Bibliography," *English Institute Annual 1941* (New York, 1942) 162.

[13]*An Apology for Actors* (London, 1612), sig. [G₄]ʳ.

consecutive page order, as one would copy a manuscript on a typewriter. Instead, Elizabethan printers sometimes were governed by the fact that the composed type for all the pages that would make up one side of a printed sheet had to be arranged in a certain systematic, but nonprogressive, order in the frame upon which the sheet was laid to receive the inked impression of the type. Thus, if "setting by formes," a compositor might first set page 6, then pages 7, 5, 8, 4, 9, 3, 10, 2, 11, 1, and 12; or if two men were working, the first would set 6, 5, 4, 3, 2, and 1, in that order, while the other set 7, 8, 9, 10, 11, and 12.

This system meant, of course, that the foreman had to "cast off" copy beforehand—that is, go through the manuscript or printed book and mark off as much copy as he expected to occupy each page of the new setting. The state of the copy naturally affected the precision with which this could be done. If the type were to be set from a printed book or a reasonably clean manuscript, an experienced printer could predict fairly accurately how much matter would go into a single page. Such would be the case, also, if the copy to be set were in verse, with its easily countable lines, rather than in prose. But, as Charlton Hinman, who made this discovery, said, "real difficulty would probably be encountered . . . in copy very untidily made up from various sources, interlined, supplied with marginal annotations partly in verse and partly in prose, and so on"; hence, "miscalculations would be inevitable and gross inaccuracy would be more likely to occur with edited than with unedited copy." To take up slack or, on the other hand, to pack more matter into a page than had been allowed for, the typesetter resorted to various typographical or outright verbal alterations—dividing a line into two, running two lines into one, omitting a word (or line) or two, and so forth. The more evidence that is found of forced expansion and compression in response to the arbitrary space requirements imposed by casting-off, the greater the likelihood that a book was set from copy that was hard to estimate and to follow.[14]

---

[14]"Cast-off Copy for the First Folio of Shakespeare," *Shakespeare Quarterly* 6 (1955): 259–73.

By similar analysis of evidence, Hinman and other modern specialists have also shown how many compositors set a given book, and for which pages or formes each was responsible. It was previously known that the tragedies in the Shakespeare First Folio were set by three compositors, one of whom probably was an apprentice (each typesetter's work has its own peculiarities). But Hinman went a step further by identifying parts of *Hamlet, Othello,* and *Lear* that the apprentice seems to have composed. His work was most inexpert, requiring constant correction before printing (the signs of which are readily evident to an expert), and Hinman concluded that because of his incompetence he was not allowed to set copy from manuscript but was, instead, limited to relatively easy-to-follow printed texts.[15]

The intricate reasoning by which specialists arrive at such conclusions is fascinating to watch, but the results are what count. Inferences derived from the practice of casting-off and from the habits and competence of individual typesetters, fitted in with various other kinds of textual evidence, are the closest we can get to establishing the nature of the copy from which a Shakespearean play was set—whether an earlier quarto (which may have been comparatively unmarked or, on the other hand, lavishly corrected), or a clean manuscript, or a much battered and amended one, or a bewildering patchwork made from two or more of these. And the nearer we come to deciding what that copy was like, the more confident can be the subsequent process of deducing, from the printed text that eventually emerged, the exact words the typesetter had before him.

The specialized knowledge necessary to study the textual history of printed books lies in the adjacent provinces of "analytical," "descriptive," and "critical" bibliography. *Analytical* bibliography has to do with the printing process, from the time of England's first printer, William Caxton (1422?–91), to the present, by which a manuscript was converted into a printed

---

[15]"The Prentice Hand in the Tragedies of the Shakespeare First Folio," *SB* 9 (1957): 3–20.

book. *Descriptive* bibliography reconstructs the printing history of a given book by examining its physical format. *Critical* bibliography applies the evidence thus obtained to problems of meaning. This last aspect of the specialty—using information derived from physical evidence to determine the author's exact language—is the one with which present-day textual criticism is most concerned. The modern phase of this discipline, as applied to the printed texts of English literary works, was called in its early years "the new bibliography." Its pioneers were four Britons, W. W. (later Sir Walter) Greg, R. B. McKerrow, F. P. Wilson, and A. W. Pollard; in the United States, Fredson Bowers of the University of Virginia was for many years Greg's most eminent, indefatigable, and influential disciple.

Greg, whose article on "The Rationale of Copy-Text" (*SB* 3 [1950/51]: 19–36) became the foundation of modern methodology, generally preferred the earliest printed text as the most authoritative, because it was closest to the writer's no-longer-existing manuscript. A reprint whose text was thoroughly revised by the author, however, seemed to Greg to have at least the same authority as did the first edition.

To one looking back from the 1990s, the first decades of "the new bibliography" were years of comparative innocence.[16] The choice a textual editor had to make was, it appeared, the simple one of "first edition" or "last edition supervised by the author." This either/or rule applied fairly well, though by no means universally, when editors were working primarily with texts dating from the earliest centuries of printing. But the changes that occurred in the printing and publishing trades since the end of the eighteenth century proved to have complicated the editor's task. It is true that the invention of stereotyping tended to stabilize a text, since there was no longer any type to be reset every time a book was reprinted, with the accompanying risk of errors. But, as in the case of Hawthorne's works, alterations

[16]They are reviewed in a series of articles in *SB* by G. Thomas Tanselle, collected under the title *Textual Criticism Since Greg: A Chronicle, 1950–1985* (Charlottesville, VA, 1987).

could be, and were, made in the plates between printings, usually not by the author.

Again, in the nineteenth century as well as the early twentieth century, many books first appeared as serials, either in the separate form of weekly or monthly numbers (the way most of Dickens's and many other Victorian novels were published), or in magazines. A number of Hardy's novels offer celebrated instances. He came to regard the serial text as only the first, tentative version, to be tinkered with on every occasion that permitted, often with important consequences to the novel's tenor and purpose as well as to telling details (the development of the idea of "Wessex" as the brooding presence in Hardy's fiction came about in this manner). As Simon Gatrell recounts in great detail in his *Hardy the Creator: A Textual Biography* (1988), by the time the first collected edition was prepared in 1895–97, "he had already had as many as five opportunities to change the English text of some of his novels," which, as we have seen, had come out in textually different American editions, and he found several further opportunities in the years to come, when the novels were reset for paperback editions in 1900 and again for the Wessex edition, beginning in 1912. Such persistent revision—and Hardy was by no means the only author to engage in creative as well as corrective alterations—is an editor's nightmare as well as his challenge.[17]

At least, Hardy's multitudinous alterations in his fiction had the simplifying virtue of being consecutive: the latest reading of a passage presumably superseded previous readings, even though all have to be recorded in a critical edition. By contrast, when he prepared two separate collections of his poems in 1909–12, the changes he made in the text of the same poems differed from one edition to the other. W. H. Auden likewise left

[17]An interesting, relatively recent case history of the changes the text of a novel underwent between serialization (in *Esquire,* 1964) and book-form publication is that of Norman Mailer's *An American Dream.* Some revisions were required during the serialization by the assassination of John F. Kennedy. See Hershel Parker, *Flawed Texts and Verbal Icons* (Evanston, IL, 1984) ch. 7.

behind half a dozen versions of "September 1, 1939," all from his own pen. Which should serve as copy text?

The farther back in literary history we go, the fewer are the surviving author's manuscripts. Lacking these, it is hard to tell how to attribute the changes between successive printed editions. The three earliest printings of the *Spectator*—the original folio sheets, the first collected edition (in octavo volumes), and the second (in duodecimo)—as Donald Bond reported, "differ widely, not only in punctuation, spelling, and capitalization, but in phrasing, in grammatical construction, and in literary style. For how many of these changes—in spelling, for example— were Steele and Addison responsible? How many were due to the style of the printing-house, or to the care—or negligence— of the compositor?"[18] Sometimes complexity is heaped on complexity by the existence of manuscript and other versions that deviate at many points from the received printed text. The editor of John Stuart Mill's *Autobiography*, for example, must cope with at least four versions: an early manuscript draft (printed for the first time in 1961), a second draft (from which the "Columbia" text of 1924 was printed), a copy prepared for the press after Mill's death (and containing over 2,650 variants from the manuscript on which it was based), and the printed first edition of 1873.[19]

Because the histories of individual books differ, it was—and is—hard to decide, therefore, which of several versions of an authorial text should be used as copy text. No single set of principles governs all cases. Editors of sixteenth- and seventeenth-century works have, for the most part, only a limited number of printed texts to compare. Few documents relating to a work's prior history, before and after it left its author's hands and went through the press, survive. But beginning toward the middle of the eighteenth century, the documentation of a text's progress into print becomes steadily more abundant, with the

[18]Bond (cited in n. 6) 112.
[19]Jack Stillinger, "The Text of John Stuart Mill's *Autobiography*," *Bulletin of the John Rylands Library* 43 (1960): 220–42.

preservation of authors' manuscripts and "foul papers" (memoranda, early drafts of passages, etc.), fair copies of the original manuscript, in-house printers' records, authors' correspondence with their printer-publishers (then usually called booksellers, who combined the two functions that are now separate). In the early years, proofs, pulled from standing type for the author to look over and correct before printing, had been routinely discarded after they had served their purpose; now they tended to be kept, at least in the case of popular authors and books. A number of years ago, the proofsheets of the first eight books of Pope's translation of the *Iliad* were discovered in the Bibliothèque de l'Arsenal in Paris. Although the proofs of books 1–4 contain Pope's corrections of typographical errors only, the remainder show him painstakingly reconsidering his artistry, "from emendations of a single word to cancellations and revisions of quite long passages."[20]

Confronted with the increased number of documents, including biographical records of various kinds that throw light on the process by which a literary work was transmitted from author to eventual reader, editors of post-eighteenth-century texts soon realized that Greg's rationale of copy text, derived only from his experience with sixteenth- and seventeenth-century books, was too simplistic. It did not allow for the numerous vicissitudes that beset a literary work as it proceeded from the author's pen to print, nor for the complications attending the idea of authorial intention. Greg did not use the term, but it was clearly implicit in his insistence that the best copy text was the one that most faithfully represented the author's words. Intentionality became the central issue in textual scholarship, and differing opinions of what it constitutes have been responsible, in part, for the tendentiousness that marks much of the recent discussion of the aims and techniques of editing.

Determining an author's intention is by no means as easy as it was, until recently, assumed to be.[21] For example, there is the

---

[20]Norman Callan, "Pope's *Iliad:* A New Document," *RES* ns 4 (1953): 109–21.

[21]For the most authoritative statements of the major opposing theories of

problem of which text, if there is more than one, best represents that intention, as in the cases already mentioned. If only one text is involved, at what point in its transmission along the chain of copyists, editors, and printers did the author cease to control what he had written—in other words, at what stage of its development did it represent his "final" intention? One possibility is that an author kept such a tight grip on the evolving text that it is difficult to decide which of many versions represents what he *really* wanted to say. Wordsworth's incessant revisions of his poems, as well as Yeats's and Byron's, are conspicuous instances of this problem. (Byron's *The Giaour* exists, as its editor, Jerome McGann, says, in "multiple manuscripts, multiple corrected and uncorrected proofs, a trial edition, [and] a whole series of early editions at least three of which are known to have been proofed by Byron" [*A Critique of Modern Textual Criticism* 31–32].)

There is also the famous case, noted in the preceding chapter, of Henry James's revision of his novels for the New York Edition of 1907–9. Which represent his true intention, the original texts or the heavily rewritten ones? This raises, in turn, the question of the point at which extensive rewriting of a work turns it into a separate artifact, to be treated on its own terms without reference to the earlier version. One of the most debated issues of the sort in recent years has been the relation of the two greatly differing texts of *King Lear*. It is now widely believed that the folio text (1623) represents Shakespeare's own revision of the quarto (1608) rather than the intervention of the printer or some other "corrector." If so, which version is more true to Shakespeare's intention?

Some theorists argue that intentionality has been overstressed, that a fetish has been made of the assumption that absolute fidelity to what the author put down on paper is the overriding concern of textual criticism. They point to Dickens's indifference to the texts of his novels: he was a poor proof-

textual editing, see Jerome J. McGann, *A Critique of Modern Textual Criticism* (Chicago, 1983) and G. Thomas Tanselle, *A Rationale of Textual Criticism* (Philadelphia, 1989).

reader to begin with, and although he "revised" the texts for successive editions, the changes he made were almost wholly cosmetic, with no effect on meaning. Ezra Pound did not object to the alterations that crept into the text of the *Cantos* as it was reprinted time after time, inferentially accepting them as part of the poem's natural growth.[22]

As investigators have delved ever deeper into the circumstances surrounding a literary work's gestation and birth, they have stressed the manifold influences that persons other than the author, from spouses to literary executors, had on the evolving text, thus beclouding the problem of authorial intention. A writer's family or friends may have persuaded him to alter (which often meant, in their eyes, "improve" according to their suggestions) a work in progress. The Romantic poets in particular were given to reading aloud lines they had just written; whether they did so to invite constructive criticism or to elicit unqualified praise must be decided on a case-by-case basis. Coleridge and Wordsworth bounced their latest poems off each other's sensibility, and Mary Shelley was not only her husband's amanuensis but his candid critic as well. Byron and Tennyson sometimes had their poems printed in "trial" editions for circulation among their friends. Bulwer-Lytton, who, as we have seen, drastically revised one of his novels to clarify his purpose as he later conceived, or alleged, it to have been, persuaded Dickens to change the ending of *Great Expectations,* so that readers could believe, if they wished, that Pip and Estella were married and lived happily ever after. (Which of these alternate endings did Dickens *truly* prefer?)

An author's intention in revising the text of a book already published may have been in response to external pressures. In preparing the text of *Typee* for its second American edition, Melville not only seized the chance to make it conform more closely to his original intention but acceded to his publisher's demand for expurgation. When editors changed a writer's text

---

[22]See Barbara Eastman, *Ezra Pound's Cantos: The Story of the Text, 1948– 1975* (Orono, ME, 1979).

before publication, or required him to revise it himself, it is often a moot question whether acquiescence represented a sincere change of intention, as in the case of Stephen Crane's *The Red Badge of Courage,* which underwent "mangling" at the hands of either Crane himself or Ripley Hitchcock, his editor at Appleton's, before it was first published in 1895. It was certainly with Thomas Wolfe's approval that Maxwell Perkins, his editor at Scribner's, quarried two large novels *(Look Homeward, Angel* and *Of Time and the River)* from the chaotic mass of drafts Wolfe had accumulated in big packing cases but was unable to shape. Whether he would likewise have found his intention respected in the three novels his later editor, Edward C. Aswell at Harper's, extracted from the even larger chaos he left after his death, can never be known.[23]

As a consequence of this increasing attention to the participation of others in the development of a text, some scholars no longer necessarily regard the contributions that intermediators made to be contaminants that must be removed forthwith. What earlier editors might have considered disfiguring errors, some present-day ones may be inclined to preserve, as making more sense in context or being more harmonious with the author's presumed but unrealized intention. This is a temptation especially when all the evidence has been weighed and there is no clear indication that reading A of a certain line has any greater authority than reading B. The editor has no recourse but to decide on intuitive grounds which seems more in accord with the author's observable practice in diction, metaphor, even details of narrative technique. Thus a certain measure of subjectiv-

---

[23]The Stephen Crane problem has been the subject of much argument; see, for a detailed (but not unbiased) account, Parker, *Flawed Texts and Verbal Icons* (cited in n. 17), ch. 6. On the question of precisely what Aswell did with, or to, the Wolfe manuscripts, the fullest treatment is in Leslie Field, *Thomas Wolfe and His Editors: Establishing a True Text for the Posthumous Publications* (Norman, OK, 1987). For another example of editorial intervention, see Arthur D. Casciato, "His Editor's Hand: Hiram Haydn's Changes in [William Styron's] 'Lie Down in Darkness,' " *SB* 33 (1980): 263–76.

ity enters into a discipline that once was credited with introducing an element of "scientific" certainty into the establishment of texts. There is the possibility, however, that in making decisions on this impressionistic basis, a textual critic may, in effect, be presumptuously second-guessing the author, substituting his or her presumably superior sense of how a line of poetry, for example, should read, for what the author unquestionably wrote.

The climate of postmodern theory has contributed to the drift away from regarding the text of a literary work as a personal artifact dominated by the author. Debate on the nature of "meaning" casts all in doubt, not least the question of intention. Even if an author assumed knowledge of his or her own mind, some maintain, there is no proof that he or she did actually know it, and therefore the meaning supposedly contained in the text is illusory. Instead of a message, there is motive: an author's discourse is that of a genial trickster, playing endless, intricate games with the reader. Or, if it is conceded that the text contains overt, intelligible meaning that the author intended to express, the important consideration is not what he or she personally meant, but the x number of meanings that x number of readers have discovered in the text. At that point, if not before, the author is dispensed with. At the farthest extreme of postmodern criticism, it is argued that meaning is not contained in language at all but is found only in nonverbal solipsistic "vision." At that juncture, the text is dispensed with also. In which case, the attempt to establish a literary text is an exercise in futility, and the present discussion has been a waste of both paper and the reader's time.[24]

It is evident from the amount of work being done in the practical editing of texts that specialists in the field are undaunted by these discouraging views of meaning and reality. Although the concept of intentionality has undergone redefini-

[24]Two articles (not for the faint-hearted) that represent current attempts to place the text-as-artifact in the ambience of postmodern theory are Louis Hay, "Does 'Text' Exist?" *SB* 41 (1988): 64–76, and D. C. Greetham, "Textual and Literary Theory: Redrawing the Matrix," *SB* 42 (1989): 1–24.

tion and the author has ceased to be the isolated central character in the history of a text, not its "onlie begetter" but simply the original creative participant in the making of what one critic calls a "social product," the work of several hands, scholarly editions continue to clarify and amplify our understanding of literary texts.

Textual criticism has been especially important on the American literary scene since the early 1980s, when its products began to be used as the texts of the ongoing Library of America editions of major American authors, distributed through trade book channels, that serve the general reader as well as the scholar. From the early 1960s until 1976, the Center for Editions of American Authors, an agency sponsored by the Modern Language Association and supported by grants from the federal government and private foundations, initiated or assisted with a series of ambitious editorial projects. What were then the latest methods of textual analysis and reconstruction were applied to the works of most leading nineteenth- and early twentieth-century writers, a partial list of whom has been given above (p. 32). When the CEAA ceased to exist in 1976, it was succeeded by the Center for [now Committee on] Scholarly Editions, also under the aegis of the MLA. Several editions have been completed; in 1989, twenty-two were still in progress.[25]

Thus far we have been talking about textual study as if it were primarily concerned with printed books and the evidence they can be made to yield about the nature of the (no longer extant) manuscript that lay before the original compositor. This kind of textual work is at present more in the scholarly limelight because of the sophistication of its methods and the dramatic results it has produced. But textual criticism of another sort is much older: the branch that deals with the history and relationships of existing, and sometimes also of hypothetical, manu-

---

[25]For a statement of the principles currently underlying the editions, see "The Committee on Scholarly Editions: Aims and Policies," *PMLA* 103 (1988): 414–16.

scripts. It began as long ago as the early Renaissance, with the humanists' attempts to determine, from a critical examination of codices (manuscripts), the oldest of which were still several centuries removed from the originals, the text of the books of the New Testament and of the Greek and Latin classics.

At the end of the nineteenth century, the techniques that had been developed in biblical and classical studies began to be applied to English literature, especially to works written before the printing press was invented and of which, therefore, a number of manuscript copies were often made. The essential problem was—and is—to establish the date and place of origin of each manuscript and thus, eventually, to construct a pedigree (technically known as a *stammbaum* or *stemma codicum*), at the top of which will stand the manuscript that presumably is closest to the lost original. Sometimes this genealogical diagram will involve hundreds of manuscripts, each with its peculiar variants of phraseology and dialect, its omissions and insertions and different placements of specific lines or passages, its obvious mistakes, and all the other idiosyncrasies that help the scholar to determine its place in the history of the author's text. Of Chaucer's *Canterbury Tales,* there are some ninety manuscripts and early printed versions, either of groups of tales or the whole sequence. An examination of the Manly-Rickert edition based on all these texts will give as impressive an idea as one could wish of the problems editors face as they seek to work back through the maze of later versions to Chaucer's own words.[26]

Needless to say, this kind of research, which ordinarily concentrates on medieval and early Renaissance texts, is not for the novice. One must be able to interpret the significance of scribal errors, dialectal variations, and other varieties of characteristic

[26]See N. F. Blake, *The Textual Tradition of the Canterbury Tales* (London, 1985), and George Kane's essay in *Editing Chaucer: The Great Tradition,* ed. Paul G. Ruggiers (Norman, OK, 1984), both of which discuss the major flaw in Manly-Rickert, its adoption of the Ellesmere manuscript as the base text. A variorum edition of Chaucer's works is now underway. For its relation to Manly-Rickert, see the preface to the volume containing the Miller's Tale.

corruptions for the sake of placing each manuscript in its appropriate chronological-genealogical slot and, more important, of suggesting emendations that will clarify meanings. In addition, an expert knowledge of paleography, a science that includes the study of medieval and Renaissance handwriting, is essential. A certain amount of the requisite knowledge and technical skill can be acquired by reading, but only experience with actual manuscripts, under firm guidance, can produce a finished textual critic.

The contributions that textual study makes to our understanding of literature, then, are twofold. One has already become apparent: an authoritative text is indispensable for the informed criticism of a work considered solely as a finished product. But a text is also an event in time. It has evolved through a number of stages represented by manuscripts, proofs, and successive printed versions, and these, well organized into chronological sequence, offer a matchless means of watching the whole process of literary creation. By presenting the three separate forms (1798–99, 1805, 1850) of Wordsworth's great autobiographical poem *The Prelude,* the Norton Critical Edition, edited by Jonathan Wordsworth, M. H. Abrams, and Stephen Gill, vividly reveals the way the poet's intellect and sensibility both mellowed and hardened over a long span of years. The Victoria and Albert Museum's rich collection of Dickens's memoranda, manuscripts, and proofsheets (including his rough working plans and passages that were discarded for lack of space) permits us to watch a great novelist at work under the new pressures of serial publication: "how he responded to and conveyed 'the feelings of the day', what methods of work he evolved as best suited to his own genius and to the demands of monthly or weekly publication, and above all, how he [learned] to combine the 'circumspection' of preparation with the immediate and intimate relation to his readers which he valued so highly."[27]

[27]John Butt and Kathleen Tillotson, *Dickens at Work* (London, 1957) 9. Additional discussion of Dickens's composing techniques can be found in three articles that focus directly on the memoranda and working plans: Harvey Peter Sucksmith, "Dickens at Work on *Bleak House:* A Critical

Equally valuable, for other reasons, is the comparison of successive printed texts in each of which the author has exercised his privilege of retouching. T. S. Eliot's *The Waste Land,* for instance, appeared in two periodicals (the *Criterion* and the *Dial*), then had a number of separate editions in book form (both British and American), and, in due course, was included in the poet's collected poems. The variant readings in all of Eliot's texts, as one scholar has noted, afford "added insight into recurrent phrasing and themes in the poems and plays and a stricter sense of their chronology and possible interrelationships," as well as "the alterations in phrasing which borrowings from other authors have undergone."[28]

Examination of His Memoranda and Number Plans," *Renaissance & Modern Studies* 9 (1965): 47–85; Paul D. Herring, "Dickens' Monthly Number Plans for *Little Dorrit,*" *MP* 64 (1966): 22–63; and Ernest Boll, "The Plotting of *Our Mutual Friend,*" *MP* 42 (1944): 96–122. The crowning achievement in this branch of Dickens studies, however, is Harry Stone's splendid *Dickens' Working Notes for His Novels* (Chicago, 1987), which reproduces both in exact photographic facsimile and in typographical approximations the novelist's "mems," as he called those notes.

[28]Robert L. Beare, "Notes on the Text of T. S. Eliot: Variants from Russell Square," *SB* 9 (1957): 21–49. A representative sampling of studies of authors' habits of composition and their revisions in manuscript and proof would include: B. C. Southam, *Jane Austen's Literary Manuscripts: A Study of the Novelist's Development Through the Surviving Papers* (Oxford, 1964); Jon Stallworthy, *Between the Lines: Yeats's Poetry in the Making* (Oxford, 1963) and its sequel, *Vision and Revision in Yeats's "Last Poems"* (Oxford, 1969); Jerome Beaty, *"Middlemarch" from Notebook to Novel* (Urbana, IL, 1960); James L. W. West III, *The Making of "This Side of Paradise"* (Philadelphia, 1983); James A. Winn, "Faulkner's Revisions: A Stylist at Work," *AL* 41 (1969): 231–50; T. C. Duncan Eaves and Ben D. Kimpel, "The Composition of *Clarissa* and Its Revision Before Publication," *PMLA* 83 (1968): 416–28; Robert Peters, "A. C. Swinburne's 'Hymn to Proserpine': The Work Sheets," *PMLA* 83 (1968): 1400–1406; and Michael Collie, "Gissing's Revision of *New Grub Street,*" *Yearbook of English Studies* 4 (1974): 212–24. Valuable discussions of current problems and methods in the editing of texts from various periods of English and American literature are found in a series of volumes originating in conferences held at the University of Toronto. See For Further Reading, pp. 268–69.

A textual editing project inconceivable before the advent of computers precipitated one of the most heated debates about authorial final intention—among other issues—in recent years. It involves Joyce's *Ulysses,* whose eventful history is replete with opportunities for corruption. The first edition was set in a French printing house, only one of whose employees knew any English (this in itself was a mixed blessing, because he, like other English-speaking printers to come, took it upon himself to "correct" Joyce's idiosyncratic language, so full of word plays and other kinds of subtle linguistic games). Joyce, nearly blind, was unable to proofread carefully, and in addition he continued to write even as his manuscript was flowing to the printers. Thus Joyce was engaged simultaneously in composing new matter (adding a third to the book's total length) and rewriting old matter time after time as fresh sets of proofs came from the printer. That was bad enough, but worse was to come. The first legitimate American edition, that of Random House in 1934, was not set from a copy of the original Dijon edition, but from one that was still worse, a totally unproofread forgery produced in 1929 for the American pornography trade. It had over eight thousand textual errors. While some of these were subsequently corrected, new ones inevitably crept in. Fortunately, in addition to the five editions published in Joyce's lifetime, an abundance of pre-printing material—manuscripts, typescripts, proofs—survives. But these successive fragmentary versions of the text were so heavily altered by Joyce (see the photoreprint *Joyce Archive* [1977–79] sixteen of whose sixty-three volumes are devoted to *Ulysses*) that no amount of unaided human labor ever could be equal to the task of relating them. Only a computer, it appeared, could determine—for the first time—the text Joyce intended his readers to hold in their hands.

The development of computer technology in the 1970s enabled Hans Walter Gabler, a scholar at the University of Munich, to set up a project designed to establish what he called a "continuous manuscript text" for the novel. Subsidized for seven years by grants that included one of $300,000 from the (then) West German government, Gabler and a team of co-workers employed sophisticated computer-assisted collation toward achieving this highly desirable, if ultimately elusive, end. In 1984 he published the novel "as Joyce wrote it" in three volumes (1,920 pages). This "synoptic text," stripped of its scholarly apparatus, was made more available in one volume, titled *"Ulysses": The Scholarly Text* (1986).

Although some scholars doubted even at first that the five thousand changes effected by Gabler and his co-workers established a text absolutely "as Joyce wrote it," the initial critical reception of *Ulysses: A Critical and Synoptic Edition* was strongly positive. The questions, criticisms, and suggestions that arose developed in a context of overall admiration for success with so formidable a task. That is, until the day when John Kidd, then a postdoctoral fellow at the University of Virginia, offered his first, strongly negative assessment. Kidd eventually devoted three years to scrutinizing the methodology and product of the Gabler team. The fullest expression of his disagreement with the editorial principles and procedures that determined this text appeared in a 173-page review in *PBSA*. The gist of these objections is found in an article in the *New York Review of Books,* where Kidd describes the Gabler edition as a "different version from what Joyce conceived, authored, and saw into print"; inordinately dependent upon facsimiles, photocopies, and microfilms—used without collation with and verification against original documents in many instances—it contains, he alleges, two thousand variant readings "not in any manuscript."[29] In this

---

[29]An overview of this debate—from an initially unbounded faith in the computer to make possible a definitive edition through the edition's favorable reception to Kidd's and others' qualifying statements—can be obtained from the following articles and books: Hugh Kenner, "The Computerized *Ulysses,"* *Harper's Magazine* 260 (April 1980): 89–95; Jerome J. McGann, *"Ulysses* as a Postmodern Text: The Gabler Edition," *Criticism* 27 (1985): 283–305; C. George Sandulescu and Clive Hart, eds., *Assessing the 1984 "Ulysses"* (Totowa, NJ, 1986); John Kidd, "The Scandal of *Ulysses,"* *New York Review of Books*, June 30, 1988: 32–39, and "An Inquiry into *Ulysses: The Corrected Text,"* *PBSA* 82 (1988): 411–584; Philip Gaskell and Clive Hart, *"Ulysses": A Review of Three Texts* (Totowa, NJ, 1989); the special issue ("Editing *Ulysses"*) of *Studies in the Novel* 22 (Summer 1990);

unsatisfactory state of affairs, Kidd recommended that scholars return to the 1961 Modern Library edition, which, though admittedly corrupt, comes closest to the last text that Joyce approved in his lifetime. Eventually a fresh "definitive" edition of *Ulysses* will have to be undertaken.

When it is, it will have the advantage of still more sophisticated electronic equipment and the experience of computer experts who have worked on similar projects. As we have seen, the capability of the Hinman Collator is confined to books printed from a single setting of type, and it can reveal only variants occurring within that narrow framework. But computers can compare texts from different settings, as with the several editions of Henry James's *Daisy Miller*, and the works of Dryden as they are being elaborately presented in the California edition. The current Thackeray edition is another case in point: the editors begin with the author's notes and preliminary drafts, which are not susceptible to computer analysis, but their chief concern is to compare electronically the texts of as many as twenty collected editions of Thackeray's works and, for individual titles, numerous separate printings. Here, the computer makes possible what could scarcely be achieved by unaided human effort alone.

It is likely that few readers of this book will become specialists in textual work. Of all the thousands of literary scholars practicing today, only a comparative handful have either the training or the occasion to qualify as experts. But because all of us reap the benefits of the discipline, we should possess a sound and accurate, if still an outsider's, knowledge of how it operates.

For many years, the standard guide to this field was R. B. McKerrow's *An Introduction to Bibliography for Literary Students* (1927). Concentrating on the early (hand press) period of book production, McKerrow showed how a reconstruction of the way a book was set in type from the author's manuscript

---

and Bruce Arnold, *The Scandal of "Ulysses"* (London, 1991), which provides a connected account of the whole tangled, controversy-ridden affair.

and then passed through the press could provide the essential information on which a study of the history of its text could rest. The most serious limitation of the volume was its neglect of most eighteenth-century developments and its total omission of the subsequent history of printing, from the beginning of the machine press era down to the present age of composition by film and computer. This gap has been filled, and McKerrow's work amplified and corrected in the light of recent research, by Philip Gaskell's *A New Introduction to Bibliography* (1972), which is distinguished by copious illustrations and an excellent reference bibliography. Every prospective literary scholar, even one with no immediate plans to do textual work, should master its contents. A more comprehensive and up-to-date work, no substitute for Gaskell but the best overview of the expanding field, is William Proctor Williams and Craig S. Abbott's *An Introduction to Bibliographical and Textual Studies* (2nd ed., 1989).

2. PROBLEMS OF AUTHORSHIP

After I. A. Richards demonstrated, through the university students' papers quoted in his *Practical Criticism* (1929), how deeply readers' judgments of a poem are affected by their knowledge of its author, some critics and theorists urged, and continue to urge, that a work's origins be disregarded altogether, that it be treated as a free-floating, autonomous artifact, isolated from all externalities and explained and judged solely in terms of itself. But—much as this view goes against the grain of some influential schools of criticism—the fact remains that as human beings we have an ineradicable and perfectly valid desire to know what fellow man or woman created the work that has attracted our attention and we want to know more intimately. The broadest kind of criticism requires that we place that work among the other productions of the same creative intelligence and use to the full the insights they have afforded both into it and into the mind that produced them all.

Knowledge of authorship, therefore, far from diverting critics from their proper business, lights the way. The research that substantiates, or corrects, this knowledge has three chief objects: to identify the author of anonymous or pseudonymous works (or of works attributed to the wrong writer); to decide which parts of a work written by two or more authors belong to each; and to remove from the received list of works whatever pieces are not the writer's, thereby purifying the canon (his or her *authentic* writings).

Certain as we are that Chaucer wrote *The Canterbury Tales,* Thackeray *Vanity Fair,* Gertrude Stein *Three Lives,* Willa Cather *My Ántonia,* and Ernest Hemingway *A Farewell to Arms,* we tend to forget how many cases of undecided authorship crowd the docket of literary history. In some ages the conditions under which literature was written often encouraged, if they did not actually require, concealment of authorship. Before the Renaissance, the poet behind the poem was of little consequence; it was the poem's content and its intended effect that counted, not the negligible human personality that happened to create it. Only during the Tudor period did readers begin to think it important to know who wrote the books they read. But this growing curiosity was frustrated in the case of authors of high social standing who, shrinking from what they considered the vulgarity of public print, circulated their work in manuscript. Such "gentleman amateurs" as Wyatt, Surrey, Sidney, Raleigh, and Donne ("lady amateurs" were virtually unknown until later in the seventeenth century) found their first readers in this form; only after their death were their poems printed for general circulation.[30]

---

[30] Donne's poems are a notable case in point. Only one is known to exist in his own handwriting; a selection first appeared in print in 1633, two years after he died. However, they circulated in more than 250 manuscripts, most at several removes from the originals, and a major task has been to relate these to the hypothetical collections that he himself made from the originals. Two manuscript verse miscellanies, discovered in 1977 at the Scottish Record Office in Edinburgh and now at Texas Tech, contain sixty-eight Donne poems, including a number not found in any of the seventeenth-century printed collections; their presence in these compan-

In the course of time, thousands of poetical miscellanies, as the genre came to be called, were compiled from the contents of these manuscripts and, like the originals, passed around among a circle of friends. In many instances from the Elizabethan age to the middle of the eighteenth century, they also were printed and sold to the public. These anthologies were fertile grounds for incorrect ascriptions, as the authorship of many poems, if it had not already been concealed or lost in the course of recopying, was now suppressed, hidden under initials, or simply misreported. The compilers matched poems and authors on grounds varying from the comparatively responsible (the existence elsewhere of a signed manuscript) to the whimsical (a fancied resemblance to the known work of the author, or a legend attributing the poem to him).

One such manuscript anthology, dating from the 1630s, in the Bodleian Library at Oxford University, was the locale of the best publicized "find" of the 1980s. In it, Gary Taylor, one of the editors of the new Oxford Shakespeare, came upon a poem beginning "Shall I dye, shall I flye / lovers baits, and deceipts / sorrow breeding," at the end of which the scribe had written "William Shakespeare." Announced in the *Times Literary Supplement* for December 20, 1985, the discovery stirred excitement that spread from the scholarly community to the mass media. Was this, or was it not, a hitherto unknown poem from Shakespeare's own pen? (Nobody, not even the people most convinced that it was genuine, claimed it was great poetry.) The whole machinery of authorship study was brought into play, dividing, for a time, the ranks of Shakespeare scholars throughout the world. Probably the most judicious conclusion is that reached by Donald W. Foster in a "post mortem" published in

---

ion manuscripts, dating from the first years of the century, not only supports the modern attribution to him but provides versions of the texts that may be closer to what he actually wrote than any other known. See *The First and Second Dalhousie Manuscripts: Poems and Prose by John Donne and Others: A Facsimile Edition*, ed. Ernest W. Sullivan II (Columbia, MO, 1988).

Shakespeare Quarterly (38 [1987]: 58–77): "If the attribution were sustained by compelling evidence, it might be credited. But the external evidence [consisting solely of the scribe's notation] is not by itself enough to carve a lasting place for this lyric among the poems of William Shakespeare."

Until at least the mid-eighteenth century, the polemicism of some of the books and pamphlets composed by leading literary figures, Dryden, Defoe, Swift, and Fielding among them, made anonymity or pseudonymity the best policy. And then, just as the repressive climate of political and religious opinion was beginning to clear, a strong new force leading to concealment of authorship appeared in the form of journalism. Since the Queen Anne period, many writers have been prolific contributors to newspapers and magazines, and only gradually, during the later Victorian age when the profession of journalism had gained respectability, did their work come to be signed as a matter of custom. Finally (though this does not exhaust the motives authors have had for dissociating themselves from their writings), there is the element of hack work. Authors of high critical stature may write potboilers or books in genres outside that in which they own their reputation, and to keep their literary personalities separate, among other reasons, they use a pseudonym. The mild deceptions occurring on the title pages of detective novels (a future Poet Laureate; an Oxford don; a Columbia University professor of English; and a biographer of Tennyson, Edward FitzGerald, and Gerard Manley Hopkins writing, respectively, as Nicholas Blake, Michael Innes, Amanda Cross, and Robert Bernard) are merely the best-known modern instances of an old practice.[31]

A rare recent case of scholarship unexpectedly adding a previously unknown title to an author's canon occurred at Queen's University, Kingston, Ontario, in 1979. The book was a novel

---

[31]An interesting earlier example is the author of *Little Women*. For details of the blood and thunder novels Louisa May Alcott wrote anonymously or pseudonymously and for the text of four of these, see Madeleine B. Stern, *Behind a Mask: The Unknown Thrillers of Louisa May Alcott* (New York, 1975).

published in 1834 as *A Year at Hartlebury; or, The Election,* the title page stating that it was by "Cherry" and "Fair Star." It made no splash at the time and sank without a trace in the history of English fiction. But researchers at the Disraeli Project at Queen's University, which is producing a complete edition of the politician-novelist Benjamin Disraeli's correspondence, discovered in his early letters references to his having written *A Year at Hartlebury* in collaboration with his sister Sarah. There is no copy of the book in Disraeli's library at his house in Buckinghamshire, and no further mention of it in his correspondence. But the evidence of his co-authorship, particularly of the chapters describing a country election, is conclusive.

The "big name" has loomed large in publishers' calculations ever since Elizabethan times. Astute eighteenth-century publishers sometimes cashed in on the current popularity of an essayist by issuing a volume, or indeed a whole "collected edition," that was padded with work lifted from other writers, but vended (and thence introduced into the canon) as his genuine production. Sterne's vogue in the latter half of the eighteenth century was responsible not only for the publication of some ninety imitations of his works, but for the outright forgery of scores of letters that were put forth as his in various published volumes.[32] The same commercial motive led time after time to the placing of the wrong author's name on the title pages of printed Elizabethan and Jacobean plays, the result being some of the most recalcitrant of all authorship mysteries. Of the fifty-two plays in the second folio (1679) of Beaumont and Fletcher, fewer than twelve actually are by the two dramatists in collaboration. The rest are by Fletcher alone or in collaboration with Massinger or with one or more of a dozen other Jacobean playwrights. Questions of authorship are no less abundant in the Restoration drama. It has been said that "Of the 678 play titles from the period 1660–1700 listed in the Harbage-Schoenbaum *Annals of English Drama* 563 have authors of

---

[32]Lewis P. Curtis, "Forged Letters of Laurence Sterne," *PMLA* 50 (1935): 1076–1106.

some sort ascribed to them. Of these 563, about 80 are significantly questionable."[33]

Despite all this mischief, remarkable progress has been made toward clarifying the record. On matters of authorship we are much better informed than our great-grandfathers were. A hundred years ago, it was still believed that Chaucer had written *The Testament of Love, The Cuckoo and the Nightingale, The Court of Love,* and other poems that had become attached to his name through the centuries. These have now been rejected, and the status of *The Romaunt of the Rose* is doubtful. On the other hand, a scientific treatise brought to light in the library of Peterhouse College, Cambridge, in 1951 is now generally accepted to be Chaucer's, though the evidence is by no means conclusive.

Estimates of the size of Daniel Defoe's canon, which was never deemed negligible, inexorably swelled over the span of two centuries. The first formal list, by George Chalmers in the 1790 edition of *Robinson Crusoe,* attributed 128 titles to him. In Walter Wilson's *Memoirs of the Life and Times of Daniel Defoe* (1830), the number was increased to 210; in William Lee's 1869 biography, it rose to 254; W. P. Trent's list in the *Cambridge History of English Literature* (1907–16), which he claimed to be "very conservative," ran to 382 items. The highwater mark was reached in John Robert Moore's *Checklist of the Writings of Daniel Defoe* (1960, rev. 1971), where no fewer than 570 books and pamphlets were attributed—15 not certainly—to the astonishingly prolific author. It was with good reason that Donald Wing, compiler of the *Short-Title Catalogue of Books Printed in England, Scotland, and Wales . . . 1641–1700,* suggested to the next person who might undertake a similar catalogue "the common sense" policy of listing all anonymous works of the early eighteenth century under Defoe. "If we keep on adding twenty or thirty a year to his corpus, wouldn't it be time-saving to admit now that he probably wrote them all?" The authors of a pun-

[33]Judith Milhous and Robert D. Hume, "Attribution Problems in English Drama, 1660–1700," *Harvard Library Bulletin* 31 (1983): 5–39.

ningly titled recent book on the history of Defoe ascriptions estimate that only 150 items, at most, can be certainly attributed to him.[34]

In recent years, a number of Coleridge's hitherto unknown essays and even a few poems have been located and identified in the periodicals to which he contributed them. Concurrently, however, more than a few pieces previously ascribed to him, sometimes on the strength of his own signature, have been shown to be by other hands.[35]

Some mysteries of attribution are not likely ever to be solved. Examples of Samuel Johnson's hack work await discovery in eighteenth-century newspapers and magazines, though in some cases this discovery in turn awaits the finding of the papers themselves, such as the missing *Birmingham Journal* for 1732–33, in which Johnson's earliest writing was printed.[36] Much of William Cullen Bryant's work is still unretrieved from the files of the *New York Post,* and William Dean Howells's journalism is distributed among the files of sixty American newspapers.

It is quite possible that, in instances like Bryant's, the labor involved in excavating his routine journalism would not be

---

[34]P. N. Furbank and W. R. Owens, *The Canonisation of Daniel Defoe* (New Haven, 1988) 173. This absorbing volume, which includes pen portraits of the men who were responsible for the inordinate expansion of the canon, applies to each alleged Defoe work the latest techniques of author attribution. The Wing quotation is on p. 3.

[35]A still unsettled attribution to Coleridge, a poem titled "The Barberry Tree," is the subject of a symposium in *RES* ns 37 (1986): 348–83. One writer claims it for him, a second for Wordsworth, and a third for—possibly—Thomas Lovell Beddoes. The three articles, taken together, well illustrate the latest techniques of author ascription.

[36]Johnson signed only a small portion of his work. For a good idea of the sources and variable reliability of Johnsonian attributions, including those by Boswell, see Donald J. Greene, "The Development of the Johnson Canon," in *Restoration and Eighteenth-Century Literature: Essays in Honor of Alan Dugald McKillop*, ed. Carroll Camden (Chicago, 1963) 407–27.

justified by the results. But sometimes the game proves eminently worth the candle. Harry Stone has added a quarter of a million words to the fringes, so to speak, of the Dickens canon in the form of essays and sketches printed in the novelist's weekly, *Household Words,* between 1850 and 1859. These are all works of composite authorship. By his extensive alterations Dickens, as editor, often made himself an informal collaborator with the author who submitted the original piece. Combining internal and external evidence, such as the *Household Words* contributors' book and Dickens's editorial correspondence, Stone was able to ascertain with a fair degree of confidence just what parts of a given essay were from Dickens's pen.[37]

Of the two kinds of evidence employed in determining authorship, internal is the more slippery.[38] The premise underlying its use is that every author's work has idiosyncrasies of style, such as preference for Latinate instead of vernacular words, or for certain turns of expression that are repeated time after time. If these characteristics are found in the writings that are unquestionably the author's, then, the argument goes, their occurrence in an unsigned or questioned work is good ground for attributing that work to him or her also. The process is analogous to fitting a piece into a jigsaw puzzle on the basis of matching colors. A noteworthy example of such a proceeding is Stuart M. Tave's *New Essays by De Quincey* (1966). We probably will never know how many of De Quincey's essays and other jour-

---

[37]Instant fame awaits the discoverer of the long-lost contributors' book for *All the Year Round*, which Dickens edited after he killed off *Household Words*. Until it surfaces, one must rely on Ella Ann Oppenlander, *Dickens' "All the Year Round": Descriptive Index and Contributor's List* (Troy, NY, 1984), which uses such evidence as an article's having been republished under its author's name and references to its authorship in other sources.

[38]The most extensive treatments of this aspect of methodology are *Evidence for Authorship: Essays on Problems of Attribution*, ed. David V. Erdman and Ephim G. Fogel; S. Schoenbaum, *Internal Evidence and Elizabethan Dramatic Authorship* (for both, see For Further Reading, p. 270, below); and Furbank and Owens, *The Canonisation of Daniel Defoe* (cited above, n. 34) ch. 3.

nalistic pieces are buried forever in the potter's field of ephemeral periodicals. The author himself forgot them once they had earned him a few pounds, and almost no external clues to their whereabouts exist. Tave, however, was able at least to identify his contributions to the *Edinburgh Saturday Post* and the *Edinburgh Evening Post* in 1827–28 by making literally thousands of cross-references from the undisputed De Quincey canon to the suspected essays in the newspapers' files. Such a feat was possible only because he had made his mind a sensitive detecting device by saturating it with De Quincey's characteristic ideas and peculiarities of style.

Methodical comparison of style (the disputed work laid alongside the settled canon) can take us some distance toward establishing authorship, but so long as it is done manually, so to speak, it can never be wholly free of impressionism. Impressionistic judgments have their place in literary study if they rest on a solid foundation of knowledge and esthetic perception. Long and intensive study of an author's works attunes the scholar's ear, as no amount of mechanical analysis can do, to his or her true and subtle accents. Scholars seeking to decide the genuineness of a literary work are in the position of art experts called in to authenticate a museum's new acquisition. Other tests proving inconclusive, they must finally rely upon their knowledge of the way the artist customarily worked. When specialists who have spent years reading and rereading an author declare that a disputed piece is genuine, their intuitive expertness must be given respectful attention. Yet no such verdict can ever be regarded as final.

It is in the hope of eliminating the uncertainty springing from subjective judgments that some scholars have turned to the new "science" of stylometry, a sophisticated computer-assisted technique now being used for a variety of purposes. The computer can analyze and classify, in whatever ways are desired, such elements of an author's style as word frequency, sentence length and structure, rhetorical and grammatical forms, metrical or other repetitive patterns, and special techniques—Chaucer's alliteration, for example, or Milton's use of names or other elements from a particular source or imagery of a specific type, astrological, biblical, historical, literary, or mythological. The basis of the attempted discrimination or identification remains the familiar cluster of characteristics that differentiate one author's style from that of others, or, conversely, reveal stylistic affinities between two or more authors. The computer method, however, is much faster and superhumanly capable of handling complicated relationships. Perhaps most important, it reduces the possibility of impressionistic conclusions.[39]

One of the latest major attempts to determine attribution has used a combination of old and new methodologies. In Martin C. Battestin's *New Essays by Henry Fielding: His Contributions to "The Craftsman" (1734–1739) and Other Early Journalism* (1989), the text of each of forty-one essays previously unascribed to Fielding is accompanied by a formidable array of "parallels" of language and idea found in works known to be his—a procedure available only to a scholar such as has just been described, one whose long immersion in the writings of the author in question has sensitized him to every characteristic turn of phrase and idea. An appendix to the book contains a "stylometric analysis" that reaches the same conclusions that Battestin reached by the subjective route, but goes beyond the listing of constant echoes of the established canon (i.e., internal parallels) to a comparison of the texts with samples of writings of other persons to whom the problematic pieces might, on other grounds, be ascribed.

The stylometric technique has figured in recent Shakespeare scholarship, where the issue of whether Shakespeare wrote certain plays in their entirety, or whether they are collaborations, has long, even tiresomely, been vexed. Semiotic surveys

---

[39]For a good exposition of computer-assisted analyses of quantifiable aspects of style, see two works on Milton by Thomas N. Corns: *The Development of Milton's Prose Style* (New York, 1982) and *Milton's Language* (Cambridge, MA, 1987). A more narrowly focused study considers ideolects in Jane Austen: J. F. Burrows, *Computation into Criticism: A Study of Jane Austen's Novels and an Experiment in Method* (Oxford, 1987).

have been made of the characteristic styles of the whole company of Elizabethan playwrights, Shakespeare's contemporaries, who might conceivably have had a hand in writing the
plays attributed to him. The result has been that the presence of
Fletcher, Middleton, Nashe, and perhaps one or two others has
been detected in half a dozen plays that are mainly Shakespeare's. The stylometric method seems also to have strengthened the case for Shakespeare's having actually been the coauthor, with John Fletcher, of one play hitherto only tentatively
attributed to him, *The Two Noble Kinsmen*. The consensus
among relatively conservative scholars is that while stylometry
promises to be of much assistance in settling questions of authorship, it will not replace more traditional approaches in the
foreseeable future.[40]

Stylometrics apart, the logic of author attribution works both
ways. A scholar's practiced ear may testify that a given piece of
writing is genuine because it "sounds like" the author in question. On the other hand, it may induce the scholar to reject the
attribution on the ground that it does not ring true. But, while
it may very well not be "like" the author as we ordinarily conceive his or her style to be, can we not assume circumstances in
which a writer's manner would markedly change? It is hardly
credible that the same poet who wrote

> O darling room, my heart's delight,
> Dear room, the apple of my sight,
> With thy two couches soft and white,
> There is no room so exquisite,

[40]The most exhaustive survey of the Shakespeare canon, including descriptions of the various authorship tests applied, is in Stanley Wells and Gary
Taylor, *William Shakespeare: A Textual Companion* (Oxford, 1987) 69–
144. In their Oxford edition of Shakespeare's works, they print the passages in the plays of contested authorship that are attributed to Shakespeare, along with the arguments pro and con. For a concise history of the
statistical study of literary style, see Anthony Kenny, *The Computation of
Style: An Introduction to Statistics of Literature and the Humanities* (Oxford, 1982) ch. 1.

No little room so warm and bright,
Wherein to read, wherein to write

also was responsible for the melancholy magic of

Dark house, by which once more I stand
  Here in the long unlovely street,
  Doors, where my heart was used to beat
So quickly, waiting for a hand,

A hand that can be clasp'd no more—
  Behold me, for I cannot sleep,
  And like a guilty thing I creep
At earliest morning to the door.

He is not here; but far away
  The noise of life begins again,
  And ghastly thro' the drizzling rain
On the bald street breaks the blank day.

But Tennyson wrote both poems, and at a remove of no more than fifteen years. Nor is an author's style consistent even within a short span of time; one day he may write prose that critics readily identify as characteristic of his ripest genius, and the next may turn out slovenly stuff reminiscent of the writer's earlier days as a penny-a-line hack. There are therefore numerous reasons why, despite our feeling that a questioned work is "uncharacteristic" of its putative author, it may nevertheless be genuine. Although the presence of features not usually found in a writer's works (or, conversely, the absence of features that are normally present) may be a point against its inclusion in the canon, we must remember that no artist is wholly consistent or predictable, and a poem or novel that has little in common with the rest of an author's work may yet be authentic.

Luckily, another kind of internal evidence—contentual—is often available to substantiate or control a judgment reached by the analysis of style. For one thing, the ideas put forth in a disputed or totally unascribed piece may closely resemble those expressed in a writer's authentic work. How much weight this similarity will carry in the total argument depends on the number of resemblances and, even more, on the degree of idiosyncrasy, the special angle and emphasis, that set this individual's opinions apart from those of others who think in generally the same way. For another, there may be intimate allusions to persons, such as patrons or close friends, which only the writer would be likely to make, or to fairly obscure authors for whom he is known to have cherished an eccentric preference; or the text may contain mention of events that have special meaning to him and that no other writer would refer to precisely as he does. Sometimes, too, there may be references to other works that are surely the author's but which were then unpublished and which he alone would have known about. These are examples of what we might call the test of unique knowledge, a sort of corollary to the test of unique style. To the stylistic question "Could any other author have written this way?" it adds: "Could any other author have known what this writer knew?"

The several kinds of contentual evidence are well illustrated by the experience of John Pitcher, a British scholar who was engaged in editing the works of the Elizabethan poet Samuel Daniel, replacing the old and defective edition of A. B. Grosart. In April 1978, while working in the Brotherton Library at the University of Leeds, Pitcher's attention was called to an untitled and anonymous seventeenth-century (1620s or 1630s) manuscript of verse epistles the library had bought at Sotheby's some years earlier and placed on display in the reading room. It was open at the first page of text. "Reading casually the first thirty lines of the Epistle to Prince Henry," Pitcher recounted later, "[I] found before me (to my surprise) the ideas, verse rhythms, phrasing, and vocabulary of none other than Samuel Daniel." This instant recognition was due, of course, to his long absorption in Daniel's known works. But intuition, however solidly based, was not enough to prove Daniel's authorship of this manuscript, and so Pitcher submitted it to the contentual test, which drew upon everything that was known of the supposed author's biography as well as his works. Such information consisted, in this case, of evidence in the text that the author had court connections and was a professional writer, that he was familiar with a prose treatise by Sir Robert Cotton, and that he was elderly and in ill health. These clues, along with self-borrowings, stylistic traits, and the presence of motifs characteristic of Daniel, convinced Pitcher that, given this convergence of clues, no other poet of the time could have written those verse epistles.[41]

Again like art experts, literary scholars trying to solve a problem of authenticity ransack external sources for possible support of their attributions. Perhaps the piece in question is referred to by the author in a private document or in another literary work—Chaucer left valuable lists of his poems in the Introduction to *The Man of Law's Tale* and the Prologue to *The Legend of Good Women*. Ordinarily, if an author says he wrote such-and-such a work, we can believe him, although writers have been known to claim books that were not theirs, and others have refused to acknowledge books that were.[42] Or, at

---

[41]See John Pitcher, *Samuel Daniel: The Brotherton Manuscript: A Study in Authorship* (Leeds Texts and Monographs, ns 7 [1981]). It might be added that in an appendix, Pitcher records the objections a fellow scholar, I. A. Shapiro, raised to his identification and his point-by-point rebuttal: a model of scholarly debate carried on with the utmost courtesy.

[42]It is advisable, though, to be sure he said what he is represented as saying. The printed text of a letter of February 1792 has Robert Burns asserting that, of the bawdy songs in *The Merry Muses of Caledonia*, "A very few of them are my own." This may be, and has been, read in two ways: either as a confession or as a denial of more than minimum guilt, depending on how one feels about Burns. But no such statement appears in the holograph; it was inserted when Burns's first biographer, Dr. Currie, printed the letter. "It is now plain," wrote DeLancey Ferguson, who discovered the original (*MLN* 66 [1951]: 471–73), "that Burns neither affirmed nor denied having enriched his collection with additions of his own. . . . The student must therefore scrutinize with new alertness every bawdy lyric which survives in the poet's handwriting, or which contemporary opinion attributed to him. The pious defenders of the Burns legend can no longer brush these compositions aside as mere transcripts of folk songs. The burden of proof is shifted: unless the defenders can show that a given song was already known in Burns's day, we must assume that he wrote it."

least as often, someone who was in a position to know recorded that a given poem or essay was written by so-and-so. (Milton's nephew and pupil, Edward Phillips, for example, left a similar list of his uncle's writings.) Such statements are useful, if true, but each must be evaluated according to the rules of evidence described in chapter 2. Was the witness in a position to know the truth? Is his statement founded on accurate knowledge or simply a report of hearsay? Any reason not to tell the truth?— and so forth.

All these kinds of external evidence were used in the compilation of the deservedly celebrated *Wellesley Index to Victorian Periodicals* (1966–89). This work identifies some twelve thousand of the writers who contributed articles printed in forty-three British quarterlies and monthlies during the great era (1824–1900) of "the higher journalism," when approximately 90 percent of the periodicals' contents were unsigned. The bibliographies of many Victorian authors have been enlarged by, in some instances, scores and even hundreds of hitherto unascribed items. The magnitude of the editors' achievement is indicated by the fact that of the eighty-nine thousand articles they list, they were able to identify the authors of some 86 percent.[43]

Even technical bibliographical evidence may help in author ascription. A number of years ago, Donald F. Bond, analyzing the typography and text matter (including advertisements) of

---

For later information, on the revised view of Burns's contributions that was made possible by the discovery of the Cunningham manuscript in the British Museum, see G. Legman's edition of *The Merry Muses* (New Hyde Park, NY, 1965). Legman's long introduction also describes the vicissitudes the collection underwent in the course of its many reprintings as a popular under-the-counter literary item.

[43]For a detailed consideration of the problem of anonymity in English periodicals, with numerous examples drawn from the Wellesley editors' experience, see Mary Ruth Hiller's chapter in *Victorian Periodicals: A Guide to Research,* ed. J. Don Vann and Rosemary T. Van Arsdel (New York, 1978) 123–48.

the folio sheets that constituted the first printing of the *Spectator,* discovered that the essay-paper was produced by two different printers, who worked on alternate issues so as to have time to strike off enough copies to meet the demand. Evidently Printer A (Jacob Tonson) and Printer B (unknown) each received the work of a different set of contributors. Since the issues Tonson printed contained almost all that have been identified of the twenty-seven papers attributed in *Spectator 555* to Eustace Budgell, it is logical to expect that Budgell's other papers, when they are identified, will be in Tonson's sequence. Discovery of this system of alternate printing, furthermore, is likely to alter the existing ascription of unsigned essays, because copy from Addison's friends seems to have gone to Tonson and that from Steele's to the other printer.[44]

On the very borderline between internal and external evidence—on the title page of a book or pamphlet, or at the foot of a periodical essay—lies the pseudonym: "Peter Parley" (Samuel G. Goodrich), "Olphar Hamst" (an anagram for Ralph Thomas), "Orpheus C. Kerr" ("office seeker": R. H. Newell), "Z" (Hannah More), "G. Forrest" (the Rev. J. G. Wood). Most pseudonyms of concern to a student of English or American literature, along with anonymous books whose authors have been identified, are listed in the standard, though not always authoritative, reference work on the subject, Halkett and Laing's nine-volume *Dictionary of Anonymous and Pseudonymous English Literature.*[45]

By now it is apparent that the certainty of an ascription is proportional to the cumulative weight of evidence, both inter-

---

[44]Donald F. Bond, "The First Printing of the *Spectator,*" *MP* 47 (1950): 164–77.

[45]Connoisseurs of adulterism, apoconyms, boustrophedons, demonyms, hieronyms, initialism, pharmaconyms, pseudandry, pseudojyns, pseudotitlonyms, stigmonyms, syncopism, telonism, translationism, and kindred phenomena will find much to occupy them in ch. 3 of W. P. Courtney's *Secrets of Our National Literature* (London, 1908) and in the introduction to the second edition of Halkett and Laing, 1: xi–xxiii. (Unfortunately, it does not appear in the new third edition, 1980–.)

nal and external. Seldom can style or content, alone or in combination, be taken as virtual proof that a questioned work was written by a particular author; and only the most unequivocal kind of external data can provide that near-proof where internal evidence is ambiguous or lacking. Rather, it is the convergence of diverse types of evidence that comes nearest to clinching an argument about authorship.[46]

The essence of what has been said in this section is illustrated by a fairly romantic story. In 1628 the London printer Thomas Walkley issued a volume of amatory poetry called *Brittain's Ida,* "written," as the title page proudly averred, "by that Renowned Poet Edmund Spenser," who had died twenty-one years earlier. In a dedicatory letter to Lady Mary Villiers, Walkley said that he was "certainly assured by the ablest and most knowing men, that it must be a Worke of Spencers, of whom it were a pitty that any thing should be lost." Nevertheless, not all students of Spenser in the following centuries were willing to believe that the poem was a sibling of *The Faerie Queene;* for one thing, Spenser's celebrity had been so great that booksellers were sorely tempted to publish under his name poems that were not his. Some editors of the poet's works omitted *Brittain's Ida* altogether; others printed it, but with reservations. A few critics, notably Thomas Warton, detected occasional stylistic resemblances to *The Purple Island* (1633), the most considerable poem by Phineas Fletcher, who was a leading imitator of Spenser. In 1869 the Reverend A. B. Grosart went a step further and tried to make a formal case for Fletcher's authorship. His fellow students of Elizabethan literature, however, were not impressed. The author of the article on Fletcher in the *Dictionary of National Biography* was noncommittal; George Saintsbury, who had read everything and sometimes gave the impression that he knew everything, maintained that there was no real evidence for the attribution; and Edmund Gosse somewhat perversely came out for Phineas's brother Giles instead.

[46]This convergence is well illustrated in William H. Marshall, "An Addition to the Hazlitt Canon: Arguments from External and Internal Evidence," *PBSA* 55 (1961): 347–70. For a later example involving the same canon, see John O. Hayden, "Hazlitt Reviews Hazlitt?" *MLR* 64 (1969): 20–26.

Forty years after Grosart's unavailing effort to add *Brittain's Ida* to the Phineas Fletcher canon, F. S. Boas tried again, founding his case wholly on the evidence in the text. In the poem, he argued, occurred passages that were remarkably similar to those in works that nobody doubted Phineas Fletcher had written. He cited scores of words that the author used in senses peculiar to Fletcher, and he showed too that many of the images were duplicated in exactly similar contexts in Fletcher's authentic pieces. But, like every argument based exclusively on stylistic resemblances, Boas's fell far short of certainty.

In the mid-1920s Ethel Seaton, rummaging through the library at Sion College, London, happened upon a manuscript volume composed of several sections bound together in fairly modern times and catalogued, vaguely, as "Latin and English MSS. on Paper, 17th Century." Its contents were variegated: mathematical calculations by some Elizabethan savants; two treatises on usury; a partial draft of a "Harmony of the Four Evangelists"—interesting pieces, perhaps, but hardly of literary importance. She turned to the last portion of the volume, badly stained by water during the Great Fire of 1666, which had destroyed part of the Sion College library. "English Pastorals," read the manuscript title. "Venus and Anchises, etc." There was no indication of authorship.

Seaton turned over the pages and quickly realized that, though she had never heard of "Venus and Anchises," she had read the poem; for here, under a title inscribed by some seventeenth-century pen, was *Brittain's Ida,* the poem Walkley had confidently attributed to Spenser. But Walkley had not printed all that the manuscript contained, and in the omitted portions lay the key to the real author. In two introductory stanzas, missing from the 1628 text, the author spoke of himself as "Thirsil" and referred to himself as writing on the banks of the Cam. As every student of early seventeenth-century literature knows, only one poet used the pseudonym of "Thirsil" time after time, and only one was so much in love with the Cam that it plays, as Seaton observes, "almost the part of a chorus" in his poetry. That one was Phineas Fletcher. Nor was this all. In the same manuscript volume, Seaton found several other poems whose authorship had never been doubted, because they had been printed in 1633, in the *Purple Island* volume. The internal and external evidence, in other words, converged upon one writer, and Grosart, in this instance, was proved right after all.[47]

3. THE SEARCH FOR ORIGINS

The possible sources of a literary work are as numerous and varied as the writer's whole experience of life. They may be people known to the author, who have served as prototypes for fictional characters; by learning all we can about those real-life models and a writer's relations with them, as has been done with much success in the cases of Thackeray, Conrad, Joyce, Hemingway, and Thomas Wolfe, among others, we can reconstruct his own view of them and thus clarify the significance of their fictional counterparts. Sources may be, as well, visual impressions, whether direct observation of scenes (a distant prospect of Eton College, or Westminster Bridge in the early morning) or graphic representations (church windows, tapestries, statues, engravings in a favorite childhood book); or they may be a combination of sight and sound (Whitman's poetry sometimes reveals the effect of his attendance at the opera); or they may be contemporary events in which a writer has participated or about which he has read (the attempt to blow up Greenwich Observatory on February 15, 1894, reflected in Conrad's *The Secret Agent,* and the British fire-bombing of Dresden, February 13–14, 1945, in Kurt Vonnegut's *Slaughterhouse Five*).

But while any kind of experience that has somehow affected the content and style of a literary work is, properly speaking, one of its sources, in practice source study concentrates on literary origins: the fund of phrase, image, plot, character, device, and idea an author accumulated through reading. This is reasonable enough, for the chief debt any work of art owes is to its predecessors in the same medium—compare music, for

---

[47]The *Brittain's Ida* story is told in F. S. Boas's edition of the *Poetical Works of Giles and Phineas Fletcher* (Cambridge, 1909) 2: xiii–xxi, and in Seaton's edition of the manuscript (London, 1926).

example, or painting. In addition, the evidence of literary indebtedness as a rule is more concrete than that of other kinds
of "inspiration," because we have, for whatever it may prove to
be worth, the testimony of printed pages laid side by side. But,
as we shall see, determining literary sources requires great tact
and caution; intelligently conducted, it is anything but the mechanical exercise it is often mistaken to be.

The whole topic of source study enters the present pages, as
it does any discussion of modern literary scholarship, trailing
clouds of stigma. During much of this century, no branch of
research brought the academic study of literature into greater
dispute among laypersons. Even before the century began, indeed, Lord Tennyson saw what was coming, and, already a
victim, deplored it on behalf of all poets—past, present, and
future. "There is, I fear," he wrote in a letter in 1882, "a prosaic
sect growing among us, editors of booklets, book-worms, index-
hunters, or men of great memories and no imagination, who
impute themselves to the poet, and so believe that *he,* too, has
no imagination, but is for ever poking his nose between the
pages of some old volume in order to see what he can appropriate. They will not allow one to say 'Ring the bell' without
finding that we have taken it from Sir P. Sidney, or even to use
such a simple expression as the ocean 'roars,' without finding
out the precise verse in Homer or Horace from which we have
plagiarized it (fact!)."[48]

Like the mythical scholarly passion for counting the commas

---

[48][Hallam Tennyson], *Alfred Lord Tennyson: A Memoir* (New York, 1897)
1:258. According to Edmund Gosse, who admittedly tended to improve
anecdotes in the telling, Tennyson later called the waspish critic Churton
Collins, who had accused him of excessive unacknowledged adoption of
other poets' language, "a louse upon the locks of literature." If the story
were true, by a superb stroke of irony Tennyson's choice of metaphor
inadvertently illustrated the very "fault" with which Collins taxed him. He
was echoing Smollett's *Humphry Clinker,* in which Matthew Bramble says
of an unnamed author he met in London, "he damns all the other writers
of the age, with the utmost insolence and rancour. One is a blunderbuss
. . . another, a half-starved louse of literature" (Ann Thwaite, *Edmund
Gosse: A Literary Landscape, 1849–1928* [Chicago, 1984] 296).

in *Piers Plowman*, the widely publicized, and admittedly all too prevalent, zeal for discovering the obscure places where a poet was alleged to have lifted his material became a symbol, to the world at large, of all that was niggling, pedantic, and futile in scholarship. While some such exercises were of indisputable value, far too many were pretentious wastes of time and misapplications of scholarly diligence. Although they were theoretically dedicated to revealing the ways of the imagination, their main effect was to disclose how little of that gift some professional students of literature themselves possessed and how inadequately they understood its operation in others. Too often, casual or unremarkable similarities were interpreted as evidence of one writer's dependence on another. Year after year, articles and monographs rested their proof that Author B had borrowed from Author A on such slender grounds as the fact that in their works both introduced precocious children or scenes in bawdy houses, or were anti-Gallic, or had a somewhat similar vein of humor, or displayed a marked familiarity with Chaucer or horsemanship, or were fond of exclamations like "By St. Paul!" and "I swear!", or had a habit of ending their sentences with prepositions.[49]

Today the criteria by which we judge the evidence of indebtedness are stricter. While the journals still occasionally print articles that are content to pinpoint a source and let it go at that, all good source study is governed by the principles laid down by Rosamond Tuve in her study of the liturgical and iconographic background of George Herbert's "The Sacrifice." The first is that "Origins are relevant to criticism only if they illuminate meaning and thus deepen feeling"—if they help to explain the meanings a poem had for "one of its greatest readers—the author." The second is that "the biography of elements in a poem . . . must follow the same stern

---

[49]These are not exaggerations or fancies. They are among the seventy-odd "types of evidence employed by scholars concerned primarily with canons, literary influence, and source relationships" that George C. Taylor enumerated in "Montaigne-Shakespeare and the Deadly Parallel," *PQ* 22 (1943): 330–37.

rules as biographical study of authors to be critically relevant."[50]

Tuve wrote long before the explicit concept of intertextuality appeared, by that name, in literary criticism, but the connection she described between the meanings (plural) that a poem had for its author and the sources he or she drew upon clearly foreshadowed it. Intertextuality in this sense refers to the significant relationship between specific and in some way similar passages in two or more authors' work, the significance residing in the way the original meaning changed as it resonated in the work of a later one, where it appeared in a new context and with some—perhaps major—difference of purpose and effect. A single passage, for example a familiar phrase or line in classical poetry, Homer or Virgil or Ovid, might turn up again in the works of poets in English from Shakespeare to Wallace Stevens, and every time it appeared, it not only was subtly colored or modified by the immediate occasion but bore whatever additional nuances it had acquired in its passage through the centuries. The critic John Hollander, himself a poet, puts it this way:

> . . . poems seem to echo prior ones for the personal aural benefit of the poet, and of whichever poetic followers can overhear the reverberations. Poets also seem to echo earlier voices with full or suppressed consciousness that, and of how, they are doing so, by accident or plan, but with the same shaping spirit that gives form to tropes of thought and feeling. Whether these figurative echoes constitute a kind of underground cipher-message for the attentive poetic ear, or perhaps a private melody or undersong during the composition by the poet as a spell or charm, matters less to me than

[50]*A Reading of George Herbert* (London, 1952) 92–93. Note also Mona Wilson's wise words (*Sir Philip Sidney* [London, 1931] 314): "The search for sources may become the dreariest form of pedantry when pursued by those who understand neither how a poet writes, nor even how an educated man reads. The literature of Italy and of antiquity was to the Elizabethans what Shakespeare and the Authorized Version became to later generations, the atmosphere they breathed, and not a topic to be got up for theses."

that the revisionary power of allusive echo generates new figuration.[51]

The reminiscence may take the form, in declining degrees of similarity, of a literal quotation from the earlier author, or of an unquoted, perhaps paraphrased allusion that the author relies on readers to recognize and, therefore, to respond to the new context, or, more vaguely, of an echo of which he or she may be unconscious. Thus source study today has acquired extra validity. Its purpose is not simply to demonstrate that Poet B "borrowed" from Poet A, but to establish the critical signifi-cance of that event in relation both to the poet's intention and to the way it affected readers.[52]

The second of Rosamond Tuve's principles, that source study must be governed by the same rigorous rules to which other kinds of literary investigation are subject, remains in effect today. In seeking to determine precisely where a borrowing or echo originated, good methodology requires us to differentiate between a direct source or borrowing, on the one hand, and a parallel or analogue on the other. When we speak of a direct source, we usually mean that certain elements in poem y are found elsewhere only in the antecedent poem x and therefore, barring independent invention,[53] must have been derived from

---

[51]*The Figure of Echo: A Mode of Allusion in Milton and After* (Berkeley, 1981) [ix].

[52]See the books listed in n. 67, pp. 131–32.

[53]Raymond D. Havens ("A Parallel That Is Not a Borrowing," *MLN* 66 [1951]: 271) cited a comment by John Henry Newman on Thomson's poetry that expresses "the same unusual idea—that poetry presents natu-ral objects with a meaning, or glory, not their own—and end[s] with the same simple but striking phrase" as did Wordsworth in *The Prelude,* book 5. (Newman: ". . . a meaning, beauty, and harmonious order not their own." Wordsworth: ". . . with glory not their own.") The obvious conclu-sion is that Newman had read Wordsworth. But Newman's essay was printed in 1829, and *The Prelude,* though the words in question were written in 1806, lay in manuscript until 1850. "The similarities," com-mented Havens, ". . . are closer than most of the parallels on which many,

x. But even if the elements that suggest the relationship are earlier found in other places besides *x*, it may still be likely that *x* was the immediate source; we may know, for instance, that the poet was reading *x* shortly before he wrote *y*, and hence the reasonable presumption is that he got his idea there rather than anywhere else. "Parallel" and "analogue," on the other hand, imply that neither internal nor external evidence is strong enough to make us confident that *y* derives from *x*. While certain features of poem *y* are indeed found in *x*, they occur fairly often in preceding or concurrent literature, and the fact that they are found in *y* may equally well—in the absence of more specific indications—be due to antecedents floating at large in the nebulous realm of literary tradition or intellectual milieu.

Here is a very elementary illustration of the problem posed by a resemblance between passages in two separate books. Douglas Bush (*The Renaissance and English Humanism* [1939] 18) speaks of "that old definition of a scholar—a siren which calls attention to a fog without doing anything to dispel it." Twenty-eight years earlier, Thomas Lounsbury (*The Early Literary Career of Robert Browning* [1911] 196) had written, "In fact, commentaries on Browning bear a close resemblance to fog-horns. They proclaim the existence of fog; but they do not disperse it." The similarity can be explained in either of these ways:

1. Bush consciously or unconsciously remembered the words he had once read in Lounsbury and could have found the remark nowhere else.

2. The quip, at the time Bush wrote, was in oral circulation, a bit of change in the petty-cash drawer of academic wit. It may have originated with Lounsbury, or it may have existed earlier and merely happened to alight in print in his book; but in either case, Bush, in writing *The Renaissance and English Human-*

----

all too many, articles submitted to learned journals are based." Yet they cannot be used to prove anything except that coincidences do occur in literary history.

ism, was drawing upon the orally transmitted version—unassignable to any one person—rather than adapting Lounsbury's.
These, then, are the several possible routes of descent:

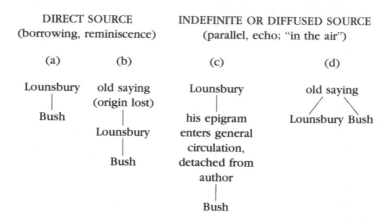

| DIRECT SOURCE | INDEFINITE OR DIFFUSED SOURCE |
| (borrowing, reminiscence) | (parallel, echo; "in the air") |

We shall not attempt to adjudicate among these possibilities—
one unsolved question is whether the epigram originally was
applied to scholars in general or commentators on Browning in
particular—but they typify some of the alternatives presented
by a question of derivation.

Of all the devices used by students of literary genetics, the
most seductive and the most laden with potential fallacy is the
parallel passage: two sequences of lines whose resemblances
are such as to suggest that the author of one sequence knew,
perhaps deliberately imitated, the other. No type of scholarly
evidence has been more frequently (and sometimes ludicrously) abused than the parallel passage, chiefly because the
desire to establish an open-and-shut case has obscured the true
subtlety of the way the creative imagination works in the midst
of a literary tradition and contemporary atmosphere. One commonsense question should accompany all attempts to establish
the direct indebtedness of one author to another on the grounds
of verbal similarities: Might not the resemblances be attributable
to the fact that both Author A and Author B were nourished by
the same culture?

In the Elizabethan age, for instance, there was a rich fund of expressions and images, originating everywhere from the classics to rural proverbial lore, which was available to and used by everybody from Ben Jonson to the earliest denizens of Grub Street. Shakespeare and his contemporaries constantly quoted or paraphrased the Bible or Ovid without much awareness of the eventual "sources" on which they were drawing. We do the same thing today when we employ phrases like "more in sorrow than in anger," "foul play," "the primrose path," "rich, not gaudy," "more honored in the breach than the observance," and "something is rotten in the state of Denmark": none of which is evidence that we have read a single line of *Hamlet*. They are merely phrases that, like innumerable lines in the King James Bible, have long since become detached from their matrix and flowed into the broad stream of everyday English discourse. To interpret a set of similar expressions as evidence of a writer's knowledge of another's works may well be to assume derivation where there is only echo—the echo of scores of other writers who were using the same forms of language simply because it was the normal thing to do. "Like this, therefore derived from this" is the commonest of all the fallacies that tempt the inquirer after sources.

Although verbal parallels are the most familiar kind of source-evidence, all other components of literary works lend themselves to borrowing. Inevitably, writers in every genre are affected by what other writers in the same genre have already done. The plot of the cheater cheated, or the tables turned, goes back at least as far as Roman comedy and has been used by dramatists and novelists ever since. Such characters as the termagant wife, the pompous pedant, the comic manservant, and the country bumpkin are so commonly encountered in literature that to assert that they owe their appearance in one work specifically to their presence in another is foolhardy, unless there are strong grounds for asserting that particular association. The author may have found a suggestion in any, or all, of a dozen other works. Dickens, as a youth, read Smollett, Fielding, Goldsmith, Cervantes, LeSage, and other comic writers; though they deeply influenced his own comic imagination, it is well-nigh impossible to say which of his episodes and habits of characterization he derived from any of them.

We are coming more and more to realize, too, how large a debt some authors have owed to the popular, or sub-literary, reading matter that stimulated their imaginations, especially in their formative years. Shelley was an avid reader of the Gothic novels of his day; the imaginative bent of Scott, Coleridge, Wordsworth, and others was shaped by their childhood reading of ballads and chapbook romances; Mark Twain's genius was affected by the tall-tale humor of the frontier, expressed and transmitted by word of mouth, in newspapers, and in obscurely printed leaflets and books. Because the materials characteristic of these popular forms were so broadly disseminated, seldom being exclusively associated with one author or work, the result of source investigations is often the statement that *"books of this sort"* suggested this manner of writing, or that kind of character, to a certain writer; to particularize is an impossibility.

And so with ideas. The literature of every age is permeated with opinions and assumptions that are nobody's, and everybody's: they are the freely circulated legal tender of a period's mind. In the past several decades historians of ideas have amply demonstrated how widely diffused in a given period were dominant ideas that once were assumed to have been more or less the property of a few influential thinkers. The Renaissance mind was replete with standard (but not necessarily uniform) notions on religion, politics, science, cosmology, and every other topic of human interest, and the literature of the time is a bountiful expression of those opinions. Shakespeare may have read Montaigne's *Essais,* but even if he had not, his frequent echoes of the French philosopher's ethical observations might adequately be accounted for by the fact that these were favorite capsules of wisdom. We cannot hope ever to identify all the books that contributed, overtly or subtly, to the poems of Milton, one of the most erudite and assimilative of English authors. He was steeped in the literature of theology and travel and science, in the classic epic, in the numerous neo-Latin, French, and Italian works that contained, in one form or another, portions of the story of the Fall of Man. The existing scholarly discussion of his sources, in fact, is a small library in itself. Some sources can be identified by author and title, but much of the material Milton drew upon was so widely distributed—the same ideas about astronomy, for instance, are found in encyclopedia after encyclopedia that he could have seen—that the only sensible conclusion we can reach is that his genius had an extraordinary power of transmuting intellectual commonplaces into great art.

The attempt to establish a particular source, again like the attempt to determine authorship, is aided by the convergence of evidence, both internal and external. The stronger the internal evidence, in nature and amount, the better the case; but the intuitive element cannot be wholly eliminated from such an argument. External evidence, therefore, has to be sought to substantiate the inferences made from a comparison of the text with its suspected source of inspiration and to serve as a check on whatever impressionism colors our thinking. The most important question to be asked is so obvious that it is sometimes overlooked: Did our author read the book from which he seems to have borrowed? If he owned a copy, as might be established by the catalogue printed when his books were sold after his death or by the survival of the copy itself, the presumption is that he did read it. But possession of a book is no positive proof of its owner's having even glanced inside it. More convincing evidence is the presence in the volume of underscorings and annotations written by the owner. Some writers had such a habit, and scholars who have followed such writers' reading, as thus marked out, have been in a peculiarly advantageous position to understand the movement of their minds and the way they transformed and incorporated the harvest of their reading into their art.[54]

[54]For some interesting examples of the scholarly work that has been done on identifying the contents of, and in some instances reassembling, great authors' libraries, see Geoffrey Keynes, *The Library of Edward Gibbon* (London, 1940), and the same editor's *Bibliography of Dr. John Donne* (3rd ed., Cambridge, 1958) 204–22; John C. Hodges, *The Library of William Congreve* (New York, 1955); Walter Harding, *Emerson's Library* (Charlottesville, VA, 1967); Allen T. Hazen, *A Catalogue of Horace Wal-*

Equally useful are the allusions authors make in their formal published work to books they have read. The letters and diaries of many writers also are replete with comments on the books they have been reading, and in addition, some authors, such as Milton, Coleridge, Shelley, and Matthew Arnold, kept commonplace books into which they copied extracts from their reading. Another avenue of investigation lies in the books an author would have had to read at school and university. The published curriculum and other contemporary school records are useful to discover these facts, though the extent and depth of an author's acquaintance with "required books" must be judged in the light of all we know of students' habits, then and now.[55]

Lacking more positive evidence, including the strong circum-

---

pole's Library (3 vols., New Haven, 1969); Chester A. Shaver and Alice C. Shaver, *Wordsworth's Library: A Catalogue Including a List of Books Housed by Wordsworth for Coleridge from c. 1810 to 1830* (New York, 1979); Alan Gribben, *Mark Twain's Library: A Reconstruction* (Boston, 1980); David Mike Hamilton, *"The Tools of My Trade": The Annotated Books in Jack London's Library* (Seattle, 1986); and Ralph J. Coffman, *Coleridge's Library: A Bibliography* (Boston, 1987). The twelve volumes of A. N. L. Munby's *Sale Catalogues of Libraries of Eminent Persons* (London, 1971–75) reproduce in facsimile the contemporary printed inventories of the books owned by a number of eighteenth- and nineteenth-century English writers.

[55]Typical of the monographs and articles that gather evidence of the books authors read, in addition to the catalogues of their libraries cited in the preceding note, are Marion Kesselring, *Hawthorne's Reading, 1828–1850* (New York, 1949); Hill Shine, *Carlyle's Early Reading, to 1834* (Lexington, KY, 1953); Floyd Stovall, "Notes on Whitman's Reading," *AL* 26 (1954): 337–62; Merton M. Sealts, Jr., *Melville's Reading: A Checklist of Books Owned and Borrowed* (Madison, WI, 1966) (see also the companion volume, Mary K. Bercaw, *Melville's Sources* [Evanston, IL, 1987]); Billie Andrew Inman, *Walter Pater's Reading: A Bibliography of His Library Borrowings and Literary References, 1858–1873* (New York, 1981) and *Walter Pater and His Reading, 1874–1877, With a Bibliography of His Library Borrowings, 1878–1894* (New York, 1990); Michael S. Reynolds, *Hemingway's Reading* (Princeton, 1981); and Robert J. DeMott, *Steinbeck's Reading* (New York, 1984).

stantial variety, we must decide whether the books would at least have been available to the author who we think levied from them. One of the main arguments of those who cannot believe that the Stratford-born actor William Shakespeare wrote the plays attributed to him is that such a man could not have known all the books the author of the plays obviously knew. But while it is true that we cannot tell precisely where or under what circumstances Shakespeare had access to them, those books were without exception available, at booksellers and in many private libraries, and there is no reason at all to suppose that a man in his position could not have read them. A more troublesome problem, where Renaissance authors are concerned, stems from the practice of circulating poems in manuscript long before they were printed. If a writer seems to have borrowed from another's works at a time when they were not yet printed but are known to have been circulating privately, painstaking biographical inquiries must be made to determine whether the suspected borrower belonged to a social circle in which one of the manuscript copies passed from hand to hand.

The most famous large-scale use ever made of this kind of evidence is John Livingston Lowes's. Beginning with the so-called "Gutch Memorandum Book," a ninety-leaf "catch-all for suggestions jotted down chaotically from Coleridge's absorbing adventures among books," and helped by such leads as the record of the poet's borrowings from the Bristol Library, Lowes followed Coleridge's trail through an incredible number of books on travel and science, emerging, finally, with a virtually line-by-line reconstruction of the way in which "The Rime of the Ancient Mariner" and "Kubla Khan" took form in the deep well of the poet's subconsciousness. The book in which Lowes described Coleridge's transmogrifying of hints found in his reading into the stuff of poetic art—and Lowes's own adventures in recreating Coleridge's—is *The Road to Xanadu* (1927). It is the most enthralling story of literary detection ever written, even though Lowes's style is too mannered to suit present-day tastes and, as more than one later scholar has observed, he does not confront the crucial problem raised by all the evidence he has collected, namely the way the esoteric "shaping spirit" that converted countless tiny bits of scattered fact and phrase into a unified work of art actually operated.[56]

The assumption of direct borrowing ordinarily can be well sustained if the internal evidence is sufficiently large and striking to rule out casual resemblance and if external evidence makes it sufficiently probable that the one author knew the other's works. But if unchallengeable dates or other circumstances make it impossible that the author should have known a certain book at the time he wrote the work in which the presumed indebtedness occurs, the case collapses. (A good example is found on page 133, n. 69.)

When our research is done, and we have defined as closely as we can the nature and extent of a literary debt, our critical faculty takes over, to infer what the material thus acquired and filtered through the author's creative intelligence meant to him, and how it accords with the rest of the artistic composition. To interpret with psychological and historical accuracy the relation between what he read and what he wrote, we seek to understand as intimately as we can the way his mind grew, the habits of his mature intellect, and the stimulation and sustenance he drew both from the literary and intellectual tradition his age inherited and from the atmosphere that prevailed while he wrote. It is not origin that matters in the long run—the literary imagination, as distinct from the historical mind, is indifferent to origins and pedigrees—but the comparison that discovery of the source makes possible. If an author derived a dominant idea from another, just how did he modify it and impress it with the stamp of his own intellect? If he took a character from the stock of a currently popular genre or, on the other hand, drew him from life, what in the process of adaptation is important to our

---

[56]In his remarkable—and controversial—*Coleridge, the Damaged Archangel,* Norman Fruman takes a darker view of Coleridge's liberal use of other men's writings (see For Further Reading, p. 263). A friend of Coleridge's, De Quincey, made equally free use of printed sources in his hack work, abstracting and abridging them and at the same time transmuting the borrowed material into what appeared to be products of his own imagination. See Albert Goldman, *The Mine and the Mint: Sources for the Writings of Thomas De Quincey* (Carbondale, IL, 1965).

understanding of his artistic technique and his attitude toward his fellow men? If his metaphors can be traced back through the generations, what meaningful differences can we discern in his use of them? "To see [a work] in relation to the tradition out of which it sprang"—quoting Tuve again—"is only to perceive with greater pleasure those leaps and those masterful ordering actions of the single human mind by which new relationships are made and new unities created."

4. TRACING REPUTATION AND INFLUENCE

To separate source study and the tracing of reputation and influence into distinct categories, as is done here for convenience, is an arbitrary division of what is in fact a single Janus-like subject, looking backward or forward, depending on one's purpose. While the investigator of borrowings and echoes moves backward in time, from the author to the sources that suggested images or ideas to him or her, the student of reputation and influence ordinarily moves forward from the author, school, or movement to examine the effect they had on their contemporaries and on succeeding generations of critics, writers, and ordinary readers. Both kinds of research are concerned with the genetics of literature, with the historical tradition that supplies a norm against which a writer's relative conformity and originality can be assessed.

Reputation and influence studies differ to the extent that the former is concerned with an author's or a given work's impact on critics and readers in general, while the latter concentrates on the effect the author or work had on particular authors, chiefly but not exclusively those in later generations.

As Lionel Trilling said, the poem is, among other things, "the poem as it has existed in history, as it has lived its life from Then to Now, as it is a thing which submits itself to one kind of perception in one age and another kind of perception in another age, as it exerts in each age a different kind of power."[57] To find everything *Paradise Lost* contains today, we must read

[57]"The Sense of the Past," reprinted in *The Liberal Imagination* (New York, 1950) 186.

it not only in the way Milton intended his first readers to do and in the various ways that modern critics suggest, but also as readers in the intervening three centuries, with their constantly changing standards of value, have done. Implicit within *Childe Harold* or *Moby-Dick* is the record of all it has meant to the intellects and sensibilities of those who have read it from the day of its first publication to our own.

That same process of historical reconstruction has other, equally valuable, functions. Tracing the course of an author's reputation helps define the critical standards and popular literary tastes that prevailed in successive eras, beginning with his or her own. Both the novelty and the traditionalism of Wordsworth's early poetry become more apparent when we read what its first critics said of it, note which poets Wordsworth was compared with—and then find out what contemporary critics and readers thought of *them,* and why. In such a fashion a whole climate of literary opinion can be re-created, with the primary aim of establishing what, given the prevailing modes and tastes, Wordsworth set out to do (his own statements in the preface to the second edition of *Lyrical Ballads* are not the whole story by any means) and how his audience interpreted both his intention and his achievement. And the subsequent fluctuations of his fame permit us to read in microcosm some of the principal trends in nineteenth- and twentieth-century taste, as well as to explain more adequately the art of those poets who found Wordsworth a rich inspiration and useful model and of those others who participated in the inevitable reaction against him.

Although the usual movement of reputation-and-influence study is chronological, the same materials and methods, applied to simultaneous phenomena, can be used to reconstruct the literary atmosphere of an age and then to account for individual aspects of literary taste and practice at the time. Once we learn, for instance, which authors of the recent or more distant past were widely read and which were out of favor in the period, we are better equipped to account for the themes and devices, the spirit and purpose, of Victorian writers and genres. Remembering the decline in popularity Fielding, Smollett, and Sterne suffered after the first third of the nineteenth century, and realizing at the same time the popularity of the historical novel during and immediately after Scott's reign, as well as of "Newgate" (crime) and "silver fork" (high society) novels, we comprehend more clearly the expectations and requirements of the audience that welcomed Ainsworth, the Brontës, Disraeli, Dickens, Bulwer-Lytton, Thackeray, and Wilkie Collins. Recalling the excitement that their discovery of Keats, after decades of neglect, caused among the young poets of mid-century, we are better able to understand the poetic ideals and techniques of two of his most gifted admirers, Dante Gabriel Rossetti and William Morris. If we know what the contemporary critical attitude was toward Chaucer, Gray, Burns, and Byron, we can gauge the degree to which Matthew Arnold, writing of those poets, was merely echoing prevailing opinion and the degree to which he was independent of it.

For the contemporary reception of most important books during the past two centuries, abundant documents are available. Heading the list are reviews, which give us a direct indication of what the arbiters of taste thought. Because there are few convenient printed indexes to such reviews in the eighteenth and nineteenth centuries, finding them may require us to examine every available periodical (monthly magazines, quarterly journals of opinion, intellectual or semi-popular weeklies, and some newspapers) for the appropriate period. For nineteenth-century works, *Poole's Index to Periodical Literature* lists some reviews but only if they are of considerable length, and in any event unsystematically. Students of the Romantic period are well served by several compilations: William S. Ward's *Literary Reviews in British Periodicals* [1789–1826] (four vols.) and Donald Reiman's *The Romantics Reviewed: Contemporary Reviews of British Romantic Writers* (nine vols.). For the Victorian period, the *Wellesley Index to Victorian Periodicals* has partially supplied *Poole's* deficiency in respect to the forty-three British periodicals whose contents it analyzes, but it does not identify reviews as such, unless the book or books under consideration are indicated in the title of the article. The twentieth-century *Book Review Digest* is helpful for reviews in popular and semi-popular periodicals. The eight-volume *Comprehensive Index to English-Language Little Magazines 1890–1970* provides easy access to reviews in some of the most symptomatic and (in the long run) influential organs in Britain and America, the so-called "little magazines."[58]

The judgments delivered in these reviews must be subjected to the same cool scrutiny that is applied to all other kinds of historical evidence. Is a certain reviewer acting as a faithful mouthpiece for the age, or does one detect a pronounced literary or political bias, or a personal dislike of the author? Many kinds of prejudice, not all of them relevant to a book's merits, affect criticism. Moreover, in various epochs, editorial policy, including political partisanship, has had a great deal to do with a critic's decision, as it still does in some quarters. Every schoolboy used to know that a Tory author could no more expect an enthusiastic welcome in the pages of the Whig *Edinburgh Review* than a Whig writer could look forward to liberal justice in the Tory *Quarterly*. Similarly, during some decades of the nineteenth century, in both Britain and America, a publisher frequently arranged for an appreciative notice of a new book. Caution is particularly desirable in the case of the periodicals owned by publishing houses; books published by the London firm of Bentley in the 1830s were extravagantly praised in Bentley's magazines, and in evaluating a notice in the *Atlantic Monthly* in the 1860s, it is useful to remember that the firm that owned the magazine also published many of the books it reviewed. Today, reviewing is much more independent, and the cruder forms of critic-influencing have almost wholly vanished. Still, it is not unknown for a friend of the author to suggest to a book review editor the name of a suitable (i.e., well-disposed) reviewer.

[58]Access to a large body of contemporary criticism of numerous English and American writers—over one hundred as of 1992—has been, and is being, made much easier through the Critical Heritage series published by the London firm of Routledge. Varying with the authors covered, these volumes generally include a survey of the writer's critical reputation and selected substantial reviews of each major work, and they may also include comments from letters and diaries of important contemporaries.

Just as important in rounding out our knowledge of how a book struck its first audience is the evidence found in the private papers left by its members—their letters and diaries and the records of their conversation. Thus we can ascertain how widely a book was discussed, by whom, and for what reasons. The farther back we go, of course, the scantier such records become. The history of sixteenth- and seventeenth-century authors' early reputations must be compiled from contemporary biographical-critical dictionaries, compilations of excerpts and criticisms (of which Francis Meres's *Palladis Tamia* [1598] is perhaps the best known), the commonplace books some readers kept (many of which are still unexamined), and scattered allusions in the imaginative, critical, and controversial writings of the time, such as Robert Greene's famous attack on young Shakespeare.[59]

Besides the quality of a book's early reception, there is its magnitude to consider. How many copies were sold? The answer, if found, will provide some indication of whether the broad public agreed with the critics and the intellectual élite. Here publishers' records are the primary source, if they are extant (many extensive and valuable archives have been lost through fire and bombing) and open to scholarly exploration.[60] The sales figures these records contain can be depended on:

[59]Two good examples of collections of allusions to earlier writers are Caroline F. E. Spurgeon, *Five Hundred Years of Chaucer Criticism and Allusion* (3 vols., Cambridge, 1925), and Gerald E. Bentley, *Shakespeare and Jonson: Their Reputation in the Seventeenth Century Compared* (2 vols., Chicago, 1945). The latter has been supplemented by the six volumes of Shakespeare criticism in the Critical Heritage series.

[60]Since the Second World War, several major publishing firms in Britain and the United States have contributed greatly to our understanding of the economic and editorial sides of publishing by donating their archives to research institutions. Thus the records of the London house of Macmillan are divided between the British Library and the University of Reading, and those of the American firm with the same name are in the New York Public Library. The papers of the long-lived Edinburgh firm of Blackwood, publishers of eminent authors ranging from Scott and De Quincey to George Eliot as well as hundreds of Scottish authors of lesser fame, are in the National Library of Scotland. In America, the Scribner archives are divided

there are no secrets between a businessman and his ledgers. Other sources purporting to give the sales figures of books and periodicals must be regarded with great skepticism, for book-trade gossip is notoriously unreliable. Hence sales figures reported in magazine articles or diary entries by people who had them from the customary "good authority" have little value unless they can be substantiated from a better source. Above all, one should not be misled by a recital of the number of editions a book went through, because an edition may consist of a few hundred or several hundred thousand copies. The number of *copies* sold is far better evidence of a book's popularity than the number of editions printed.[61]

The same observation applies to the subsequent publishing record of a book. Scholars sometimes point to the number of reprints a classic like *The Vicar of Wakefield* went through in the nineteenth century as a sign of its enduring popularity. Actually, practical considerations, such as the publishers' desire to get their full money's worth out of their investment in plates and stock, may well have caused certain old standbys, such as Dryden, Pope, Goldsmith, Johnson, and Cowper, to overstay their welcome. Thus economic expediency (as well as the empty dignity of received reputation), rather than genuine popular interest, often accounts for the year-in, year-out sale of many books.

It is instructive, also, to go through anthologies of contempo-

---

between Princeton and the University of Texas; the Holt papers (420 cartons) are at Princeton, Harper's at the J. Pierpont Morgan Library in New York, Random House's at Columbia University, and Bobbs-Merrill's at the Lilly Library, Indiana University. An ambitious series undertaken by the British firm of Chadwyck-Healy has made available in microform the records of eleven publishing houses, including Longman, Macmillan, Harper, and the Cambridge University Press.

[61]Probably the most exhaustive use so far made of publishers' ledgers and other records in respect to a single author is represented by Robert L. Patten's table- and chart-laden *Charles Dickens and His Publishers* (Oxford, 1978).

rary poetry and essays to study the selections that the editors, who presumably were good judges of what their readers wanted, made from authors who were in fashion. And, in the case of extremely popular writers like Byron and Dickens, the number and nature of adaptations that were made of their books, particularly dramatizations, plagiarisms, imitations, and spurious "continuations," are a valuable measure of the public's insatiable appetite for their work, even if what was offered under their names had never been touched by their pens.

Obviously, the largest body of evidence bearing on critical fortunes in subsequent years is found in the books and articles that deal with or simply mention an author and his or her works. From these materials, which for major authors can be bewilderingly abundant, can be constructed an imaginary graph that will reveal the ascents and declines their reputations have undergone. Prominent among such books are ones that are specifically about the writers—critical and interpretive studies and biographies (which often contain revealing, if sometimes oblique, glimpses of current critical opinion). In periodicals can be found not only formal articles but what in many instances are equivalent to critical essays: reviews of new biographical and critical volumes and editions of the author's works.

In addition to these books and articles devoted specifically to the topic, the majority of which can be found without too much trouble by consulting the standard bibliographical tools, a wealth of incidental comment is to be found simply by wide reading in the critical literature of whatever era one is concerned with. A general article on the English humorists may contain a suggestive paragraph on Ned Ward, and a book on Emerson, written in 1900, may prove to have a long digression that throws light on the way people at that time regarded Thoreau.[62]

---

[62]See *Toward the Making of Thoreau's Modern Reputation,* ed. Fritz Oelschlaeger and George Hendrick (Urbana, IL, 1979), which prints the correspondence of five figures who influenced the development of that reputation, 1889–1907.

Some bibliographies of individual authors and books are so broad in their coverage that they serve as shorthand histories of the author's critical and popular fame. The Garland Dickens bibliographies, each volume devoted to a single novel, include sections on that novel's contemporary literary reception; stage, film, musical, radio, and television adaptations; parodies, plagiarisms, "pictorial representations" apart from the illustrations in the original edition, and every other form of evidence bearing on the novel's reception and subsequent fame except artifacts, which are within the range of only a few truly all-embracing bibliographies. A recent bibliography of *Alice in Wonderland,* in addition to a large section on "Alice in the Arts" (including spoken recordings, film strips, musical adaptations, and ballets), documents the presence of Lewis Carroll's heroine in advertising, tote bags, belt buckles, calendars, cartoons, chess sets, dolls, games, puzzles, coloring books, soaps and toiletries, tea towels, wrapping paper, posters—the list goes on and on.[63]

Before leaving the topic of literary fame, we must notice the recently widened scope and increasing sophistication of reputation studies, a development stemming from a belated recognition of the important conceptual issues they involve. While the strictly literary attributes of a work may determine the various ways it has been and is now regarded—the esthetic factor—its reputation is also a social product, as much subject to changes in the social and cultural climate as is our interpretation and

[63]This is Charles C. Lovett and Stephanie B. Lovett, *Lewis Carroll's "Alice": An Annotated Bibliography of the Lovett Collection* (Westport, CT, 1990). It is, of course, books like Carroll's, which engage the enthusiasm of collectors and cults, that produce so many spinoffs—solid evidence of their lasting popularity among portions of the general public. A similar compilation is Ronald Burt de Waal's *The International Sherlock Holmes* (Hamden, CT, 1980), which, in addition to the categories already mentioned, catalogues Sherlockian comic strips, door knockers, license plates, postcards, stained glass windows, tobacco jars, and wallpaper. No one has yet had the temerity to attempt a comprehensive catalogue of all the physical objects that attest to Shakespeare's fame across the centuries and around the world.

evaluation of the work itself. What is more, the received image of the author as a person is often reshaped by the prevailing forces of taste, ideology, and psychological theory. "All reputations each age revises," observed Emerson in his journal in 1839.[64]

During a span of no more than three years (1988–90) appeared several case histories of authors' reputations that illustrate the differing approaches used in this newly vivified and provocative branch of scholarship. One author (Lawrence H. Schwartz, in *Creating Faulkner's Reputation: The Politics of Modern Literary Criticism* [1988]) traced the process by which, in the brief period 1946–50, Faulkner was transformed from an obscure author of grotesque and sordid stories laid in a mythical Mississippi county into a giant of modern American literature. The motive force was the new esthetic sensibility of the moment, a product in turn of "the intelligentsia's accommodation to a changed political order." Faulkner's publishers joined a small but fervent group of New Critics (the ascendant school of criticism in the America of the day) and New York intellectuals in mounting a campaign on behalf of his just fame. Prominent among these was Malcolm Cowley, whose *Portable Faulkner,* issued at a propitious moment (1946), was probably the single most influential contribution to the novelist's almost overnight canonization.

Politics of another kind, on a much larger scale, was at the heart of George Orwell's evolving fame both before and after

---

[64]Much recent scholarship in this area has centered upon British and American women authors in the seventeenth and, particularly, the eighteenth centuries. One may acquire quick orientation to the range and achievement of this activity by consulting the introductory essays in Janet Todd's *A Dictionary of British and American Women Writers 1660–1800* (Totowa, NJ, 1987) and Roger Lonsdale's anthology *Eighteenth-Century Women Poets* (Oxford, 1989). For an excellent example of the heretofore underacknowledged (by literary history) reputation and influence of women's writing in the following generation, see Stuart Curran's "Romantic Poetry: The I Altered" in *Romanticism and Feminism,* ed. Anne K. Mellor (Bloomington, IN, 1988).

his death in 1950. In an ample and densely documented study, *The Politics of Literary Reputation: The Making and Claiming of "St. George" Orwell* (1989), John Rodden took up the case of a writer who "has been both an extraordinarily popular serious writer and a critically acclaimed one." His books, above all *1984,* appealed to a diversity of audiences, whose response was inevitably, in the nature of the case, deeply affected by their respective political orientations. He was an intellectual hero to several distinct bodies of opinion—a rebel to one, the avatar of the common man to another, a prophet to a third, a secular saint to a fourth. Accordingly, there was an anarchists' Orwell, the Soviet Union's Orwell, West Germany's Orwell, the feminists' Orwell, and more besides. Evidence for all these guises of a protean figure is found in sources ranging from the ideological literature of each constituency to school reading lists and television adaptations. Since his works can be read from so many different angles, agreement on who was the "true" Orwell is still to be reached; perhaps it never will be.

The public conception of Thomas Hardy is undergoing similar re-examination. For decades even before his death in 1928, argued Peter Widdowson in *Hardy in History: A Study in Literary Sociology* (1989), his identity was fixed by an increasingly influential—and uncritically accepted—cliché, which held that he was "a tragic humanist-realist, marred by 'flaws,' but represented by six or seven 'masterworks' which rank, in their grasp of the (universal) human condition, with other great literature in English." This assumption was reflected and reinforced by educational syllabi and in due course by the entertainment media, which put the best-known Hardy novels and short stories on film and television. The notional Thomas Hardy thus created replaced the "real" flesh-and-blood person in the popular view. Concurrently, a revision of the relative standings of Hardy's novels is also underway, the preeminence of such works as *Tess of the D'Urbervilles* and *The Return of the Native* being questioned in favor of such "minor" novels as *The Hand of Ethelberta.*

In his wide-ranging *Reinventing Shakespeare: A Cultural History, from the Restoration to the Present* (1989), Gary Taylor described "the mechanisms of cultural renown"—the ways in which, for over three centuries, the image of Shakespeare has been constantly refashioned by the changing assumptions and practices of performance, criticism, scholarship, and editing. The seventeenth-century "Shakespeare" under whose aegis the actor Betterton performed was remade into the eighteenth-century one whose works Samuel Johnson edited, then into the nineteenth-century demigod in tribute to whom Coleridge wrote rhapsodies, and, most recently, the late twentieth-century practical man of the theater conceived of by such producers as Peter Brook.

Sometimes the popular and critical history of a single book can be seen to constitute "an on-going myth," as Peter Davis showed in *The Lives and Times of Ebenezer Scrooge* (1990). The original "Christmas Carol" as Dickens wrote it quickly became a malleable "culture text" that in the past century and a half has been interpreted, rewritten, and illustrated in response to the ever-shifting requirements of popular taste. Each generation of readers has interpreted the Scrooge story differently and selectively, as the colorful, indeed curious record of its adaptations as children's stories and stage, film, television, and even operatic versions attests.

An author's work not only evokes response from critics and common readers as it passes down through time; as has been noted, it also affects new generations of writers. In measuring the effect writers have on their younger contemporaries and successors, we re-enter to some extent the territory briefly surveyed in the pages on the search for origins. But there is this difference: although the terms "source" and "influence" are sometimes used almost synonymously, the latter refers to the wider, more profound, more subtle and intangible effects that a knowledge of one writer's works has upon another, whereas "source" designates specific borrowings that may or may not be related to that larger debt.

In tracing influences we find ourselves dealing not only with the relationship of one author to another (Sir Thomas Browne to Lamb, Ruskin to Proust) but, to a greater degree than is true

in source study, with generalized forces—conventions (Pe-
trarchism), genres (the pastoral elegy), schools and movements
(the Scottish Chaucerians), clusters of ideas (New England Transcendentalism)—at both the transmitting and the receiving
ends. The author of an interesting theoretical discussion of the
subject[65] notes that the emanators of influence may include, in
addition to specific authors and works, "climate, mores or locale of a people"; historical events such as the Armada and the
American Civil War; "some particular style or literary convention"; "a particular theory or idea"; a specific thinker; and a
literary movement. Similarly, the influence may be exerted
upon such broad entities as the age at large, the cultural tradition, or a literary movement.

As a leading American Shakespeare scholar has observed,
"The concept of 'influence' is multifaceted, ranging from the
practice of wholesale plagiarism (as when a hack like William
Heminges, son of Shakespeare's close colleague John Heminges, pillaged unassimilated chunks of Shakespeare's plays
to construct his unspeakably bad revenge tragedy *The Fatal
Contract*) to a kind of spiritual discipleship, through which (as
with Keats) Shakespeare becomes an informing vision that
permeates and enriches, while it complements, a major writer's
voice. . . ."[66]

Research into the transmission of literary influence has been
freshly legitimatized by developments in theory and criticism
since the 1970s. First, W. Jackson Bate, in *The Burden of the
Past and the English Poet* (1970), and then, more sensationally,
Harold Bloom in *The Anxiety of Influence: A Theory of Poetry*
(1973) argued—Bloom largely on psychoanalytic grounds—
that modern (post-Miltonic) poets have been haunted by the
achievements of their great predecessors. Their admiration

[65]Ihab H. Hassan, "The Problem of Influence in Literary History: Notes
Towards a Definition," *Journal of Aesthetics and Art Criticism* 14 (1955):
66–76.

[66]G. Blakemore Evans, preface to a collection of essays by various hands,
Shakespeare: Aspects of Influence (Harvard English Studies 7; Cambridge,
MA, 1976).

turns first to despair ("What is there left to do, when Shakespeare and Milton have done it already, and unmatchably?")
and then to a grim struggle to free themselves from the incubus
of past glories, as Sindbad the Sailor sought to unburden himself
of the Old Man of the Sea. An earlier generation, parroting an
Adlerian catch term, would have called the poet's neurosis an
inferiority complex, but Bloom preferred the concept of anxiety, of an Oedipean confrontation between living genius and
hallowed super-genius, the resulting poetry being, therefore,
the product of the clash between adversaries.

Another, more history-oriented school of thought took a
brighter view. Far from being malign, it maintained, the influence of revered masters upon writers in later generations or
centuries was wholesome. Putting aside Freudian considerations, the relation of a poet to his or her great precursors was
one of respect and healthy rivalry. Scholars repeatedly invoked
the doctrine of *imitatio*, which the English Renaissance had
inherited from classical literary theory and now embraced on its
own behalf and that of the following two centuries: the idea that
the monuments of past poetic achievement should serve not as
models to be slavishly imitated (as was done by unoriginal
versifiers) but as a treasury of literary art to be drawn upon for
inspiration—a stimulus to imaginative craftsmanship and an
invitation to originality. *Imitatio* involved challenge, not anxiety, and it was under its auspices that most of the great poetry
of the seventeenth and eighteenth centuries as well as the Romantic period was written.[67]

[67]"Though it may seem attractive to us to imagine that every writer's life is
filled with literary anxiety, and that his relationships with his predecessors
are intense, charged, and highly conflicted, I do not find this to be true of
writers in the age of Dryden, Pope, and Johnson. Indeed, I find instead a
sense of detachment, friendly rivalry, and literary personality" (Dustin
Griffin, *Regaining Paradise: Milton and the Eighteenth Century* [Cam-
bridge, 1986] ix). Other books that represent the scholarly reaction to the
"anxiety of influence" theory are Robert F. Gleckner, *Blake and Spenser*
(Baltimore, 1985); Jonathan Bate, *Shakespeare and the Romantic Imagination* (London, 1987); R. S. White, *Keats as a Reader of Shakespeare*

It was with good reason that André Morize wrote, "Influence by its very nature does not always declare itself by precise and well-defined signs; its study does not admit of the same exactness as, for instance, the investigation of sources. Frequently, it consists in following the capricious, unexpected meanderings of a stream whose waters are led hither and thither by the accidental contour of the ground and take their color from the various tributaries and the soil through which they flow—at times even disappearing from view for a space, to reappear farther on."[68] Thus diffusion, cross-currents, the inextricable mingling of numerous impalpable elements in the literary and intellectual atmosphere make the tracing of influence a delicate and uncertain business, most especially where generalized forces are involved.

Since source and influence studies use the same highway for much of their distance, the same common-sense rules of the road prevail, and the same caution signs are posted. Confining ourselves to the kind of influence study most commonly practiced—that involving the impact of a single author or work on a later group or succession of writers—we need to ask three main questions: Is there enough solid evidence to permit us to convert our supposition of influence into a probability? If so, by what means, such as general diffusion or transmission through a series of identifiable intermediaries, was it carried down, and how widely was it felt? Finally, and most pertinent for the intentions of criticism, what was the precise nature of that influence as revealed by the literary works where it can be detected?

The first question can be answered by the techniques discussed above, on pages 112–14. As always, similarity does not

---

(London, 1987); and Edwin Stein, *Wordsworth's Art of Allusion* (University Park, PA, 1988). Bate, Gleckner, and Stein discuss at some length the definition, taxonomy, and functions of allusions as they integrate authors into the literary tradition. All these books might just as pertinently have been cited in connection with the pages on source study, along with the works on authors' libraries and their reading (see nn. 54 and 55 above).

[68]*Problems and Methods of Literary History* (Boston, 1922) 229.

necessarily mean causal relationship, and once in a while a tempting case involving source or influence is ruined by one or more inconvenient facts. In two great Victorian novels of the 1840s, *Vanity Fair* and *Dombey and Son,* are memorable passages describing the sale by public auction of the luxurious household goods of a wealthy man who has lost his fortune—a modern version of the old "fall of princes" theme. Might not Thackeray and Dickens have been inspired by what they read in the newspapers of two widely publicized sales of the kind, the dispersal of the contents of Stowe House, palatial home of the bankrupt duke of Buckingham, and of Gore House, site of the London salon presided over by the now equally destitute countess of Blessington? The idea is almost irresistible. But alas, the dates destroy the hypothesis. The pertinent chapter of *Vanity Fair* (17) was published in May 1847; that of *Dombey and Son* (59) in April 1848. The Stowe House and Gore House sales occurred in August–September 1848, and May 1849, respectively. Thackeray, therefore, could have had neither sale in mind; and while Dickens would have read of Stowe House's being taken over by bailiffs at the end of August 1847, his description of the dispersal of Dombey's property could have owed nothing to the actual Stowe sale. Both novelists, we must conclude, simply drew upon their—and their readers'—knowledge of what, after all, were quite common events, given the risks of early Victorian business life. The dates and other bibliographical and biographical facts must, therefore, certify that the supposed influence could have occurred.[69]

The second of our major questions, that of the breadth and intensity of an author's influence and the way it was transmit-

[69]Dates are notoriously difficult to keep straight, and they are the single type of information that most requires checking and re-checking in the course of a scholarly argument. Even the most careful of literary reference-book compilers sometimes nod. In the *Stanford Companion to Victorian Fiction* (Stanford, 1989), John Sutherland, writing (p. 565) of G. A. Sala's novel *The Seven Sons of Mammon* (1862), says, "It is clear that in writing it he had a recollection of Dickens's *Our Mutual Friend.*" But *Our Mutual Friend* was published only in 1864–65.

ted, can be answered in large part by the methods of reputation study.[70] We can show, for example, how many writers or schools of writers were affected by the author's style, formal techniques, attitudes; and how many critics, sitting on the sidelines of literary creativity, urged their contemporaries to emulate him or her. But as we seek evidence of influence in a given period or down through the centuries, our eagerness to prove a thesis may dull our sense of caution and discrimination. Granting that many ideas and artistic devices, once introduced into the air of an age, gain wide circulation, we run the risk of thinking we detect influence where the resemblances are, in fact, unremarkable and probably fortuitous. Here is one of the many situations in research where tough-minded skepticism must hold a tight rein on the human tendency toward all-out enthusiasm.

If the evidence assures us that A's influence on B is no figment of the overeager imagination, we must try to decide whether it was exerted directly or in diffused or intermediary fashion. Eighteenth-century poetry often has a markedly Miltonic style. If we put aside the possibility that the resemblances are due to both Milton's and the eighteenth-century "Miltonists" ' drawing upon a common fund of heroic style, two explanations are available: the eighteenth-century authors were intimately acquainted with Milton's works, and the influence was therefore exerted directly from him to them; or they were simply echoing the idiom and tone that are found in the poetry of their numerous predecessors who imitated him.

---

[70]Representative recent studies of literary influence, in addition to some cited in n. 67, are: Howard Schless, *Chaucer and Dante: A Revaluation* (Norman, OK, 1984); Ann Thomson, *Shakespeare's Chaucer: A Study in Literary Origins* (Liverpool, 1978); David Staines, *Tennyson's Camelot: The "Idylls of the King" and Its Medieval Sources* (Waterloo, Ont., 1982); Loralee MacPike, *Dostoevsky's Dickens* (Totawa, NJ, 1981); James E. Miller, *The American Quest for a Supreme Fiction: Whitman's Legacy in the Personal Epic* (Chicago, 1979); and Robert Emmet Long, *The Great Succession: Henry James and the Legacy of Hawthorne* (Pittsburgh, 1979). See also For Further Reading, pp. 271–72.

Seldom is a clear-cut answer possible. It is not a matter of "either/or," but far more likely of "both"; in which latter case, our job is to estimate, as best we can, the relative proportions of direct and of indirect influence in the relationship between one writer and another. It is a moot question how much of the unmistakable Browningesque element in T. S. Eliot's technique is traceable (despite his own disclaimer) to his reading of Browning's poetry itself and how much to his acknowledged indebtedness to Ezra Pound, whose early work, in turn, as Pound often said, was deeply influenced by Browning. A third possibility, which does not exclude the other two, is that Eliot's use of the dramatic monologue and of colloquial diction is simply one evidence of the influence Browning had upon poetic technique in general during the first decades of the twentieth century.

While the complex and elusive quality of literary influence makes any confident answer suspect, it is far from idle to raise such questions. The very attempt to decide whether an influence was direct or secondhand, or both—or indeterminate—forces us to examine more intently the nature of that influence, which, after all, is our final concern. By seeking to establish *how* and *why* it happened that one writer had an important role in the making of others, we come face to face with the problem of exactly *what* happened. And the quality of that influence is affected, obviously, by the channels through which it was transmitted. No two cases are the same. The results are as various as the number of personalities that have assimilated certain of Writer A's artistic idiosyncrasies and ideas in their own work, modifying them as the conditions of their era and their temperamental bent required, and the number that they, in turn, have influenced.

5. CULTIVATING A SENSE OF THE PAST

Most questions of the kind discussed in the preceding sections—what is the best text of a work? who wrote it? what were its sources? how was it received, and what influence has it had?——can be answered from the materials associated with *literary* history. And it is with literary history, obviously, that as researchers we are most concerned. It enables us to place the author or work or tendency we are studying among all the other authors, works, and tendencies belonging to its time and, perhaps, to the preceding eras as well. The better our knowledge of literary genetics, the more surely can we distinguish between the individual, the original, the innovative on the one hand, and the commonplace and conventional on the other.

But the present chapter has, at the same time, implied another, closely related, point. Surrounding the specifically literary current of history have always been the manifold currents of ideas, the other arts, and everyday habit that constitute the milieu of a work of literature at the time of its creation. "To judge rightly of an author," wrote Dr. Johnson in his "Life of Dryden," "we must transport ourselves to his time, and examine what were the wants of his contemporaries, and what were his means of supplying them." Or, as a more recent writer has put it, a little less succinctly, "The literature of every country and of every time is understood as it ought to be only by the author and his contemporaries. . . . The task, therefore, of one who lives in another age and wants to appreciate that work correctly, consists precisely in rediscovering the varied information and complexes of ideas which the author assumed to be the natural property of his audience."[71]

The applications of historical knowledge to literary scholarship range in size from the minute to the panoramic, and their variety is endless. Acquaintance with the ideas and customs of an era may be drawn upon to explicate a tiny topical allusion. When a character in a Victorian novel is said to have taken a "Shillibeer," did he swallow it, board it, or sniff it? If we are to be genuine authorities on the whole body of an author's works, or on the literary productions of a certain epoch, we must not

[71]*The Making of Homeric Verse: The Collected Papers of Milman Parry* (Oxford, 1971), quoted by Jerome J. McGann, *Historical Studies and Literary Criticism* (Madison, WI, 1975) 8.

only take into consideration the knowledge that was then current, but synthesize it into an entity that represents our personal, well-informed reconstruction of "the medieval [or Restoration, or Augustan, or Victorian, or early twentieth-century American] mind." To know what the lines of Shakespeare's plays probably meant to their first audiences, we need a practical acquaintance with Elizabethan medicine, religion, costume, superstitions, crafts, political theory, ornithology, music, law, sport, table manners, military and naval practices, and scores of other topics. Similarly, in studying sixteenth- and seventeenth-century poetry, our specifically literary orientation (knowledge, for instance, of the medieval conventions that survived into Tudor times, and of the classics that affected the whole face and spirit of Elizabethan poetry) has to be supplemented from many nonliterary fields. No sphere of current intellectual interest was alien to those restless, questing poets, who wove ideas from everywhere into their pages: the Ptolemaic, and then the Copernican, cosmology that permeated the thought of Spenser, Donne, and Milton; Neo-Platonism, most particularly as it affected the poets' idea of human love; the philosophical symbolism of musical harmony, exemplified in Sir John Davies's "Orchestra," Milton's "At a Solemn Music," Dryden's "A Song for St. Cecilia's Day"; alchemy, somewhat discredited intellectually but a prolific source of metaphor, as in Donne; the whole system of medieval-Renaissance psychology and physiology (the theory of the humors, the "passions," and so forth).

But our historical lenses must, like those of television cameras, be capable of different ranges. Not only are literary works products of a long age: they are, far oftener than we customarily recognize, products of a decade, even of a year or a month. In studying many authors, both the long view and the short are indispensable to adequate comprehension. Milton O. Percival's *William Blake's Circle of Destiny,* which traces the age-old esoteric systems of thought upon which the poet-artist drew, is complemented by David V. Erdman's *Blake: Prophet Against Empire,* which focuses on the contemporaneity of Blake's message in the politically and socially critical years of the French Revolution.

Consider how much of the multiplex allegory of *The Faerie Queene* is overlooked if, by concentrating on the wider set of ethical and philosophical themes, we fail to see how immediately topical Spenser's religious and political shadow-references were to readers in the 1590s. Joyce's *Ulysses* is, among many other things, a colossal feat of retrospective journalism, preserving in the amber of its Homeric myth the streets and people of Dublin as they existed on June 16, 1904. One of the most noteworthy recent contributions historical scholarship has made to the explication of a major literary work has been the joint effort of many researchers who have combed newspaper files and interviewed virtually every surviving old-time Dubliner, for the sake of explaining Joyce's almost countless topical and local allusions.[72]

Of peculiar importance to a valid reading of English literature in some epochs is a knowledge of contemporary politics. Research in the writings associated with Dryden, Defoe, Swift, Pope, and the pamphleteering Henry Fielding calls for a good working knowledge of who was who and what was what in court and Parliament during the Restoration and the early eighteenth century. Such data are not easily obtained, because politics, religion, economics, and personalities were perhaps never more desperately entangled than in the years from the end of the Commonwealth to Sir Robert Walpole's administration.[73]

[72]See, for example, Weldon Thornton, *Allusions in "Ulysses"* (Chapel Hill, NC, 1968); Don Gifford, *"Ulysses" Annotated* (Berkeley, 1988); and Roland McHugh, *Annotations to "Finnegans Wake"* (Baltimore, 1980). The Dickens Companion series published by Allen and Unwin, now in progress, exhaustively annotates Dickens's fiction, devoting a volume to a single novel.

[73]A number of massive recent biographies of these figures attest to the necessity of such in-depth knowledge: James A. Winn's *John Dryden and His World* (New Haven, 1987); Paula R. Backscheider's *Daniel Defoe* (Baltimore, 1989); Irving Ehrenpreis's *Swift: The Man, His Works, and the Age* (3 vols., London, 1962–83); Maynard Mack's *Alexander Pope: A Life* (New York, 1985); and Martin and Ruthe Battestin's *Henry Fielding: A Life* (London, 1989). Not that the political history of earlier or later periods is

Yet neither the controlling assumptions nor the point of individual passages in the writings of some of the age's greatest authors—not to speak of the mass of historical documents surrounding them—can be comprehended without such knowledge. This is true, above all, of the period's satire, whose subject generally is the moment and its fleetingly spotlighted inhabitants. A superficial acquaintance with the political and literary feuds behind the *Epistle to Dr. Arbuthnot* and *The Dunciad* may enable one to appreciate the broad swipes of Pope's satirical weapon, but only a much closer knowledge of the personalities and the petty gossip of Grub Street garrets and fashionable drawing rooms at the very time Pope wrote can make available the far more numerous, and subtle, dagger thrusts we find in these poems as well as in *The Rape of the Lock*.[74] In American literature, similarly, the humor of Irving's *History of New York* and Lowell's *Biglow Papers* is largely lost without an appreciation of the contemporary persons and events that called it forth.

Probably the most fundamental necessity, and the hardest to satisfy by any systematic means, is mastery of an era's vocabulary. We have to learn the language of the past before we can accurately grasp its ideas. Denotations offer little trouble: we can quickly find out what obsolete or otherwise puzzling words meant, at a given time, by going to the *Oxford English Dictionary,* the *Dictionary of American English,* or more specialized lexicons such as those of slang and trade argot. But much more vital to understanding are the intellectual implications and the emotional connotations borne by words that epitomize dominant ideas and strains of opinion in various epochs. In the

---

irrelevant to the study of literature from those periods. David Bevington's *Tudor Drama and Politics: A Critical Approach to Topical Meaning* (Cambridge, MA, 1968) and Carl Woodring's *Politics in English Romantic Poetry* (Cambridge, MA, 1970) are representative studies in those fields.

[74]For a stimulating exposition, based on a wide variety of sources, of all that "Grub Street" meant, literally and figuratively, to Pope's readers, see Pat Rogers, *Grub Street: Studies in a Sub-Culture* (London, 1972).

literary criticism of the sixteenth, seventeenth, and eighteenth centuries, key words like *wit, imagination, fancy, imitation, genius, irony, sublime, picturesque,* and *invention* had complex and unstable significance, and much research has gone into examining their histories and reinterpreting the critical documents accordingly. A substantial volume could be assembled of articles dealing with the word *romantic* alone. *Nature,* a word that for centuries was one of the main links between metaphysics and esthetics, has had an even more complicated, and by now intensively examined, career.

Terms with political or religious references—*deist, Puritan, Tory, Jacobin*—usually are laden with feeling, the nature of which depends on the period, the user, the immediate circumstance. Whether examining a literary text or a historical record, the scholar is obliged to determine and take into account the aura of connotation surrounding such a word (mere description or heavily charged epithet?) wherever it occurs. In *Absalom and Achitophel* (lines 519–26), the succession of the words *cant, zealous,* and *inspiration* suggests to the alert student of Restoration attitudes, who recognizes their strongly derogatory implications, Dryden's feelings about Dissenters:

> Hot *Levites* Headed these; who pul'd before
> From th'*Ark,* which in the Judges days they bore,
> Resum'd their Cant, and with a Zealous Cry,
> Pursu'd their old belov'd Theocracy.
> Where Sanhedrin and Priest inslav'd the Nation,
> And justifi'd their Spoils by Inspiration;
> For who so fit for Reign as *Aaron*'s Race,
> If once Dominion they could found in Grace?

From the time of the French Revolution down to at least the middle of the nineteenth century, the word *democrat* in English usage was heavy with prejudicial connotations; it suggested a far-out radical who advocated such causes, anathema to most upper- and middle-class people, as a society in which class distinctions and privileges were largely abolished and the nation was ruled by a government elected by "universal" (i.e., manhood) suffrage. Such words as *Papist* and *Romish,* in a predominantly (and officially) Protestant nation, had their own inflammatory connotations, and Dickens's intended effect in the employment office scene in *Nicholas Nickleby* (ch. 16) is intelligible to us only if we realize that to his contemporary readers the word *serious,* which he uses with irony-filled itera-tion, designated the members of the Evangelical sect, whose sanctimonious attitudes and ways he detested.

The ability to hear the overtones in a document—not only what it says to us but what additional meanings its original readers found in it—is indispensable no matter in what way one is applying historical knowledge to the study of literature. But such an ability is particularly valuable in dealing with the materials of intellectual history, the discipline that once had the longest common border with literary history.

The chief difference between the two fields is that the history of ideas utilizes a work of literature as an intellectual document rather than as an example of art; it is more interested in the substance of the work and in its relationship to other writings in the same philosophical current than in its literary characteris-tics. But the eventual gain to critical understanding is great, for when wisely and sensitively managed, the tools of intellectual history can dramatically enlarge, in fact can even transform, our interpretation of a poem or essay. Moreover, by combining a historically oriented analysis of a work's content with a close examination of its structure and idiom, we often realize how subtle and intricate is the interplay between statement and form. What a certain poem *is,* we discover, depends largely on what it *means*—and vice versa.

The diversity and fruitfulness of the branch of scholarship that examines the history of literature and of ideas through a single glass are exemplified in the work of three figures whose study of philosophical tendencies has had marked pertinence to literary history: A. O. Lovejoy, Basil Willey, and Marjorie Nicol-son.

Lovejoy's classic work, *The Great Chain of Being* (1936), traced a cluster of philosophical concepts, presided over by the religious-metaphysical-political idea of hierarchy, from Greek

times down to the nineteenth century, both in literature and in
nonliterary works. Lovejoy's principal beneficiary has been the
student of eighteenth-century philosophical prose and poetry,
who has been enabled to view certain controlling ideas in, say,
Pope, both as characteristic of Pope's age and as the product of
two thousand years of evolution—thus, in effect, placing
Pope's poetry more firmly in the eighteenth century and at the
same time more expansively relating it to a long tradition.[75]

Basil Willey's major concern was to examine the interplay of
epistemology and theology, on the one hand, and literature on
the other, from Bacon to Tennyson. His series of volumes,
beginning with *The Seventeenth Century Background* (1934),
analyzes the way the poets of each age gave eloquent, and
sometimes impassioned, utterance to the prevailing doctrines
that were also set forth in learned treatise and sermon.

Marjorie Nicolson's specialty was, to borrow the title of her
1956 volume, "science and imagination"—that is, the impact of
seventeenth- and eighteenth-century natural science, theoretical and applied, upon the imaginative vision of poets and prose
writers. By examining, side by side with the actual literature of
the time, the voluminous writings of the scientific speculators
and experimenters, Nicolson showed how manifold were the
effects of the invention of the microscope and the telescope, of
Newton's treatise on optics, and of the insistent dreams of voy-
ages to the moon, upon the language, imagery, and assumptions of contemporary literature.

These are but three of the many learned men and women
who have demonstrated the relevance of intellectual history to
the study of literature.[76] Although some of their work has subse-

---

[75]The profound influence of Lovejoy's work was recognized in five essays
marking the fiftieth anniversary of the book's publication: "Lovejoy, the
Great Chain, and the History of Ideas," *Journal of the History of Ideas* 48
(1987): 186–263.

[76]Another was Ronald S. Crane, who, in addition to his original research,
was distinguished for his insistence on rigorous methodology in intellectual history and its application to literary studies. His searching reviews, in
the earlier issues of the *PQ* annual bibliography of eighteenth-century

quently undergone critical examination and required fine-tuning, they were seminal figures to whom all later explorers of the ideas behind, and in, works of literary art are deeply indebted. An outstanding example of their received legacy is Carl Woodring's magisterial *Nature into Art: Cultural Transformations in Nineteenth-Century Britain* (1989).

Under such auspices, specialists in medieval religion and philosophy have helped clarify meaning in hundreds of passages in Chaucer; students of Renaissance theology have related *Paradise Lost* to the fervid religious climate of Milton's era; while in American studies, F. O. Matthiessen, for instance, interpreted the literature of Emerson's, Hawthorne's, and Thoreau's generation in terms of the derivative yet persistently adventurous New England mind, and Henry Nash Smith, drawing upon a fund of historical evidence that reached from poetry to political speeches and dime novels, described how the myth of the West as an earthly paradise and the settler as an ennobled yeoman—a theme that pervaded much nineteenth-century American literature—flourished, then faded.

Just as pertinent to literary study as intellectual history is social history, whose scope, as G. M. Trevelyan wrote in the introduction to his *English Social History* (1942), "may be defined as the daily life of the inhabitants of the land in past ages: this includes the human as well as the economic relation of different classes to one another, the character of family and household life, the conditions of labour and of leisure, the attitude of man to nature, the culture of each age as it arose out of these general conditions of life, and took ever-changing forms in religion, literature and music, architecture, learning and thought."

As Trevelyan implies, the three disciplines—the history of literature, of ideas, and of the conditions and habits that set the tone of everyday life in any given period—are inseparable. Social history to a great extent reports the way that ideas have

studies and elsewhere, are required reading for every student who proposes to deal with the history of ideas.

been translated into attitudes, customary behavior, and physical environment. Much imaginative literature does essentially the same thing through the agency of art: it gives ideas a local habitation and a name, expressing them, illustrating them, working out their consequences through metaphor, character, situation, plot, setting, and whatever other devices serve to make them comprehensible to the writer's intended audience, who are people firmly rooted in place and time. Intellectual history explains the ideological themes of a literary work and relates it to other works in the same intellectual tradition; social history explains its temporal milieu, its reflection of the social attitudes, the manners, the visual surface of its age. All three kinds of history can be applied to a book like *Tom Jones*— literary history to suggest the meanings in its epic, picaresque, and theatrical elements, the history of ideas to expose its embodiment of characteristic eighteenth-century philosophical assumptions, and social history to explicate it as a Hogarthian version of English life in the 1740s.

Like that of the source student, the social historian's most important contribution to criticism is to provide the data by which we can gauge the nature and extent of the artist's accomplishment. We do not read literature as authentic history; between the facts of experience and the substance of a poem or novel, a creative intelligence has intervened, to transmute the historically real, which is transitory, into the imaginatively real, which, once brought into being, is preserved through the centuries. By establishing the way people in general were feeling and acting at the precise juncture of time and in the precise locale that served as a matrix for a great book, the social historian reassembles the factual materials and the prevailing spirit that were poured into the alembic of the writer's imagination; with this aid, the critic is better able to describe and assess the distillate.

Since the 1930s, for instance, much attention has been paid to Dickens's novels as incisive, often acidulous, criticism of the Victorian culture, with its pursuit of profit and its sacrifice of individual dignity to the demands of faceless institutions. A cluster of books and articles, typified by Humphry House's *The*

Dickens World (1941), has studied the conditions and events that lay behind the novelist's growing disillusionment with contemporary society and, some feel, with the nature of mankind itself. From the bulky reports of parliamentary investigating committees that exposed some of the more dreadful social abuses, the journalistic and fictional literature of protest, and a host of other sources, researchers have brought evidence that makes it possible for us to compare Dickens's fictional vision with the actuality.[77]

At the same time, the social historian deepens our understanding of the artist himself. Whether conforming to it or rebelling against it, every writer has inescapably been molded by the social environment, and to know what manner of person an author was—and thus to account, in part, for the kind of literature he or she wrote—we need an accurate sense of what that environment was like and the impact it would likely have had on various kinds of temperament. In his *Mark Twain's America* (1932), Bernard DeVoto, a scholar extraordinarily knowledgeable about all that related to the history of the country west of the Mississippi, drew from the materials of social history a devastating counterblast to Van Wyck Brooks's psychoanalysis of Twain, in *The Ordeal of Mark Twain* (1920), as a potential Shelley nipped in the bud by the harsh American climate.

Another important aspect of what is often called "the sociology of literature" is the history of the profession of authorship. Except for the hacks who fed the press at minimum rates from the sixteenth century onward, people seldom wrote for money from the public until Dr. Johnson's time. At that point, the patronage system, whereby authors were subsidized by the nobility, gradually gave way to the modern system in which literature is a commercial commodity, with authors deriving their living in the form of royalties from their publishers. Insepa-

---

[77]Dickens has been particularly well served by research of this type. Excellent studies subsequent to House's, also dealing with the social reality behind the fiction, include Philip Collins's two volumes, *Dickens and Crime* (London, 1962) and *Dickens and Education* (London, 1963), and Norris Pope's *Dickens and Charity* (New York, 1978).

rable from the expansion of the reading public (or "market"), the emergence of authorship as a money-making profession worked profound changes in the aims and methods of literature. Increasingly, the people who paid the piper called the tune—and the piper, if he wished for a living wage, had to take into account their expectations and desires. The materials of social history, used in conjunction with authors' biographies and publishers' account books and editorial correspondence, document this vital relationship between authors and their public.[78]

Social history combines with intellectual history to open still another avenue by which a work may be interpreted and judged, because the two in conjunction help account for an era's taste. Taste, or fashion, emerges from the interaction of various intellectual tendencies and social conditions, and it manifests itself on many levels, from grave treatises on esthetics to popular demand for circulating-library novels, and in many fields of artistic expression, of which literature is but one. It is scarcely possible, for instance, to be at home in either the poetry or the criticism of the eighteenth century without a command both of contemporary literary theory and of the theory and practice of the other arts, from "Capability" Brown's gardening to Sir Joshua Reynolds's portraits, and without recognizing the reasons why, in landscape architecture, painting, and literature, the inclinations of artists and connoisseurs alike were increasingly divided between placid pastoralism and the romantically irregular and "sublime."

In late years, indeed, a growing number of literary scholars have been exploring hitherto neglected aspects of the many-

---

[78]For a general study of this subject in nineteenth-century England, see John Sutherland, *Victorian Novelists and Publishers* (London, 1976). The American relationship is considered in William Charvat, *Literary Publishing in America, 1790–1850* (Philadelphia, 1959); *The Profession of Authorship in America, 1800–1870: The Papers of William Charvat,* ed. Matthew J. Bruccoli (Columbus, OH, 1968); and James L. W. West III, *American Authors and the Literary Marketplace Since 1900* (Philadelphia, 1988).

sided relationship between literature and the visual arts, which have frequently adopted a common vocabulary and even similar techniques. Medievalists are expanding our appreciation of the literary art of Chaucer's time by studying the iconography and architecture that played a constant, if normally subliminal, role in people's everyday experience and thus colored their imagination. Specialists in the Renaissance are analyzing the "literary pictorialism" of poets like Spenser, and showing, too, how the manneristic fashion in painting had its reflections in poetry. A full-length study has revealed how deeply Keats's consciousness was permeated with memories of the paintings, prints, sculpture, and stained glass he had gazed upon with delight and awe.[79]

In America, literary scholarship has profitably examined the interest that writers like Cooper and Bryant had in contemporary native painting, especially the Hudson River school, and it has laid bare the affinity and indebtedness that prevailed between certain writers and painters of that epoch. In a quite different vein, a whole new field of investigation has been opened by recent demonstrations that, far from being casually

[79]See, respectively, V. A. Kolve, *Chaucer and the Imagery of Narrative: The First Five Canterbury Tales* (Stanford, 1984); John B. Bender, *Spenser and Literary Pictorialism* (Princeton, 1972); and Ian Jack, *Keats and the Mirror of Art* (Oxford, 1967). Other representative studies include Norman K. Farmer, Jr., *Poets and the Visual Arts in Renaissance England* (Austin, TX, 1984); Murray Roston, *Renaissance Perspectives in Literature and the Visual Arts* (Princeton, 1987); Roland M. Frye, *Milton's Imagery and the Visual Arts: Iconographic Tradition in the Epic Poems* (Princeton, 1978); Jean Hagstrum, *The Sister Arts: The Tradition of Literary Pictorialism and English Poetry from Dryden to Gray* (Chicago, 1958); Morris R. Brownell, *Alexander Pope and the Arts of Georgian England* (Oxford, 1978); Ronald Paulson, *Book and Painting: Shakespeare, Milton, and the Bible: Literary Texts and the Emergence of English Painting* (Knoxville, TN, 1982); Hugh Wittemeyer, *George Eliot and the Visual Arts* (New Haven, 1979); Joan Grundy, *Thomas Hardy and the Sister Arts* (London, 1979); Estella Lauter, *Women as Mythmakers: Poetry and Visual Art by Twentieth-Century Women* (Bloomington, IN, 1984); and Adeline R. Tintner, *The Museum World of Henry James* (Ann Arbor, MI, 1986).

placed embellishments, the illustrations in the first editions of some nineteenth-century novels were meant to be closely integrated with the text, amplifying and giving finer point to what the novelist was attempting. Sometimes, notably in the case of Dickens, the novelist worked closely with the illustrator to make sure that the pictures, to be inserted at specified places in the text, would have a complementary rhetorical effect.[80]

Inseparable from questions of taste are those of the attitudes and opinions on nonartistic matters held by the people to whom writers have addressed themselves. Much present-day criticism recognizes the advantage of considering literary works as implicit dialogues between writer and reader, their effect residing, to a greater or less degree, in the tension between the writer's announced or presumptive purpose and the reader's preconceptions and expectations concerning the subject under discussion.

Comprehension of an author's purpose (to entertain? instruct? condemn? inspire? dissuade? soothe? . . .) and the means adopted to achieve it is increased if we can find out what conception of the prospective audience the artist held. But if this specific evidence is lacking, we still can discover much about the audience. Here again the diverse and often scattered and obscure data of social history are invaluable. Alfred Harbage's books, *Shakespeare's Audience* (1941) and *As They Liked It* (1947), and more recently Andrew Gurr's broader study, *Playgoing in Shakespeare's London* (1987), have done much to clarify our hitherto hazy or misinformed notions of the

---

[80]For a full account of Dickens's collaborative relationship with his principal illustrator, Hablôt K. Browne, see Michael Steig, *Dickens and Phiz* (Bloomington, IN, 1978) and the more comprehensive study by Jane R. Cohen, *Charles Dickens and His Original Illustrators* (Columbus, OH, 1980). Among other recent works in the field of book illustration may be cited Robert Halsband, *"The Rape of the Lock" and Its Illustrations 1714–1896* (Oxford, 1980); John Harvey, *Victorian Novelists and Their Illustrators* (New York, 1971); N. John Hall, *Trollope and His Illustrators* (London, 1980); and Michael Hancher, *The Tenniel Illustrations to the "Alice" Books* (Columbus, OH, 1985).

social distribution of the clientele that attended the Shakespearean playhouse, the nature of its education and moral attitudes, and its expectations, whether of entertainment or of edification, as it paid its pennies at the entrance. The development of a mass reading audience, beginning in the eighteenth century, has been shown to be the result of many forces—educational, political, economic, religious—which combined, though often at cross purposes, to stimulate the reading habit among ordinary people.

All the kinds of inquiry suggested in the present section require data lying off the usual path of literary investigation. Seeking to unravel problems associated with the size, shape, and topographical orientation of the second Globe theater, John Orrell consulted mathematicians, astronomers, and the classic *De Re Architectura* by Marcus Vitruvius Pollo (first century B.C.), reaching, as one of his conclusions, the hypothesis that the Globe was "a theatre designed according to a system which incorporates the unmeasurable quantity of the ratio between the square and its contingent circles, a mystery which fascinated artists and scientists alike in the Renaissance, and which through Vitruvian theory was seen to link the human body to the ideal proportions of the cosmos. . . . Here surely is the true English Theatre of the World." Interpreting the underlying satirical intention of Ben Jonson's poetry and plays requires one to delve into the records of the early seventeenth-century English court and of the noble families who populated it. Students seeking to reveal the esoteric relationships between Blake's poetry and his handmade illustrated books must acquire expertise in the art of engraving. Our understanding of Wordsworth's early poetry and *The Prelude* is enhanced when we have at our fingertips as much as can be learned, at this late date, about the people he knew as a youth in the Lake District, the local traditions, and the small details of everyday life in that time and place. To assess the possible effects Keats's experience as a medical student had on the images and ideas in his poetry, it is necessary to establish the exact content of medical education in early nineteenth-century London and the information Keats would thus have acquired in such fields as chemistry, pathology, and materia medica. Coleridge's opium addiction, which had so momentous an influence on his personal life, is better understood if we resort to the literature of toxicology, including evidence of the way the use of narcotics was viewed in Coleridge's time by both physicians and laypersons.[81]

Apart from the information and vivid period-sense it provides, such free exploration of the sources is the surest means by which the scholar can build up relative immunity against the most common errors of literary-historical study. Some of these fallacies and oversights are peculiar to intellectual and social history; others, as we have seen, imperil the incautious in the various fields of specifically literary inquiry as well. They are:

1. *Unwarranted generalization.* This, probably the commonest of all perils, has the most varied origins. The instinctive preference most minds have for simplicity and uniformity when coping with large concepts or tendencies tempts us to make sweeping statements and unqualified assumptions where no such easy reductions are permissible. Generalizations cannot, of course, be avoided, but in adopting them, scholars must ask themselves, and satisfactorily answer, such questions as these:

(a) Have I taken adequate account of the complexity of the phenomenon I am describing or using as the basis of

[81]On these respective topics, see John Orrell, *The Quest for Shakespeare's Globe* (Cambridge, 1983); David Riggs, *Ben Jonson: A Life* (Cambridge, MA, 1989); Joseph Viscomi, *The Art of William Blake's Illuminated Prints* (Manchester, 1983); T. W. Thompson, *Wordsworth's Hawkshead,* ed. Robert Woof (Oxford, 1970), the product of the avocation, for sixty years, of a schoolmaster who died in 1968; Donald C. Goellnicht, *The Poet-Physician: Keats and Medical Science* (Pittsburgh, 1984); and Mollie Lefebure, *Samuel Taylor Coleridge: A Bondage of Opium* (London, 1974). Lefebure, it might be noted, came to literary scholarship by an unusual route: for six years she was private secretary to the British Home Office pathologist and the head of the Department of Forensic Medicine at a leading London hospital. "Since we were largely dealing with criminal cases in our daily work," she writes, "I learned a considerable amount about drugs and poisons."

my argument? (The spread of the reading habit in the eighteenth and nineteenth centuries, for instance, was a cultural development with so many ramifications, limitations, and exceptions that every reference to it must be carefully qualified.)

(b) Have I allowed for opposing tendencies or doctrines? (The Renaissance was accompanied by a counter-Renaissance, and in every age that cherished the idea of progress there was a concurrent tendency to deny that very idea. Because the Romantic movement dominates the history of English literature from 1800 to 1830—arbitrary dates in any case—we are prone to overlook the fact that eighteenth-century structures of thought and literary tastes were still predominant, the Romantics being only part-time innovators.)

(c) Were the attitudes, presuppositions, values in question prevalent *at the particular time* I am talking about? And were they peculiarly characteristic of that era? (Climates of thought are constantly changing. The intellectual orientation of an "Elizabethan" writing in 1570 was not the same as that of another "Elizabethan" writing in 1600. By the same token, some of the strains of moral and social bias that are facilely called "Victorian" were already in the air, and influencing thought and ways of life, decades before Queen Victoria came to the throne in 1837.)

(d) Have I allowed for the variant forms a doctrine or concept may take (though it may be called by the same name) under the auspices of different writers or in different eras? (No two authors interpreted in precisely the same way the doctrine of "benevolence"—which, incidentally, was widespread before its reputed author, the third earl of Shaftesbury, was born—and the doctrine itself was modified with the passage of time.)

(e) Is the body of evidence large enough to justify a general statement, or am I mistaking the unusual and the exceptional for the normal? (Remember Montesquieu's newspaper-reading roofer.)

(f) Am I unconsciously accepting clichés and stereotypes handed down from previous writers who have failed to ask themselves the above questions? (It is an exaggeration to say flatly that the neoclassicists "distrusted" the imagination; the Middle Ages were no more characterized by serene and universal "faith" than the eighteenth century was unexceptionally an "age of reason"; and the notion of a once-existent "merrie England" where everybody, from lord to serf, gorged himself on plum pudding, wassail, and good fellowship, is a figment of sentimental sociology.)

2. (Vice-versa.) *Unwarranted specification.* The pitfall we have already noticed in connection with attribution and source-hunting also awaits the careless student of cultural history: that of mistaking for a novelty, a unique peculiarity at a given period, or in one author, what was in fact a commonplace of thought with a long previous history.

3. *Failure to allow for prejudice and emotional distortion in the sources.* Here close and sympathetic reading is important. Anyone can see at a glance that the Puritans' descriptions of the riotousness that they alleged typified both conditions in the playhouses and the private lives of the players are of dubious worth as sober history: the frenetic language gives them away. But unreliability is not always so apparent, and language that is notably judicious and restrained may muffle the sound of a grinding ax. It is the scholar's business to cultivate a knowledge of historical situation and person that will facilitate detection of whatever partisanship or animosity, selfseeking or championship of a cause, lurks in a superficially objective document.

4. *Unhistorical or oversimplified reading of language.* The meaning of many of the key words used in the documents of intellectual and social history constantly shifted as discussion of the ideas they represented progressed, and some also possessed several meanings at once. Accurate interpretation of evidence and the making of a sound case require the scholar to determine the precise intended meaning of a word each time it occurs. As Raymond Williams showed in *Culture and Society 1780–1950*

(1958), the key words *industry, art, culture,* and *class* either entered common usage or acquired new meanings in the late eighteenth and early nineteenth centuries, and all study of the discussion, dating from that period or later, of the role of culture and the arts in an industrial, democratic society must take account of these semantic shifts and their reflection of contemporary thought.

5. *The attribution of modern judgments to another age.* In reconstructing the attitudes and responses an event (or a poem) would likely have evoked in its time, we must exclude any reaction of our own insofar as it is conditioned by the time and place in which we live. To a certain extent, of course, human nature is changeless, and we react to the elementary situations of life—love and hope and grief and fear—as members of every other generation have. If this were not so, much literature of past ages would say nothing to us. But we must recognize the historical differential that sets each generation apart from every other: the ethical, religious, political, and other attitudes that are not for all time but of an age.

The anachronistic fallacy, as it can be called, may take the form either of attributing present-day attitudes to a past society or of reproaching that society for *not* sharing our values. Until relatively recently in both America and Britain, as elsewhere, people sincerely subscribed to attitudes, especially relating to justice and equality, that are anathema to us now. Even authors who came to oppose some of those strains of social and political thought had acquired them in the first place from the prevailing ethos. Those societies may have been, in our view, sexist, bigoted, stupid, unfeeling, ignorant, hypocritical, narrow-minded—whatever adjective best fits the individual case—but they did not know they were. In discussing literary works from the past, we must consider them in the framework of history; their authors may have been unconscious of issues that are of great concern to us. Nowhere in literary studies is the necessity for historical perspective more urgent than where ideological disagreement is involved. But once we have successfully eliminated modern bias, there remains the task of deciding, so far as we can, which of several historically possible attitudes

or responses would have been most probable in the circumstances.

These fundamental rules can be found, amply illustrated,
expanded, and supplemented, in various treatises on historical
method. But what they amount to, for the purposes of literary
study, is very simply expressed. They are among the empirical
lessons learned by many generations of inquirers after truth.
With their aid, the historian, including the historian of literature,
reads more accurately the record of human life; they enable him
to determine with increased confidence what really happened,
and why. And to this inherited realism of approach scholars add
what is at least as valuable, the intelligence they personally
bring to their task: an intelligence sharpened by their own direct
experience and observation. No textbook, no long shelf lined
with textbooks, offers any substitute for the intellectual keen-
ness gained from living and watching. In the last analysis, it is
this combination of received and privately cultivated wisdom
that makes literary research an effective instrument of learning.
It is the application of the testimony of life to literary assumptions—not only to what a work seems to assert, but to what its
author's purposes and achievement are reputed to be.

Let the last words, in summary, be those of A. N. Wilson,
writing of C. S. Lewis's *The Discarded Image:*

> . . . old books must be read with delicacy; with a sense that
> if we go blundering into them, assuming that they mean what
> we mean by words like *sky, earth, history,* or *nature* we shall
> get everything wrong. If we read the books in *their* way—
> whether we are reading Dante, or Chaucer, or Isidore of
> Seville—we will get something from it. The more we soak up
> their way of looking at things, their method of understanding,
> the more we shall get.[82]

---

[82]*C. S. Lewis: A Biography* (New York, 1990) 64.

CHAPTER FOUR

Finding Materials

Knowledge is of two kinds. We know a subject ourselves, or we know where we can find information upon it. When we enquire into any subject, the first thing we have to do is know what books have treated of it.

— Samuel Johnson, before dinner at Mr. Cambridge's house, 1775

T his chapter deals with the basic tools of literary research, which enable scholars to take the utmost advantage of all existing printed or unprinted sources. This, of course, the standards of our profession obligate us to do. We must always lead, as the diplomatic jargon has it, from a position of maximum strength; our statements must rest on a sure knowledge of all the relevant facts. And only thoroughness can insure us against one of the most painful blunders a researcher can commit—trumpeting as a fresh "discovery" some information that was scholarly news when we were in grade school. Apart from the time we have wasted, we suffer the acute embarrassment of being proved not to have done our bibliographical homework satisfactorily. Listen again to Dr. Johnson's trenchant words:

By the Means of Catalogues only can it be known, what has been written on every Part of Learning, and the Hazard avoided of encountering Difficulties which have already been cleared, discussion of Questions which have already been decided, and digging in Mines of Literature which former Ages have exhausted.

How often this has been the Fate of Students, every Man of Letters can declare, and, perhaps, there are very few who have not sometimes valued as new Discoveries, made by themselves, those Observations, which have long since been published, and of which the World therefore will refuse them the Praise; nor can that Refusal be censured as any enormous Violation of Justice; for, why should they not forfeit by their Ignorance, what they might claim by their Sagacity?[1]

It is said that there once was a time when a scholar could carry all the bibliographical information needed under his or her hat. But the good old days ended at least three-quarters of a century ago. The gross (inter)national product of English and American literary scholarship has reached staggering proportions. In the three years preceding the preparation of this freshly revised edition, the average annual count of books and articles on Chaucer was 141; on Milton, 138; on Shakespeare, the undisputed leader, 588; on Emily Dickinson, 55; on Faulkner, 111; on Joyce, 219; on Virginia Woolf, 63. To find one's way through the ever-thickening jungle of print in pursuit of a topic becomes a steadily more formidable task.

The exact procedure to be followed in using bibliographies, and the number of bibliographies that have to be consulted, differs with every problem.[2] Ordinarily the most direct way to find what has been written about a strictly limited topic (the boar in *Venus and Adonis,* the game of ombre in *The Rape of*

[1]"An Account of the Harleian Library," *Gentleman's Magazine* 12 (1742): 637.

[2]Except in a very few great libraries, which contain virtually everything printed on a topic, and for special limited problems, a library catalogue is not a tool of scholarly bibliography. Since it is only a location-directory to a particular stock of books and analyzes the contents of relatively few of these, it should never be resorted to for the guidance that thorough research requires.

the Lock, the influence of Persian poetry on Emerson's work) is to go to the appropriate one of the two basic bibliographies in our field: the *New Cambridge Bibliography of English Literature* (with the caution noted below, pp. 161–62) or the *Literary History of the United States (LHUS),* whose now dated bibliography is being superseded by the sixteen-volume *Bibliography of United States Literature* (1991–). In one or the other of these tools, you may find references to the precise books or articles that will give you the information you want, or, failing that, it may direct you to a specialized bibliography on the subject, which will contain the desired references. In either case, once you have obtained your information, you are finished—almost. For one precaution is necessary. There is a chance that the information you have found has subsequently been modified, amplified, or challenged. By consulting more recent bibliographical sources (to be mentioned on pp. 162–63), you can make sure that you are abreast of the very latest state of knowledge.

Many research projects, however, are of larger scope, requiring the use of not one but several, perhaps even a dozen or more bibliographies. Since we want to enjoy a fairly wide view of the bibliographical landscape, in the rest of this chapter we shall assume a topic of quite ambitious dimensions, always with the understanding that no two projects are ever conducted in exactly the same manner and that very few call into play all the kinds of bibliographies we shall be mentioning.

At the outset, it should be noted that there are two large-scale compilations that are indispensable to work in any field of literary interest. One is James L. Harner's *Literary Research Guide: A Guide to Reference Sources for the Study of Literatures in English and Related Topics* (1989); the other, which appeared almost simultaneously after being in preparation for many years, is Michael J. Marcuse's *A Reference Guide for English Studies* (1990). Although Harner calls Marcuse's work "a valuable complement" to his own, for most purposes a researcher need consult one or the other, seldom both. Each of the thousands of entries in both volumes includes a detailed descriptive, and in some cases evaluative, annotation. Harner's book is slightly more up-to-date, Marcuse's cutoff point being 1985. The two differ in degrees of comprehensiveness: Marcuse's wider scope, embracing as it does much peripheral material, may well be as much a hindrance as a help in most investigations. On balance, Harner's book is to be preferred, not only because it is physically easier to handle and more efficiently organized and indexed but because its low price, as an MLA not-for-profit publication, enables it to be bought as an ever-handy book for home use.

Every researcher has to decide which reference tools, among the multitude listed in Harner and Marcuse, have possible relevance to the work in hand, and in what order it would be most efficient to use them. Usually it is best to break the ground of a large-sized enterprise with one of the two "first-help" guides already mentioned—the *NCBEL* or *LHUS,* supplemented, in the former case, by T. H. Howard-Hill's *Bibliography of British Literary Bibliographies* (vol. 1 of his *Index to British Literary Bibliography*). From there the next move is to specialized bibliographies. A paper on the medieval lyric, for instance, would call for Carleton Brown's *Register of Middle English Religious and Didactic Verse,* the later Brown and Robbins *Index of Middle English Verse* (and supplement), and John Edwin Wells's *Manual of the Writings in Middle English,* in the revised and enlarged edition by J. Burke Severs and others. Other specialized bibliographies—literally thousands of them, including compilations relating to very recent and contemporary writers such as Gwendolyn Brooks, Flannery O'Connor, Phillis Wheatley, Langston Hughes, James Baldwin, Zora Neale Hurston—are devoted to individual authors. Some of these bibliographies ("primary" ones) are limited to works *by* the author, often with minute details of publication, subsequent editions, and so forth. Some ("secondary") are devoted instead to lengthy lists of the factual and critical material that has been published *about* the author. Some cover both areas. At their best, they are so full as to obviate the need to consult other bibliographical sources, except to bring the record up to date. But relatively few are so gratifyingly exhaustive; most simply provide the easiest starting point for further investigation.

What if the topic is a literary theme (the Danaë myth in English poetry), the history of a technique (stream of consciousness before Joyce), the relation of a genre to the thought of a given period (the familiar essay and the concept of "romanticism"), or some other general subject? The *NCBEL,* Howard-Hill, and *LHUS* are again the best starting places, though some time and patience are required to round up the needed references; the researcher may find what is wanted under "General," "Literary Movements," "Social Background," "Intellectual Relations"—it all depends on the classifications and headings the editor has adopted. Beyond these specifically literary guides, there is a wide range of general "subject bibliographies" that will be glanced at on pages 176–77.

Several groups of the Modern Language Association have sponsored extremely useful "guides to research" in the English romantic poets and essayists (two volumes, one edited in the current edition by Frank Jordan, Jr., and the other by Carolyn W. and Lawrence H. Houtchens), the Victorian poets (Frederic E. Faverty), Victorian fiction (two volumes, the earlier edited by Lionel Stevenson, the more recent by George H. Ford), the major Victorian writers of nonfictional prose (David J. De Laura), Victorian periodicals (two volumes by J. Don Vann and Rosemary T. Van Arsdel), and Anglo-Irish literature (Richard J. Finneran). Five volumes should be checked for American writers: eight major nineteenth-century ones (current edition by James Woodress), twelve additional nineteenth-century ones as well as Edward Taylor, Jonathan Edwards, and Benjamin Franklin (Robert A. Rees and Earl N. Harbert), sixteen twentieth-century authors (Jackson R. Bryer), American women writers (Maurice Duke, Jackson R. Bryer, and M. Thomas Inge), and black American writers (Inge, Duke, and Bryer). These thirteen bibliographies take the form of evaluative essays, each written by a specialist, surveying and assessing the bibliographical, editorial, biographical, and critical work that has been done on the authors treated. The experts, by calling attention to topics that have hitherto been neglected, often provide suggestions for fruitful research.

As you work through one bibliography after another, the law

of diminishing returns is bound to set in. Most of the references found have already been noted. But there is always that "plaguy hundredth chance," as Browning's Bishop Blougram put it, that in the next bibliography you open, an obscure item, overlooked by all the others, will change the whole direction or complexion of your project. Time-consuming though the chore may be, there is really no alternative to canvassing every bibliography that shows even the faintest promise of having something for you.

To this all-important survey of the existing books and articles on a given topic must be brought not only the proverbial fine-tooth comb but also a constant awareness that bibliographies and reference works vary greatly in authority. This has always been a fact of scholarly life, but it has become more evident—and more of a problem—in the years since the 1950s, which witnessed the proliferation of academic libraries large and small, on new university campuses and in community colleges. Several publishers, scenting rich profits in supplying reference materials to this suddenly expanded market, commissioned and produced hundreds of such books, often without having them pass the inspection of qualified authorities. This lack of quality control has placed numerous third-rate author bibliographies, for example, on the same shelves as the most reliable works of the sort, and unless one consults reviews in scholarly journals, it is often difficult for one to decide whether a certain bibliography can be relied upon. Reviews in the library press seldom apply scholarly criteria to publications meant for scholarly use. And the inadequacies of older bibliographies are not regularly indicated in such librarian's bibles as Sheehy's *Guide to Reference Books* (see below, p. 176).[3]

If your project involves the Gothic novel, for instance, it is well to handle one of the more obvious tools, Montague Summers's *A Gothic Bibliography,* with great caution, for it is ex-

---

[3]See Richard D. Altick, "Bibliographies: How Much Should a Reviewer Tell?" *Literary Reviewing,* ed. James O. Hoge (Charlottesville, VA, 1987) 68–79.

tremely careless in regard to titles and dates. Never trust appear-
ances or the assurances of the compiler or the publisher; the
façade of a bibliography may be noble and its dimensions imposing, but closer inspection may well reveal serious defects of
bibliographical workmanship. The accuracy and thoroughness
of every such guide can be determined only by reference to
authoritative reviews and practical experience in using it.

The number of absolutely complete bibliographies is negligible, if, indeed, any such exists. The compilers may have deliberately been selective or otherwise limited their range of coverage; or they may not have had access to libraries in which they
could have discovered many more titles; or they may simply
have overlooked some items. One old vellum-bound folio
owned by the Bodleian Library is not entered in its printed
catalogue for the sufficient reason that during the whole process of compilation, the editor was sitting on it.[4]

Seldom do bibliographies adequately "analyze" (distribute
under all relevant subject-headings) the contents of a book that
has numerous distinct topics. At best, they provide a certain
number of cross-references to the main entry. Normally a book
or article is listed, as it should be, under the topic announced in
its title. It may, however, contain valuable material on another
topic—the very one you are investigating. Hence it is prudent
not to limit oneself to the most directly relevant subject-heading
but to look also under related headings that might harbor items
of tangential value. The more you read around in bibliographies, the more you discover.

Most bibliographies compiled by groups of contributors are
bound to be uneven and to some extent inconsistent. The
NCBEL, whatever its considerable virtues, is notorious for the
unequal treatment it apportions to various authors; some sections are thorough, others are superficial. Although in most
cases the *NCBEL* is the best place to begin research into a topic
in English literature down to the middle of the twentieth cen-

---

[4]William Dunn Macray, *Annals of the Bodleian Library Oxford* (2nd ed.,
Oxford, 1890) 388n.

tury, it should never be relied upon for complete lists either of an author's works or of the scholarly and critical work that has been done on them, or for accurate titles, dates, or lists of editions.

Bibliographies are prime examples of inherent obsolescence. Even when they are confined to the works of an author published, say, in his lifetime and the first century after his death, they are subject to revision in the light of newly found editions or new data on editions already recorded. If they list secondary material, the progress of scholarship and criticism renders them incomplete from the moment the editor sends his copy to the printer. Therefore, it is essential to continue the search down to the present minute, beginning not with the actual year when the bibliography was issued but two or three years earlier, which may be nearer the time when the manuscript was finished. For this vital purpose, among others, serial bibliographies have been established, the oldest dating from the time of the First World War. Three annual lists cover English literary studies: the _MLA International Bibliography,_ which is also strong on linguistics;[5] the _Annual Bibliography of English Language and Literature,_ published by the Modern Humanities Research Association, the British-based counterpart of the MLA; and _The Year's Work in English Studies,_ which makes no attempt to be exhaustive but whose chapters conveniently review, with summaries and (usually) brief critical comments, the more important books and articles published during the year.

In addition, specialized bibliographies appear in the pages of various learned journals.[6] The major ones in English literature,

[5]The _MLAIB_ is now accessible online from 1964 (eventually, from its beginning in 1921). Since 1981, each volume contains a subject index, and information is accessible further via CD-ROM through key-word searches.

[6]This moment is as appropriate as any to point out that it is a _faux pas,_ no less deplorable than eating peas with a knife, to speak of our professional publications as "magazines." Magazines are publications of miscellaneous content for the lay reader: _Time_ and _Smithsonian_ are magazines. The proper generic term to use is _periodicals;_ if the periodicals are devoted

published annually, cover the Restoration and eighteenth century (formerly in *PQ*, now published as a monograph with the title *The Eighteenth Century: A Current Bibliography* under the auspices of the American Society for Eighteenth Century Studies), the Romantic movement (a monograph entitled *The Romantic Movement: A Selective and Critical Bibliography*, formerly in *ELH*, *Philological Quarterly*, and *English Language Notes*), the Victorian age (formerly in *Modern Philology*, now in *Victorian Studies*), and the twentieth century (in *Twentieth-Century Literature*). A selective annotated list of important articles—not books—on American literature appears in each quarterly issue of *American Literature*. This can be supplemented, especially in respect to books, by the annual *American Literary Scholarship*, which is analogous to *The Year's Work in English Studies* but more authoritative.[7] Other serial bibliographies list work in such areas as Old English studies, folklore, Shakespeare, the Keats-Shelley circle, Afro-American (also American Indian, Hispanic American, and Jewish American) literature, Australian (and Canadian, Caribbean, etc.) literature, literature and psychology, literature and science, film, short fiction, popular culture, fantasy, science fiction, women's studies, prose style, bibliographical studies, and modern drama. All of these inevitably overlap; a book or article with wide ramifications may be listed in as many as half a dozen bibliographies. But that is all to the good, because such duplication reduces by just so much the chance that a scholar will miss the very item most needed.[8]

---

mainly to research, they are *journals;* if to criticism, *reviews.* But never "magazines."

[7]The very first of these specialized period bibliographies, the Renaissance one in *Studies in Philology,* was concluded with the issue for 1969, but its file of course remains useful.

[8]Scanning a whole run of a serial bibliography is a tiring business, but the publication of collected and indexed volumes has minimized the toil in several cases. The *PQ* bibliography of Restoration and eighteenth-century studies is collected 1925–70 in six volumes; the *ELH-PQ-ELN* Romantic, 1936–70, in seven volumes; the Victorian, 1932–85, in five volumes; the

Not the least important of the services rendered by some of these compilations (among the general ones, the MHRA *Annual Bibliography,* which in this respect is clearly superior to the *MLA International*) is their practice of listing reviews of new scholarly and critical books in their respective fields. Whether one is using a book in direct connection with a research project or reading it to broaden one's knowledge of a subject, e.g., in preparing for an M.A. or a Ph.D. general examination or a thesis or a dissertation, it is always good to find out what reception it has had among the experts. Acquaintance with the scholarly notices may save one from trusting what is actually an unreliable book. Thus the register of reviews in the annual bibliographies (which should be consulted for at least three years after the book's publication because reviews of scholarly books are often late in appearing), supplemented by the list of reviews included in each issue of the *Humanities Index,* constitutes our professional equivalent of the index of more popular reviews contained in the *Book Review Digest.*

An ideally thorough survey of all that has been written on a topic includes dissertations. By no stretch of the charitable imagination can some of them be regarded as having any value for research. On the other hand, many unpublished dissertations contain factual and bibliographical material that is not found elsewhere or critical interpretations that fully deserve to be absorbed into the mainstream of literary study. One should begin with McNamee's *Dissertations in English and American Literature,* which brings the record down to 1973. This computer-produced listing of dissertations accepted at American, English, and German universities is limited in general to those written in departments of English. Because McNamee's cutoff date is 1973 and because dissertations of substantial importance to literary studies are also occasionally written in other disciplines such as drama, philosophy, and history, it is essential to

---

twentieth century, 1954–70, with thousands of additional items, in seven volumes; and American literature, 1900–75 (articles only, but with many additions), currently in three volumes, with a supplement in preparation.

go to the lists, covering all fields, in the *Comprehensive Dissertation Index 1861–1972* (1973), with its annual supplements (cumulated 1973–82).

Now comes the question of how to locate printed material that is not in your headquarters library. Thanks to the highly developed services and guidebooks of American librarianship, this task is not difficult. One basic tool to refer to, once you have ascertained that the book you need is not in your library, is the 685–volume *National Union Catalog: Pre-1956 Imprints* (and supplement of additions and corrections, volumes 686–754), which indexes in a single alphabet the holdings of over two thousand libraries in the United States and Canada. The largest single publishing enterprise ever undertaken down to its time (528,000 pages!),[9] it has rendered obsolete the older printed Library of Congress Catalog, which listed the books on the LC shelves down to 1956 and gave locations for some books in some other libraries as well. Along with its open-ended continuation, which lists titles acquired by all participating libraries since 1956 (but has been published only in microfiche since 1983), the *NUC* provides a master key to the contents of most American libraries of research importance and constitutes the only national union list of books in any country in the world.[10] It is supplemented, for books published since the early 1970s, by the OCLC (Online Computer Library Center), the computerized network that currently records over 20 million titles of books and other materials in nine thousand affiliated libraries,

---

[9]For sheer number of volumes, the prize now goes to the New York Public Library, whose 10 million deteriorating catalogue cards have been published in eight hundred volumes as well as on microfilm. See the *Dictionary Catalog of the Research Libraries of the New York Public Library, 1911–1971* (New York, 1983).

[10]For a full description of the range of research needs addressed by the *National Union Catalog*, see Thomas Mann, *A Guide to Library Research Methods* (New York, 1983) 106–16. In addition to their chief function, the locating of copies of a given work, the *NUC* and OCLC are often useful for verifying titles and dates of publication.

including the LC. It may be searched by using terminals at any of the subscribing libraries (see below, p. 179).

Another aid to locating books is Robert B. Downs's *American Library Resources,* a bibliography of printed catalogues, inventories, exhibition lists, and other guides to individual library collections. By referring to the local lists cited by Downs, you can often locate nearby copies of the books you need. Particularly useful in this search are the general catalogues that various American libraries—the Boston Athenaeum, the Peabody in Baltimore, and so on—issued in the nineteenth century before card indexing replaced the former system of cataloguing a library's whole collection in printed volumes.

In addition, some scholarly bibliographies give at least one, and as many as five or ten, locations for each book they list. Among the multivolume standard works, the *Short-Title Catalogue* (of English books printed through 1640) locates copies, as do Donald Wing's continuation of the same catalogue to 1700, and now the *Eighteenth-Century Short-Title Catalogue,* a machine-readable bibliography and union list of materials in any language printed in Britain or its territories and in North America or printed in English anywhere in the world between 1701 and 1800; Joseph Sabin's *Bibliotheca Americana;* and Charles Evans's *American Bibliography.* So do many more specialized bibliographies, such as Carl J. Stratman's *Bibliography of Medieval Drama,* W. W. Greg's *Bibliography of the English Printed Drama,* and William H. McBurney's *Check List of English Prose Fiction.*

The *Union List of Serials* and its continuation, *New Serial Titles,* serve the same purpose for periodicals. Once you become accustomed to the abbreviated system of entry, which is not difficult, you can discover which American libraries have files of the periodical you need to examine and exactly how extensive those files are—beginning when, ending when, and lacking which volumes.

Before going to the trouble of borrowing the books or periodical volumes you need, however, it is well to make sure that they have not already been reproduced in microform (a generic term that includes microfilm, microcard, microprint, and microfiche). In recent decades the development of the several different microreproduction processes has enabled even libraries of fairly modest proportions to acquire immense quantities of rare books and periodicals. Every pre-1641 English book (called, for short, an *"STC"* book), and a large selection of those from 1641 to 1700; thousands of English and American plays; complete files of hundreds of literary periodicals and of newspapers, ranging from the London *Times* to small-town Iowa weeklies; every American imprint listed in Evans's *American Bibliography,* beginning with the "Bay Psalm Book" of 1640 and reaching down to 1800; thousands of the nineteenth-century English and American novels listed in the bibliographies of Michael Sadleir and Lyle H. Wright; numerous author manuscript collections, library and government archive collections; doctoral dissertations written since the Second World War; and many other kinds of source material, totaling tens of millions of pages, are available in microform in the library of nearly every institution that offers graduate degrees in the humanities. Entries for certain classes of microtext, such as *STC* books, files of periodicals, and pre-1800 American imprints, usually are found in their alphabetical places in the library's main catalogue. But some other classes are not so catalogued, and in any event, practice differs from library to library. Furthermore, because of budgetary limitations not all libraries receive all the microtexts that are issued. If you are in doubt whether the books you want are available in your library in microform, ask a librarian.

Microtext series are projects to which many cooperating libraries subscribe, just as they do to periodicals and other kinds of serials. Numerous firms now prepare and sell microforms of books, journals, and other materials; their stocks are listed in the annual *Guide to Microforms in Print.*

Much additional material, such as miscellaneous out-of-the-way books, pamphlets, newspapers of local interest, and obscure journals, has been reproduced by individual libraries and other agencies on special order. The masters from which prints can be made are located in the serial *National Register of Microform Masters.*

Thus no scholar nowadays has to be limited to what is to be

found in the book stacks; the thousands of little boxes filed in another part of the library building contain material whose originals would otherwise occupy miles of shelf space, and would cost the library, if they could be obtained at all, the price of several NASA space shuttles. Infinite riches in a little room, indeed! And modern technology has given researchers one more boon. If they must work constantly with a certain rare item, and convenience and concern for their eyes make it undesirable to spend many hours at a microtext reader, full-sized photocopies can be made.

Sometimes a research task involves a particular copy of a book—one that contains, for example, annotations by its author or by a subsequent reader, such as Keats's copies of Shakespeare or Melville's copy of Arnold's poems. Leads to the present whereabouts of such books can be found in certain author bibliographies and the catalogues and other guides to special collections listed in Downs's *American Library Resources*. If these prove of no help, results can sometimes be obtained by tracing the movements of the book from the time it left its owner's library. Countless annotated books and "association" copies, prized because of their unique literary and sentimental interest, have passed from collector to collector, frequently by way of a bookseller's auction.

For reconstructing this pedigree of successive ownership, which can, with reasonable luck, reveal the book's present location, the basic tools are the printed catalogues of various private collections (Ashley, Britwell Court, Huth, Newton, etc.) in the nineteenth and early twentieth centuries; two histories of book collecting, Seymour De Ricci's *English Collectors of Books and Manuscripts (1530–1930)*[11] and Carl L. Cannon's *American Book Collectors and Collecting*; and the files of the several annual records of book sales, such as *Book-Prices Current*. If the book you are looking for appears to have turned up last in

[11]On the incredible De Ricci, a walking data processing machine whose brain held the exact history of ownership and present location of several million books and *objets d'art,* see E. Ph. Goldschmidt's obituary article in *The Library* 4th series 24 (1944): 187–94.

a bookseller's or auction house catalogue, write the seller. Although some firms are reluctant to divulge the names of purchasers, you may succeed in learning who bought the volume. Often the paper trail will end at a library, where, ordinarily, the book will be made available to you; if it ends at the doorstep of a private collector, there is no harm in writing to ask whether, in the interests of research, you might be allowed to examine it.[12] Many collectors willingly cooperate, but some regard their literary treasures as chattels whose main value resides in their prospective sale price or in their uniqueness. (It is reported that when the political scientist Harold Laski tried to see one of the manuscripts of John Stuart Mill's *Autobiography,* the owner, reputedly Lord Rosebery, "sent an unsigned note saying the pleasure of possessing a manuscript consisted in the fact that nobody else could see it.")[13]

Locating manuscripts calls for the same general techniques and, sometimes, the same bibliographical tools. Although some authors' personal archives, like their libraries, have been kept intact down through the years, dispersal has been much commoner, with the result that their books and papers are now scattered in scores of British and American libraries and private collections. To locate a particular item requires knowledge, ingenuity, patience, and persistence, in approximately equal, and generous, parts.[14] One should certainly check three major

[12]A good illustration of the technique of running down particular copies is found in two narratives by Sir Geoffrey Keynes (*TLS*, March 8, 1957: 152, and May 3, 1957: 277) in which he describes his protracted but eventually successful search for Blake's annotated copies of Bacon and of Dante's *Inferno.*

[13]Jack Stillinger, "The Text of John Stuart Mill's *Autobiography,*" *Bulletin of the John Rylands Library* 43 (1960): 224n.

[14]For several copious examples of how widely a body of manuscripts may be dispersed, see Mary C. Hyde, "The History of the Johnson Papers," *PBSA* 40 (1951): 103–16; Kenneth N. Cameron (ed.), *Shelley and His Circle* (Cambridge, MA, 1961) 2: 892–913; and D. Anthony Bischoff, "The Manuscripts of Gerard Manley Hopkins," *Thought* 26 (1951): 551–80,

location tools—Philip M. Hamer's *Guide to Archives and Manuscripts in the United States,* now largely but not entirely superseded by a publication of the National Historical Publications and Records Commission, *Directory of Archives and Manuscript Repositories in the United States;* the Library of Congress's *National Union Catalog of Manuscript Collections* (a continuing series, also available in many libraries on alphabetically arranged cards); and *American Literary Manuscripts: A Checklist of Holdings in Academic, Historical, and Public Libraries, Museums, and Authors' Homes in the United States* (a project of the Modern Language Association's American literature group; revised edition, 1977). These have made it possible to discover in a few minutes which United States libraries have collections of individual American and English writers' personal papers, annotated books, and manuscripts of their published and unpublished works. It is also advisable to look into Downs's *American Library Resources;* there you can learn if a library has issued some sort of description or catalogue of its special collection of an author in whom you are interested. If it has, by tracking down the catalogue you can often discover the extent of the manuscript holdings. Additional valuable suggestions for tracing manuscript material in the United States are contained in the introduction to *American Literary Manuscripts,* just mentioned.

Finding a specific manuscript, as distinguished from broad collections, requires additional tools. The ones mentioned in the preceding paragraph, naturally, are first steps: there is a good chance that the document you seek may be found among the collections listed there. If it is not listed in the printed guides

---

supplemented by the preface to *The Journals and Papers of Gerard Manley Hopkins,* ed. Humphry House, completed by Graham Storey (London, 1959). An exciting narrative of the patient regathering of the manuscript of Frank Norris's *McTeague,* which had been broken up, page by page, to adorn sets of an expensive edition of Norris's works, is given in James D. Hart, "Search and Research: The Librarian and the Scholar," *College and Research Libraries* 19 (1958): 365–74.

to the collections that you suspect might contain it, bear in mind that most libraries have unpublished calendars (inventories) of their manuscripts, and a letter to the librarian or curator of the collection would settle the matter. For older manuscripts there is Seymour De Ricci and W. J. Wilson's *Census of Medieval and Renaissance Manuscripts in the United States and Canada*. For later manuscripts especially, follow the procedures outlined above in connection with finding specific copies of books.[15]

Researchers in English literature need to be equally at home among guides to British resources. Robert B. Downs's *British Library Resources* is useful for orientation. But since the British Library[16] is the richest research center in the United Kingdom, its 360-volume *General Catalogue of Printed Books to 1975,* with 8.5 million entries, is the supreme everyday tool—not only for locating books but for many bibliographical purposes.[17] There are many printed catalogues of special collections and classes of books in the library, such as incunabula, romances, seventeenth-century controversial pamphlets (the famous Thomason tracts), and pre-1641 books.

In respect to periodicals, the British are as well served as we are; their *British Union-Catalogue of Periodicals* and its partial successor, *Serials in the British Library,* are the equivalent of our *Union List of Serials* and often supplement the *ULS* by locating files of extremely rare or obscure periodicals that are not to be found in the United States.

---

[15]Lewis Carroll is known to have written nearly 103,000 letters. For the strategies used in a comprehensive effort to locate as many of these as possible, see Morton N. Cohen and Roger Lancelyn Green, "The Search for Lewis Carroll's Letters," *Manuscripts* 20 (Spring 1968): 4–15, and Cohen's more informal reminiscences, "Serendipity in Research," *Literary Research Newsletter* 9 (1984): 28–37. The product of this search was his two-volume collection, *The Letters of Lewis Carroll* (New York, 1979).

[16]The name since 1973 of the former British Museum Library. Obviously, the old title occurs in all pre-1973 books and articles that refer to materials in that vast collection.

[17]This catalogue is accessible online and via CD-ROM. Supplements are cumulated 1976–85; from 1986, these are on microfiche.

There are hundreds of printed catalogues of manuscript collections in the British Isles. The British Library has a number of "named" collections (Sloane, Egerton, Harleian, Cottonian, Stowe, Arundel, Lansdowne, etc.), most of which are richest in medieval and Renaissance material, and for which there are printed catalogues, though some are both ancient and inaccurate. But by far the biggest British Library collection is the so-called "Additional Manuscripts," into which have been funneled all the miscellaneous bequests and purchases of the past century and a half. The "Additionals" are most important to literary students because of the masses of papers they contain relating to British literary figures of the eighteenth, nineteenth, and twentieth centuries. The MS of Hawthorne's *The Marble Faun,* acquired in 1936, has the numbers Add. 44,889–44,890; the several MSS of *Finnegans Wake* are Add. 47,471–47,489. The *Index of Manuscripts in the British Library* in ten volumes (1984–86) consolidates more than thirty of these indexes and catalogues and lists in one alphabetical sequence all acquisitions down to 1950. For acquisitions after 1950, one should first check M. A. E. Nickson, *The British Library: Guide to the Catalogues and Indexes of the Department of Manuscripts* (1978) and the lists cumulated every five years since 1960.

Outside the British Library, the greatest concentrations of manuscripts are at the two old universities. The Bodleian at Oxford has a seven-volume *Summary Catalogue* of manuscripts, completed in 1953—a not wholly satisfactory compilation, but better than none at all. At Cambridge, the manuscripts owned by the various colleges have been catalogued in many volumes by Montague Rhodes James, provost of Eton and well-known author of ghost stories.[18] For a descriptive catalogue of specifically *literary* manuscripts of British writers, one should check the *Index of English Literary Manuscripts.* These four volumes (and a fifth volume index) (1980–), locate the manuscripts of the British and Irish writers from 1450–1900 who are found in the *Concise Cambridge Bibliography of English Litera-*

[18]See Michael Cox, *M. R. James: An Informal Portrait* (New York, 1983).

ture. The alphabetical entries exclude letters (though important collections are noted), but include marginalia in books as well as typescripts, notebooks, diaries, and so forth. Each entry begins with an introduction describing the extant manuscripts and the scholarly issues pertinent to them.

Then there are the catalogues of manuscripts held at other ecclesiastical and educational centers—Lambeth Palace, Westminster Abbey, cathedrals (Durham, Lincoln, Hereford, etc.), and the ancient public schools. Most of these manuscripts date from the Middle Ages and represent but a pathetic fragment of the wealth the religious foundations contained before the depredations of Henry VIII. Of frequent usefulness to literary scholars, also, are the many volumes of reports of the Royal Historical Manuscripts Commission, established in 1870 to make inventories of all archives in institutional and private hands to which access could be gained. Through the ensuing decades, inspectors of the Commission labored in the muniment rooms of old castles, the archives of municipal corporations, and the libraries of (mostly) aristocratic families. The results of these canvasses were printed in the capacious, small-type reports, which are in part simply calendars but which also contain great expanses of summaries and direct quotations from the documents examined. The long series is a rich mine of primary material for students working in any period down to the beginning of the nineteenth century. As Allan Nevins once pointed out, "Many of the searches of the Commission were made in the nick of time. . . . Numerous collections of family papers, especially those containing autographs of value, have been sold piecemeal; others have been bought in bulk and transported abroad" (i.e., to America), and others have been destroyed.[19] Thus the series often contains the only available excerpts and summaries from important historical documents that are now lost.

Supplementing the services of the HMC is the National Register of Archives, founded in 1945. It is a kind of union catalogue-*cum*-information clearing house for the contents of the various

---

[19]*The Gateway to History* (Boston, 1938) 106.

county record offices, which have grown more numerous and active in recent years, as well as of the private collections that have been inventoried by agencies other than the HMC. The so-called NRA Reports—manuscript, mimeographed, or printed indexes, analyses, excerpts, and summaries—facilitate access to the contents of over thirteen thousand archives. But the largest effort to supply a name and subject index to unpublished finding aids to British archives and manuscript collections is the *National Inventory of Documentary Sources in the United Kingdom,* an open-ended series produced on microfiche, which covers county record offices, university and public libraries, and private repositories. All this information is joined with similar data from the (American) *National Union Catalog of Manuscript Collections* and the catalogues of such major collections as the Folger and Huntington Libraries to form a master list that indicates at a glance where the papers of a given person or family are located.

With the HMC and NRA reports we cross the boundary between the tools designed for the student of literary history and those that serve more specifically historical research. As we saw in the final section of chapter 3, the literary investigator often needs information that lies within the province of the general historian. To find that information he must usually consult the general historian's tools. But specialized literary bibliographies are still of frequent assistance. For subjects immediately adjacent to literary history, such as the history of English education, printing and publishing, and the social backgrounds of some periods, the lists in the *NCBEL* are invaluable. So too are those on "Literature and Culture" and "Movements and Influences," which occupy half of the bibliographical volume of the *LHUS.* For very recent books and articles on historical subjects, the sections headed "Economic, Political, Religious, and Social Backgrounds" (or something similar) in the serial bibliographies devoted to particular periods of English and American literature are the best place to go. In some of these serials, to be sure, the coverage of nonliterary history is skimpy, but others, notably that for 1660–1800 in *The Eighteenth Century: A Cur-*

rent Bibliography and that for the Victorian era in *Victorian Studies,* are so full that they are as useful to professional historians as to literary students.

For topics in British history there is an older series of period bibliographies that begins with Wilfrid Bonser's *Anglo-Saxon and Celtic Bibliography* and Edgar B. Graves's *A Bibliography of English History to 1485.* The ensuing centuries are well covered in five more recent bibliographies, compiled by Conyers Read (supplemented by Mortimer Levine, *Tudor Britain*) for 1485–1603; Godfrey Davies (supplemented by J. S. Morrill, *Seventeenth-Century Britain*) for 1603–1714; Stanley Pargellis and D. J. Medley for 1714–89; Lucy M. Brown and Ian R. Christie for 1789–1851; and H. J. Hanham for 1851–1914. The record can be brought virtually down to date through Alfred F. Havighurst's *Modern England 1901–1970,* continued by the Royal Historical Society's annual bibliography of British and Irish history.

On American historical subjects, there is Henry P. Beers's list of *Bibliographies in American History* (1942), which can be supplemented for more recent material by the *Harvard Guide to American History,* by the American sections of the *American Historical Association's Guide to Historical Literature,* which is worldwide in scope, and by Francis Paul Prucha's *Handbook for Research in American History.*

Indispensable to historical research, less for their bibliographies (which are outdated, though often useful for leads to older sources) than for their factual information, are the two fullest ready-reference sources of biographical data: the *Dictionary of National Biography* (for Great Britain) and the *Dictionary of American Biography,* published in 1885–1900 and 1928–37, respectively. Each now has several supplementary volumes listing people who died after completion of the main alphabet, and a volume of the *DNB* now in preparation will contain articles on figures such as Gerard Manley Hopkins, who were overlooked in the main set. Though works of such magnitude are bound to have some errors, both the *DNB* and the *DAB* (now being revised and updated for publication in 1996 as *The American National Biography*) have a well-deserved reputation for accuracy. (It should be remembered, of course, that the articles in the original sixty-three volumes of the *DNB* were written a century ago, and subsequent research has often corrected or amplified their statements. The *DNB* should be cited as a source only when the information in question has not, to your knowledge, been amended by later writers.) Use of these volumes should be supplemented by the on-going series on writers, critics, publishers, and literary-historical movements in the *Dictionary of Literary Biography*.

But when the scholar must go beyond history into other areas of human interest that bear on literature, such as the fine arts, psychology, philosophy, religion, sociology—what then? There are no standard procedures; once again, every problem must be attacked in its own terms. Where he begins depends partly on the thoroughness with which he wants to acquaint himself with the topic. If he simply wishes to orient himself in a general way, or find a fact that might reasonably be expected to appear in a standard reference work, the best thing to do is consult the latest edition of Eugene P. Sheehy's *Guide to Reference Books* and its British counterpart, A. J. Walford's *Guide to Reference Material*. These contain well classified and annotated lists of the best bibliographies, histories, manuals, and encyclopedias in every field of learning. The lists are, naturally, not exhaustive for any one field, but somewhere among the half-dozen books to which one is referred may well be all the material needed. In addition, the researcher might consult the concise bibliographies appended to the longer articles on his topic in the *Encyclopaedia Britannica* and, even better, in specialized encyclopedias such as the *New Catholic Encyclopedia,* the *International Encyclopedia of the Social Sciences,* the *Encyclopedia of Philosophy,* the monumental *New Grove Dictionary of Music and Musicians,* and the *Encyclopedia of Religion.*

For more intensive study in fields outside one's home territory, requiring as many books as can be located, it is best to begin either with subject indexes (bibliographies that classify books under topic) or with bibliographies of bibliographies. Here again the choice is determined by the nature of the individual project; the former are more convenient, in that they involve one less step, but the latter (bibliographies raised to the second power!) offer better insurance against missing anything. The main subject indexes are those of the British Museum, which classify the books the Museum received between 1881 and 1950 (for books received before 1881, see R. A. Peddie's *Subject Index,* uneven but sometimes helpful), and the Library of Congress's subject catalogue of newly published books, 1950–1983 (continued since 1983 as *NUC: Books: LC Subject Index*). Researchers conducting subject searches should also check through the Research Libraries Information Network (RLIN), particularly, and also the Online Computer Library Center (OCLC); each is discussed below, on page 179.

Much material is published in periodicals, of course, finding its way into books, if at all, in synthesized or fragmentary form. The bibliographies in some of the volumes found by the procedure just described enumerate at least a scattering of articles but seldom can be relied on for full coverage. To supplement them, *online* use the *Humanities Index,* which since 1916, under other, earlier titles, has efficiently analyzed the contents of many scholarly journals in areas related to literature. For older material that the bibliographies in standard works may have overlooked, *Poole's Index* to nineteenth-century English and American periodicals should be consulted.

Maximum thoroughness, however, requires using the fourth edition (1965–66) of Theodore Besterman's *World Bibliography of Bibliographies,* which lists about 117,000 bibliographies on every conceivable subject. (Note that Besterman cites only bibliographies that have been separately issued; he omits those that appeared as parts of larger works, as well as some other classes of bibliographies, such as booksellers' catalogues and general library catalogues. Hence, even with 117,000 entries, his work is by no means exhaustive.) The scholar should copy Besterman's list for the topic in which he or she is interested; then find the individual bibliographies mentioned therein; then, as a final step, find the books *they* list—bringing him or her within sight of the desired information. The easiest way to bring Besterman down to date is first to use the update of Alice F.

Toomey, *World Bibliography of Bibliographies, 1964–1974,* and then to consult the *Bibliographic Index,* a continuing publication, begun in 1938, which records newly published bibliographies, both those appearing separately and those included in larger works.

Using these and similar tools in whatever combination and sequence seems most feasible, you soon will amass a list of books and articles that will be adequate for your purposes. It is true that when you find yourself adrift for the first time on strange seas of learning, you will feel somewhat bewildered and helpless. But the scholarly intelligence and resourcefulness that serve you well in your home waters, assisted by bibliographical charts of the kind just touched upon, may be depended upon to bring you safely to port. The fundamental techniques of finding material are the same, no matter what the subject matter may be, and exploring unfamiliar reaches of knowledge is not the least adventurous part of research.

From time to time in these pages, we have referred to the computer's great usefulness in performing complicated tasks of textual collation and applying stylistic tests to works of unestablished or debatable authorship. In a field adjacent to the latter, experiments, not yet wholly successful, are being made in computer-assisted studies of literary influence and indebtedness; the computer is called upon, for example, to determine the extent to which a given work, say *Prometheus Unbound,* bears significant resemblance in style and idea to a preceding one, such as *Paradise Lost.* We have also noted that some major bibliographical tools—the *MLA International Bibliography*, the British Library catalogue, and the *Eighteenth-Century STC,* to name only three—can be searched electronically. But these applications of computer science, advantageous as they are in themselves, represent only a small portion of the benefits the so-called electronic revolution has already conferred, and promises to confer, on literary scholarship.

Computers excel at all kinds of bibliographical and informational work. They can establish and cross-reference great lists. They can compile bibliographies of books and articles on any topic as well as break down, under any desired system of classification, the contents not only of the bibliographies themselves but also of the individual books and articles they list. They can add new dimensions to existing reference works, such as the author index generated for the often frustrating *Poole's Index to Periodical Literature*. Indeed, this indexing function has become a common scholarly aid, particularly for the wide range of archival materials—library holdings, publishers' records, authors' manuscripts—now being made available in microform.

And, perhaps most importantly, the computer offers access to increasingly varied databases, e.g.:

1) The Online Computer Library Center (OCLC) and the Research Libraries Information Network (RLIN) for identification of journals, manuscripts, and other printed materials and of separately published works of an author (including editions and translations of a specific title) and locations. The OCLC is the world's largest bibliographical database, listing materials in English and 468 foreign languages, and functioning as a union list, an invaluable resource when interlibrary loan is required. The RLIN, with eighty-seven research library affiliates, though less comprehensive than OCLC, offers greater international coverage and more flexibility in subject searches, information on special collections, access to certain other databases, such as the *Eighteenth-Century STC,* and, in cooperation with the Modern Language Association and selected journals, a prepublication listing of works accepted and grants funded by the NEH Research Programs Division.

2) Dialog and WILSONLINE for databases of secondary materials important to literary research. They offer access to numerous indexes, such as *American Library Directory, Bibliographic Index, Biography Index, Cumulative Book Index, Humanities Index,* and *Readers' Guide.*

Much is being done toward the computerization of raw data found outside literary works and bibliographies. An ambitious enterprise involving this kind of material is the "information bank" at Lawrence University, Wisconsin, in which are stored the hundreds of thousands of tiny individual facts contained in the eleven-volume *London Stage 1660–1800* (1960–68)—box office receipts, dates of performances, casts, lists of actors' roles, authors' payments, details of scene design, musical accompaniment, advertising—and which can sort out and assemble them in whatever categories and combinations are necessary for a particular line of research. Every similar hoard of information (Chambers's *Elizabethan Stage,* Bentley's *Jacobean and Caroline Stage,* Allardyce Nicoll's handlists of English plays) might be stored in computers in the same way.

Progress is being made on many fronts: with complete records of English and American publishing houses, their editorial correspondence and accounts (much is now available in microform, with access to its broad contents facilitated by various computer indexes); with content analyses, following the principles of the *Eighteenth-Century STC,* of all the books listed in the Pollard-Redgrave and Wing *Short-Title Catalogues,* which cover the preceding centuries, and in Evans's *American Bibliography* (which, along with its supplements, will soon be superseded by the North American Imprint Program database of the American Antiquarian Society).[20]

Another form of database stores and produces, on command, words as such, in whatever combination is needed. The whole of the *Oxford English Dictionary* is accessible by CD-ROM. In fact, the computer may be said to thrive on lexical tasks, organizing and giving words and phrases back in the form of dictionaries, indexes, glossaries, phrasebooks, and, particularly important for literary study, concordances to the corpus of an author or to individual works. The list of concordances, produced with far less labor than when the unit of data was an index card, and with great gains in accuracy and flexibility, grows yearly. Already in existence, with many more to come, are exhaustive concordances or word indexes to (for example)

---

[20]One can remain current with database developments by checking the quarterly *Directory of Online Databases.*

Beowulf, Chaucer, Gower's *Confessio Amantis,* Skelton, Shake-speare,[21] Sidney, Milton, Herbert, Swift, Johnson's poems, *Robinson Crusoe,* Blake, the 1798 and 1800 editions of *Lyrical Ballads,* Byron's *Don Juan,* Arnold, Hopkins, D. H. Lawrence's poetry and short stories, Dickinson's poems, James's *Daisy Miller,* Frost, Faulkner's *As I Lay Dying,* Joyce's *Finnegans Wake,* Beckett's *Molloy,* and Shaw's, Yeats's, and O'Neill's plays.

When contemplating the wonders that computers can and do accomplish, however, one must never forget the old adage that "if something seems too good to be true, it probably is!" Computers are not the key to all knowledge on any topic, least of all one that has so high and irreducible an element of subjectivity, and in the last analysis is so unquantifiable, as the art of literature. No matter how sophisticated it may be, electronic storage is not likely to usher in the bibliographer's or scholar's nirvana. Thomas Mann, general reference librarian at the Library of Congress, points out the disadvantages of computer searches as compared with the use of printed sources:

Published bibliographies will never be replaced by machine searches because . . . they often reach materials that human compilers can find but that lie beyond the reach of databases. And, further, a printout is generated only in response to specific words being typed in, whereas a published list is compiled according to the ideas in a human mind without rigid verbal criteria of exclusion. Published bibliographies, in other words, can often present perspectives on the literature of a subject that cannot be duplicated by machine searches. And the published lists will continue to be valuable in any event because they provide the best access to records dating to the period before the advent of database coverage.[22]

---

[21]Oxford University Press has produced for the personal computer an electronic edition of its modern-spelling *William Shakespeare: The Complete Works* and a companion software package for creating word lists, indexes, and concordances of any Shakespeare work.

[22]*A Guide to Library Research Methods* (cited above, n. 10) 73–74. A

These sobering observations could be applied to the entire realm of computer-assisted research—the stores of stylometric data, the concordances, the collation machinery, and databases of numerous kinds. (A particular limitation, because arbitrary, is the use of key words in some kinds of searches.) The crucial missing factor is the creative intelligence that inspires and guides all scholarship that transcends the merely mechanical. High-tech software, however time- and effort-saving, can only serve, not replace, the imagination that detects relationships and significances that cannot be contained in electronic circuitry. Research conducted before a display terminal can take an investigation just so far.[23] After a certain point, the human mind, the seat of all originality, must take over. Once full use has been made of the available databases, the scholar must, so to speak, switch to manual mode. To make sense out of the data—that is, to contribute to the store of genuine knowledge—the "little grey cells" of Agatha Christie's Hercule Poirot must be brought into action.

---

common-sense and informative discussion of the methods and limitations of computer searches can be found in Mann's ch. 9; see particularly pp. 89–102.

[23]Probably the best way to keep up with the rapid developments in computer-assisted literary research is to consult the articles and bibliographies in the journals *Computers and the Humanities* (1966–) and *Literary and Linguistic Computing: Journal of the Association for Literary and Linguistic Computing* (1986–). See also Robert L. Oakman, *Computer Methods for Literary Research* (Columbia, SC, 1980; rev. ed., Athens, GA, 1984).

CHAPTER FIVE

Libraries

How much . . . are all we bound, that are Scholars, to those munificent Ptolemies, bountiful Maecenases, heroical Patrons, divine spirits . . . that have provided for us so many well furnished Libraries as well in our publick Academies in most Cities, as in our private Colleges!
—Robert Burton, *The Anatomy of Melancholy* (1621), part 2, section 2, member 4

The amount of information stored in even the largest computerized databanks is minuscule compared with the wealth of unsystematized information enclosed in the books shelved in any research library. A knowledge of the history, strengths, and facilities of the major libraries that serve scholars in the humanities is as indispensable as a command of the bibliographical tools that are the primary keys to their contents. "Houghton," "Berg," "Huntington," "Folger," and "the British Library" are terms that figure in the shoptalk of scholars wherever they gather. What, and where, are these libraries? What do their major collections contain? Above all, which have the greatest wealth of books and manuscripts relating to one's particular field of interest?

Unfortunately, there is no such convenience as a literary scholar's Baedeker. Printed information on the growth and holdings of research libraries, though fairly abundant, is scattered through various kinds of books and periodicals. Important new acquisitions are announced in the annual reports of the various libraries' directors and in the periodicals issued by some libraries. These sources are often supplemented by the grapevine that connects the librarian's world with the scholar's. Apart from consulting the printed sources, including those mentioned in the preceding chapter, the way to locate your own bibliothecal paradises, as Erasmus called them in a letter to Bishop Fisher in 1524, is to note where the leading researchers in your field go to do their work, and as you read their books, observe, in the prefatory acknowledgments and footnotes, where the material was gathered. Make a habit (it is easily cultivated, and a pleasant one) of storing away information about the history of book collecting, because most of the contents of the fabulous collections that were amassed and sold in the past century or so (Church, Hoe, Devonshire, Halsey, Quinn, Kern, Bixby) have by now found their permanent homes in institutional libraries. You can trace their migrations, down to recent decades, with the aid of De Ricci's and Cannon's books mentioned on page 168. Moreover, a little knowledge of academic history comes in handy. It is no accident, for example, that the Yale Library is supreme in eighteenth-century literature; the university's English Department has been famous for its eighteenth-century specialists, typified in an older generation by Chauncey Brewster Tinker and Wilbur Lucius Cross. The University of Texas traces its Pope collection to the long presence on the faculty of the poet's bibliographer, R. H. Griffith. University library strengths are frequently memorials to the ambition, tenacity, and resourcefulness of scholars; to the same qualities in librarians, who found the money and knew how to spend it; and, far from least, to the generosity of wealthy alumni and other friends of libraries, who signed the checks.

Thanks to all these people, American literary scholars are in a fortunate position. It is only to be expected that most of the documentary materials for the study of any aspect of American literature are to be found in the continental United States. But it is much more remarkable that America possesses so large a portion of the books and manuscripts needed for research in

English literature. Ever since the late nineteenth century, the buying power of certain great American fortunes, exerting itself during years when the British purse was steadily shrinking, resulted in a massive movement of literary treasures across the Atlantic. Today, by an irony that a few of them understandably fail to relish, English scholars often must come to American libraries to study their own country's great authors.

Only in a large book could justice be done to the wealth of rare books and manuscripts that American scholars have at their disposal in their research libraries. In these few pages, we will single out a handful of the Meccas to which scholars gravitate. Our tour of the gold mines of research will take us from Massachusetts to California.

Harvard's is the undisputed monarch of academic libraries. The Widener Library, built as a memorial to the scion of a wealthy Philadelphia family who at twenty-eight, when he went down on the *Titanic*, was already known as "the Marcellus of the race of book collectors," houses Harvard's general collection. In addition, it contains certain specialized ones, such as the folklore material gathered by Francis James Child and his students, the poetry collection (a pioneer in the recording of poets reading their own works), and the theater collection, whose hundreds of thousands of playbills, programs, prompt books, photographs, manuscripts, and books associated with the history of the stage make it one of the Big Three in this field, the other pre-eminent American collections being at the New York Public and Folger Libraries.

Most of Harvard's rarities, however, are housed in the adjacent Houghton Library. Its wealth ranges over the whole of English and American literature, but one of its particular strengths is its collection of seventeenth-century English books. The hundreds of stack sections devoted to manuscripts house, among other treasures, the largest single parcel of papers by and associated with Keats (the merging of collections formerly owned by the marquess of Crewe and Amy Lowell). More recently, the Houghton bought from Sir Charles Tennyson a large portion of the extant papers of his grandfather, including many unpublished drafts of the Laureate's poems. Among the manuscripts of other English authors, there are the holographs of novels by Conrad, Disraeli, Hardy, George Moore, Trollope, and D. H. Lawrence, and quantities of letters and manuscript literary works of such diverse figures as De Quincey, Max Beerbohm, Kipling, Ruskin, and Thackeray. The roster of American authors whose papers are concentrated in the Houghton's vaults is as long as it is lustrous; the names range from Melville to J. P. Marquand. Thomas Wolfe's famous packing cases, crammed with the chaotic products of his creative seizures as well as his college lecture notebooks, exam papers, checkbooks, and royalty statements—for Wolfe never destroyed anything—came to Harvard, where he took his M.A. Henry James's papers are here, as are those of Emerson (10,000 letters to him, and 140 volumes of journals), Lowell, Longfellow, Holmes, Howells; and in the Houghton a large portion of Emily Dickinson's manuscripts, long the subject of bitter dispute among her survivors, has found a final home.

Yale's Sterling Library is the headquarters of a whole complex of literary industries, among them the "Boswell factory" (producing complete editions of Boswell and Johnson), a branch of the "Walpole factory" (main plant at Farmington, Connecticut, where the late Wilmarth Lewis pursued his lifework of issuing the complete correspondence of Horace Walpole), the "Franklin factory," and "the More factory," from which the definitive edition of St. Thomas More is emerging. The storehouse from which these editorial enterprises derive the multitude of facts they need is Yale's book collection. Annotating Boswell's journals or Walpole's letters, for example, requires an array of printed aids that will supply dates, identify allusions, provide biographical sketches of obscure persons, and perform the thousand other services that such work requires. Innumerable county and local histories, maps, town directories, biographies and memoirs, files of contemporary magazines and newspapers—nothing that is germane to the English eighteenth century is foreign to the Yale Library. In the nineteenth century, Yale is especially strong in first editions and manuscripts, some of them still unpublished, of Carlyle, Ruskin, Mill, Arnold, George Eliot, Meredith, and Stevenson, and the library's lively interest in preserving the papers of twentieth-century authors is symbolized by its possession of Gertrude Stein's manuscripts (11,500 pieces), Edith Wharton's (5,000), and Sinclair Lewis's (1,000). It also holds the largest extant collections of Eugene O'Neill and Ezra Pound materials.

At Fifth Avenue and Forty-Second Street, New York City, stands the nation's second largest library, after the Library of Congress. The heart of the "New York Public" is its research collection of over 6.3 million volumes, thoroughly covering all but a few fields of humanistic and scientific interest. Its several specialized collections are of significant scholarly importance. The manuscript division, which owns more than 13 million manuscripts and 3.6 million microform pieces, is especially rich in the papers of writers associated with New York (Walt Whitman and Washington Irving, for instance), and the theater collection, housed separately in the Lincoln Center for the Performing Arts, is, as noted above, one of the largest in the nation.

But the library's jewel, as far as literary research is concerned, is the Berg Collection. Its creation gave the New York Public Library the added distinction of being one of the three or four richest rare-book treasuries in the United States. Henry W. and Albert A. Berg were two New York physicians, under whose care, happily for the future of literary study, came some of the nation's most eminent millionaires. When Doctor Henry died in 1938, his brother gave to the library, in his memory, 3,500 rare books and manuscripts, a nucleus that was especially strong in nineteenth-century English and American writers. A little later, two larger collections came up for sale: those of W. T. H. Howe, president of the American Book Company (16,000 volumes, also concentrated in the nineteenth century) and Owen D. Young, the head of General Electric (over 10,000 items, ranging from the fifteenth to the twentieth centuries, and rich not only in first editions but in association copies, autograph letters, and manuscripts of literary works). Dr. Albert Berg forthwith bought them for the library, too, with the result that in a span of only fifteen months the Berg Collection increased tenfold. Upon his death in 1950 he left a large endowment that permits the constant enlargement of the collection.

Though the representation of eighteenth-century English literature is imposing enough by any ordinary standards (Pope's draft of the first three books of the *Essay on Man,* fifty letters each by Gray and Dr. Johnson, a mass of Burney papers), the Berg Collection's supreme strength resides in its first editions of all major nineteenth-century American and English authors, including such rarities as Browning's *Pauline,* Poe's *Tamerlaine,* and the Bristol edition of *Lyrical Ballads,* and literally thousands of letters and literary manuscripts by such writers as Coleridge, Thackeray, Dickens, Kipling, Hawthorne, and Whitman. Many of these prizes, among them Thoreau's nature studies (1,700 manuscript pages) and some of the fifty Mark Twain manuscripts, are as yet unpublished. In recent years much Berg money has gone into the purchase of the first editions and personal papers of twentieth-century English authors, most notably Arnold Bennett, Joseph Conrad, John Masefield, Bernard Shaw, and Virginia Woolf, the great bulk of whose manuscripts are here. T. S. Eliot is another star of the collection; the surfacing in the Berg of the long-lost typescript of *The Waste Land,* dense with comments and alterations by Ezra Pound, was a headline event. (Published in facsimile in 1971, this is one of the most fascinating documents of modern literature.)

Walking a few blocks down Fifth Avenue and then east on Thirty-Sixth Street, one comes to the Pierpont Morgan Library (given to the public in 1924), which is dedicated exclusively to rarities. Its founders, the elder and younger J. P. Morgan, were bidders in auction rooms during the decades when the transatlantic cables pulsed with virtually carte blanche orders from American collectors to their London agents. As a consequence of one of their hobbies, the library has an array, unmatched in this country and rivaled by few in Europe, of ancient and medieval manuscripts, especially masterpieces of the illuminator's art, as well as of finely bound books. It has the richest collection of Caxtons in America (some seventy, one of which is the only known perfect copy of the first edition of Malory's *Le Morte d'Arthur*). The library's first editions, especially of authors like Dickens, who were fashionable in collecting circles during the peak of the Morgans' buying, are superb.

But for literary researchers, probably the heart of the collection lies in the almost bewildering range of authors' manuscripts: the first book of *Paradise Lost* (in the hand of Milton's amanuensis), Keats's *Endymion* and his sonnet on Chapman's *Homer,* Lamb's "Dissertation upon Roast Pig," one hundred poems of Burns, ten novels of Scott, Rossetti's "The Blessed Damozel," many Byron poems (including cantos 1–5 of *Don Juan, The Corsair,* and *Manfred*), Thackeray's *The Virginians* and a portion of *Vanity Fair,* Dickens's *A Christmas Carol* and *Our Mutual Friend,* Ruskin's *The Stones of Venice* and *Modern Painters,* Meredith's *Diana of the Crossways,* Browning's *Dramatis Personae,* Elizabeth Barrett Browning's *Sonnets from the Portuguese,* Stevenson's *Dr. Jekyll and Mr. Hyde,* Mark Twain's *Life on the Mississippi.* To say nothing of personal papers: thirty-eight volumes of Thoreau's journals, ninety letters of Pope, over thirteen hundred of Dickens, hundreds by Burns, Byron, Carlyle, and scores of other celebrated authors. Perhaps the inclusiveness of "the Morgan's" interests is best suggested by the fact that under the same roof are cherished one of the finest collections in existence of William Blake's illustrations and the nation's largest mass of scores, programs, manuscripts, and other memorabilia relating to Gilbert and Sullivan.[1]

What the New York Public and the Morgan are to New York, the Library of Congress and the Folger are to Washington. The Library of Congress, appropriately, as the national library, is the possessor of more books than any other in America. In 1990, it owned 23 million books and pamphlets. In addition, it had over 3.2 million pieces or reels of microforms, and 11 million photographic negatives, slides, and prints. The rare-book division alone has more than 575,000 volumes on its shelves. Since the passage of the first effective copyright law in 1870, the library has received two copies of every new American publication, be it a book, periodical, piece of sheet music, photograph, motion picture, phonograph record, or a copyrighted advertisement for

---

[1]For a fuller description see Israel Shenker, "J. Pierpont Morgan and the Princely Library He Founded," *Smithsonian* 10 (September 1979): 77–83.

a dictionary.[2] But these acquisitions are responsible for only a few of its many strengths. It is one of the very first places to go for any piece of Americana regardless of date; its holdings in numerous areas of English literature are extensive; and it has over 40 million pieces of manuscript. The latter are, for the most part, the papers of public men, the "makers of the nation": presidents, congressmen, diplomats, cabinet members, generals, scientists, explorers. Although comparatively few of its author-archives are as extensive or as important for the study of literature as those in several other libraries, hundreds of American writers and journalists, including some still living, are represented by at least a few boxes of papers.

Across the street from the Library of Congress since 1932 has been the Folger Shakespeare Library, the monument to the lifelong hobby of a shy, almost reclusive Standard Oil executive, Henry Clay Folger. As a youth—he graduated from Amherst in 1879, and under the terms of his will the library is administered by the college—he read Emerson's eulogy of Shakespeare in the essayist's "Saturday Club Address" and forthwith dedicated all his leisure and his (prospective) fortune to collecting Shakespeareana. For decade after decade, Folger and his wife devoted their evenings to poring over sale catalogues and sending off purchase orders to dealers and the special agents they had stationed in the principal bookselling centers abroad. When Folger died in 1930, he owned the greatest hoard of Shakespeare material in the world. Ironically, he never saw most of it, because as soon as the boxes arrived, he had them carted, unopened, to bank vaults and Brooklyn warehouses, where they remained until the library building in Washington was finished. Then a heavily guarded procession of trucks, loaded with three thousand of the most precious packing cases in literary history, moved down U.S. Route 1 to Washington, and the Folger was in business.

[2]Before 1870, the Library of Congress was one of several copyright depositories designated by law and as such received many new publications, but loopholes in the earlier acts, widened by languid enforcement, prevented it from receiving all publications automatically, as it did after that year.

"Here," wrote the first librarian, Joseph Quincy Adams, "in almost unbelievable fulness and richness, are assembled books, pamphlets, documents, manuscripts, relics, curios, oil-paintings, original drawings, water colors, prints, statues, busts, medals, coins, miscellaneous objects of art, furniture, tapestries, playbills, prompt-books, stage-properties, actors' costumes, and other material designed to illustrate the poet and his times. The Library is thus more than a mere library; it is also a museum of the Golden Age of Elizabeth, and a memorial to the influence that Shakespeare has exerted upon the world's culture."

The subsequent growth of the Folger has turned Adams's exuberant claim, which may have seemed slightly hyperbolic at the time, into something approaching understatement. Thanks to the income from the well-invested endowment and the vision and energy of the library's staff, the Folger's scope has steadily widened. Its center, of course, remains Shakespeare: out of some 240 known copies of the First Folio, the Folger has seventy-nine (the British Library has five); over two hundred copies of the quartos, including several unique ones, such as the 1594 *Titus Andronicus* that surfaced in Sweden in 1904, was sold at auction, and then submerged again—in one of Henry Clay Folger's warehouses; thousands of association copies of Shakespeare's works, and scores of thousands of books in which Shakespeare is simply alluded to; and virtually all the collected editions and editions of separate plays, in whatever language and from whatever period.

The Folger Library's Shakespeareana, then, is almost boundless; but Shakespeare was a man of the theater, and so the library is, as well, a treasure house of stage history, with prompt books, playbills (over a quarter million), manuscripts, and other memorabilia of thousands of actors and producers, reaching from Elizabethan times to the present. Shakespeare was also a man of the Renaissance, so the Folger has built up a magnificent collection of books and manuscripts from, or relating to, that era. Every year hundreds of Renaissance and drama specialists from all over the world, working on subjects that have nothing to do with Shakespeare, come to the Folger for material they could find elsewhere with great difficulty, if at all.

At the University of Virginia in Charlottesville is the Clifton

Waller Barrett Library covering American literature from 1775 to
1950: a collection of well over a quarter-million first editions
and manuscripts that aims at comprehensiveness down to 1875
and thereafter concentrates upon the major writers. All told,
some five hundred authors are "collected in depth"—that is,
everything by them or relating to them, whether in manuscript
or print, is sought and preserved. Here, for example, are letters,
counted in the hundreds for each author, of Irving, Longfellow,
Hawthorne, Whitman, Mark Twain, Edwin Arlington Robinson,
and Theodore Dreiser, as well as the largest collection of Willa
Cather's; four hundred pieces of the manuscript of *Leaves of
Grass;* a large portion of the Alcott family papers; the largest
Robert Frost collection in existence; and the manuscripts of
Hemingway's *Green Hills of Africa* and Steinbeck's *The Grapes
of Wrath.* At Virginia also, though not in the Barrett Library, are
the papers of William Faulkner.

   Although the Eastern seaboard possesses the greatest con-
centration of literary research facilities (both general collections
and assemblages of rarities), the nation's interior, once known
as a cultural wasteland, is dotted with a number of splendid
libraries. Only a few can be cited here, and inadequately at that.
Because it is perhaps the least famous of the major American
research libraries, the Newberry, on Chicago's near north side,
has a special claim to mention. Though the library contains
fewer of the classic, headline-making rarities than its sister institutions on the East and West coasts, and its holdings of literary
manuscripts are not especially noteworthy (though the papers
of Sherwood Anderson, for instance, are here), its general collections in literature, history, biography, philosophy, folklore,
music, and allied fields make it as useful to scholars in the
Midwest as Harvard and the New York Public are to their Eastern colleagues. Its periodical files are especially extensive. In
addition, the Newberry has many special collections, among the
most notable being the Wing Collection relating to the history
of printing, which is a gorgeous gallery for the student of typography, illustration, and related arts, and the Ayer Collection of
books and other material dealing with the American Indian. In
English literature, the Newberry's greatest strength lies in books

of the sixteenth and seventeenth centuries, but in recent years it has been purchasing heavily in the later periods.

Two major university libraries cannot be omitted from even the briefest survey of the Midwest and Southwest. In 1960 Indiana University dedicated the beautiful building that houses the Lilly Library, a private collection amassed and given to the university by an Indianapolis pharmaceutical manufacturer, Josiah K. Lilly, Jr. In addition to a wealth of Greek and Latin classics, books on the history of science and thought, and the literature of Europe, the Lilly collection of first editions and manuscripts runs the entire gamut of English and American literary history from the introduction of printing (two Caxtons) through Shakespeare (all four folios), Walton (all five editions of *The Compleat Angler* printed during his lifetime), and Burns (a remarkably extensive array) down to the manuscripts of Bennett's *The Old Wives' Tale* and Barrie's *Peter Pan*. For many first-rank American authors, from Poe to Hemingway, there are complete sets of first editions. And the collection is constantly being added to. Among other noteworthy purchases made since it was transferred to the university have been eight tons of Upton Sinclair's papers, Louis Untermeyer's comprehensive collection of modern English and American poetry, and nine hundred titles of rare early American fiction. The research potentialities residing in the Lilly's seventy-five thousand rare volumes and 1.5 million pieces of manuscript will not soon be exhausted.

At the University of Texas at Austin, the rare book collection in the Harry Ransom Humanities Research Center, initially built up over many years by the indefatigable Miss Fannie Ratchford and liberally supplied with books and purchase funds from oil, grain, and other fortunes, is richest in English literature of the past three centuries. Because of its holdings of Dryden, Defoe, Swift, Fielding, and Pope, as well as its files of periodicals from the era, it serves students of the Queen Anne and early Georgian period as adequately as Yale serves those concentrating in the second half of the eighteenth century. Moreover, it is one of the country's leading places for the study of the English Romantic poets. Its Byroniana rivals that in the Morgan Library (one of the principal scholarly works based on Texas's Byron manuscripts is the variorum edition of *Don Juan*). Another pronounced strength is in the late nineteenth and early twentieth centuries; among other authors of whom Texas has extensive collections are Lawrence, Hemingway, Shaw, Joyce, Beckett, O'Neill, and Henry Miller.

In recent years Texas has devoted untold amounts of money to purchasing manuscripts of contemporary writers, of both major and minor rank. It now possesses rough notes, first drafts, and finished manuscripts and printer's proofs of such writers as Arthur Miller, Tennessee Williams, Lillian Hellman, Jack Kerouac, Allen Ginsberg, Graham Greene, and Vladimir Nabokov. Over the years, Texas's voracity has become something of a cynical joke in England, where even minimally famous writers have known they could always get a grub stake by selling off the contents of their desk drawers to Austin. Most of this material has not been intensively used, and indeed much is not yet fully catalogued. So wide and deep is its scope that among students of twentieth-century literature a working axiom is that the two most likely places to find primary sources for authors in whom they are interested are the Ransom Humanities Research Center and the Berg Collection in New York.

The golden years of American book collecting centered in the epoch before and just after the First World War, when the Morgans and Folger, among others, were reaping the harvest of London auctions and of sale (as the delectable English expression goes) "by private treaty." A monarch even among such titans was Henry E. Huntington, who built much of Southern California's transit system and at one time sat on no fewer than sixty boards of directors. The nucleus of Huntington's library was the collections of three other bibliophiles, E. Dwight Church, Robert Hoe, and Beverly Chew, which he bought in 1911–12 and which were particularly noteworthy for their early editions of Shakespeare, Spenser, Milton, and other seventeenth-century poets. To these he soon added the Kemble-Devonshire collection of 7,500 English plays (the library now contains a printed copy, film, or photostat of every known pre-1800 play), the Frederic R. Halsey library of 20,000 rare volumes, including twenty Shelley first editions, and the

Bridgewater House Library of sixteenth- and seventeenth-century literature, which contained numerous literary manuscripts of the period. When the library that Huntington built at San Marino, adjacent to Pasadena, was completed in 1920, the collection was already especially strong in the earlier centuries of English literature, and it has remained so through subsequent purchases. It owns more incunabula than any other library in the Western hemisphere, and its assemblage of *STC* books is exceeded only by the British Library's. Surrounded by over two hundred acres of botanical gardens and groves, and having as near neighbor a gallery with a rich collection of British paintings, this library has an ambiance unmatched by any other major research center.

The Huntington's manuscripts, contained in some 450 collections, number over 1.5 million leaves, and range from 230 Middle English literary texts (including the Ellesmere Chaucer, the Towneley Plays, the Chester Cycle, and four manuscripts of *Piers Plowman*) to rich assemblages of the manuscripts and correspondences of nineteenth-century English authors: Lamb (228 pieces), Southey (over 1,300), Ruskin (626), Thackeray (316), Dickens (1,250), the Rossetti circle. . . . Nor are American history and literature neglected. One of the founder's special interests was Americana, from the New England of Cotton and Increase Mather to the exploration of the Pacific Northwest. The representation of first editions and manuscripts by celebrated American authors is the most extensive west of the Alleghenies: there are some 45,000 pieces of manuscript by 330 authors. Their scope includes the papers of James T. Fields, the Boston editor and publisher (among them 5,300 letters to and from luminaries like Whittier, Longfellow, Lowell, Holmes, Emerson, and Hawthorne) and the Jack London collection of 60,000 pieces. The Huntington also has several thousand copies of Beadle's Dime Novels, and—to further illustrate its diversity—it possesses many papers of Conrad Aiken and Wallace Stevens.

A more comprehensive survey of American libraries that are of constant, and sometimes prime, usefulness to literary scholars would include the Boston Public Library ("New England-ana" and rare books, especially of the Renaissance, collected by properly wealthy Bostonians a century ago); Cornell University (a magnificent Wordsworth library, now complemented by an equally important James Joyce collection); the Lockwood Library at Buffalo, which specializes in the working drafts of modern writers—"poetry in process"; and the William Andrews Clark Library of the University of California at Los Angeles, which is most famous for its three thousand manuscripts relating to Oscar Wilde and the *Yellow Book* nineties and for its English literature from the Commonwealth to the mid-eighteenth century—a period in which the neighboring Huntington Library is (relatively!) weak.

As has been noted in the preceding chapter, the British Library, in the Bloomsbury section of central London, is the British equivalent of our Library of Congress and one of the two or three greatest libraries in the world. In its circular reading room (headquarters of the Department of Printed Books), countless books have been prepared for, or in some cases, such as *Das Kapital* and Samuel Butler's *The Way of All Flesh,* actually written; and in the adjoining Department of Manuscripts scholars have, for generations, pored over the papers of hundreds of famous authors. In the period 1991–96, the British Library, in the "largest move in library history," plans to transfer 11 million volumes from eighteen different locations around London to a single site, "where over 300 linear kilometers of shelving will accommodate them."

One reason, among many, for the library's pre-eminence is that until 1989, when the sheer quantity of intake forced it to abandon that function, it was the principal British copyright depository. Like America, Great Britain long had laws making copyright contingent upon the sending of copies of all newly published matter to several libraries. But only about 150 years ago, at almost the time the American law began to be rigorously enforced, did the energetic librarian, Sir Anthony Panizzi, take similar measures. The result is that the British Library has the most comprehensive collection of books and periodicals published in Britain in that period.[3] But, again like the LC, the BL is

---

[3]Although most of the material necessary for research in American literature is obtainable in major American libraries, even in this sphere the

just as capacious a storehouse of older material. Ever since it was founded in 1753, it has acquired, by gift or purchase, books, pamphlets, periodicals, and manuscripts relating to every conceivable subject, literary or nonliterary. Its collection of material by and about most British authors is the richest in the world, and its holdings in peripheral areas—history, art, philosophy—make available to literary students all the tools they need to elucidate incidental allusions and supply whatever background information is lacking. From the fabled *Beowulf* manuscript fragment down to files of papers for schoolboys, it is all there.[4]

Second in importance to the British Library is Oxford's Bodleian Library, founded in the seventeenth century, and today a fascinating medley, in both outward appearance and contents, of the old and the new. The original portion, "Duke Humphrey's Library," is the very exemplification of the pursuit of knowledge under difficulties: dark aisles of shelves, ponderous folios, some of them chained to the desks, cold readers' cubicles that obviously were modeled after monastic scriptoria; and at the entrance, the charming admonition, which every library should copy,

Tread Lightly and Speak Softly

But the reading rooms in both the "old" Bodleian and its modern "extension," a block away, are spacious, light, uncluttered; and in the new building, the storage areas, most of them underground, are thoroughly Americanized with their concrete and steel stacks, adequate lighting, and air conditioning. On the

---

British Library sometimes proves indispensable. It has been pointed out that whereas the Library of Congress lists 384 editions of Longfellow, the BL holds 531.

[4]The library's loss of about 150,000 volumes in the Second World War did not seriously affect its strength in literary and related subjects. But the bombing of its newspaper warehouse in a northern suburb, followed by a week of heavy rain, turned some 30,000 bound volumes of irreplaceable newspapers into sodden pulp.

open shelves in the stacks, unguarded by grills and marked by no other special distinction, are the priceless "named" collections—the tall brown folios and squat quartos redolent of pioneer English antiquarianism, philosophy, and other learning that figure in countless volumes of literary scholarship.

Because the Bodleian's one catalogue of its book holdings, unlike the British Library's *General Catalogue,* is for internal use only and is not available elsewhere, it is often hard for researchers to decide whether they could work more profitably at Oxford than in London. In general, it is well to remember that the book collection, while smaller than that of the British Library (it could scarcely be bigger), has the particular value of greater age; the Bodleian, after all, was a hundred and fifty years old, and well stocked even then, when the British Museum was founded. Moreover, it too is a copyright depository, though it now receives only the newly published books it specifically requests; and its manuscripts are multitudinous, ranging from treasures from the Middle Ages to, for instance, papers of such relatively modern figures as Shelley.

For the literary scholar, Cambridge offers somewhat smaller opportunity, partly because it has traditionally been the seat of the sciences rather than of humane learning. But the University Library contains well over a million and a half volumes and some ten thousand manuscripts. The Trinity College Library, a gem of Wren architecture, is rich in English literary manuscripts, including, for example, many of Tennyson's and Macaulay's. And at Magdalene College is housed Samuel Pepys's private library (including the incomparable diary), preserved in exact accordance with the provisions of his will.[5] In Edinburgh, the National Library of Scotland is the natural *pied-à-terre* of anyone working on a topic with Scottish bearings.

[5]American students should perhaps be reminded that, because the two ancient English universities are composed of autonomous colleges (Trinity, Corpus Christi, All Souls, Balliol, Pembroke, Gonville and Caius, Peterhouse, St. John's, and the rest), many of the most precious books and manuscripts in Oxford and Cambridge are found not in what we would call the "main library" (the Bodleian or the Cambridge University Library) but in the dim religious light of the individual college libraries.

Though its contents—some fifty million pieces of manuscript—are primarily of interest to specialists in English history,
the Public Record Office in London's Chancery Lane (always
called the "PRO") claims a place in even the briefest account of
British institutions the literary student must know.[6] It is there
that a scholar goes if the writer in question had any contact,
direct or indirect, with some branch of the national authority—
criminal and civil courts, diplomacy, military affairs, law enforcement, and so on—from the Middle Ages downward. More
or less the counterpart of the National Archives in Washington,
the PRO houses about three-quarters of the surviving records of
eight hundred years of such activity. Among these thousands of
tons of documents are many of importance to literary history:
deeds and depositions signed by Shakespeare; the coroner's
report that, when discovered in the mid-1920s by Leslie Hotson,
revealed the circumstances of Christopher Marlowe's murder;
Shelley's letters to Harriet Westbrook. Army records throw light
on "Silas Tomkyn Comberbacke's" (i.e., Samuel Taylor Coleridge's) discharge from the ranks of the dragoons, in which he
had ill-advisedly enlisted in 1793, and Home Office papers
authenticate and fill out the story Coleridge tells in chapter 10
of his *Biographia Literaria*. It is quite true that, as he says, he
and Wordsworth were shadowed by a government agent as
they walked and made philosophical conversation in the Quan-
tock Hills in 1797; the pair were suspected by some of their
neighbors of engaging in subversive conspiracies. But the most
piquant detail of the story, that the detective thought they were
aware of his lurking presence because, as he reported to his
control in London, he overheard them speaking of "Spy-nosy"
(Spinoza), seems to have been Coleridge's invention.

The very diversity of the public records is guarantee enough
that they often repay searching by biographers and other literary historians. The Revels Accounts and other classes of docu-

[6]See A. D. Harvey, "The Public Record Office in London as a Source for
English Literary Studies." *Études anglaises* 43 (1990): 303–16. The author
cites the presence there of biographical documents, and even previously
known literary texts, relating to Yeats, Conrad, Pinter, Joyce, D. H. Lawrence, Wilde, Byron, and Fielding, among others.

ments have provided a great deal of information on the history of the Elizabethan and Restoration drama.[7] The records of the Admiralty may throw light on the careers of seagoing authors like Smollett and Marryat (and, as we have seen, they have provided a valuable check on Trelawny's incurable romancing); the archives of the various courts of justice and the so-called "state papers domestic and foreign" contain the answers to nobody knows how many literary puzzles—because they are so extensive, and so complicated in their arrangement, that many sections have never been explored.

For biographical work, it is often necessary to consult local records. In Britain, there are the registers of births, marriages, and deaths kept across the centuries by the thousands of parishes that formerly constituted small, autonomous governmental units, and the administrative and legal documents generated more recently by the governments of towns and cities. Some classes of such records have now been brought together in the archives of the respective counties, but others remain in the places where they originated. (For assistance in locating these, see above, pp. 173–74.)

A noteworthy recent instance of how useful public documents can be in solving a literary mystery involved the "morganatic" family of the Victorian novelist Wilkie Collins. Collins never married, but he was known to have left behind an adopted daughter (his first mistress's by a former marriage) and three children of his own by his second mistress. After his death, these offspring vanished from view, and Collins's biographers made little if any effort to trace them. Not until the 1980s did the husband of Collins's great-granddaughter set out to find the

---

[7]Among all the scholars who have seined the Public Records for data bearing on theatrical history, C. J. Sisson has probably drawn up the fullest nets. For an absorbing account of the way in which records of early seventeenth-century lawsuits enabled him to reconstruct the plots of two lost plays, Chapman's *The Old Joiner of Aldgate* and the Dekker-Rowley-Ford-Webster collaboration, *The Late Murder in Whitechapel, or Keep the Widow Waking,* see Sisson's *Lost Plays of Shakespeare's Age* (Cambridge, 1936).

novelist's other descendants. By consulting, among other sources, the records at St. Catherine's House, London (the central registry of deaths and wills) and church records at a fishing village on the Norfolk coast, he succeeded in identifying and locating them and received from them the handed-down reminiscences of their famous forebear, thus largely dissipating what Dorothy Sayers, who once set out to write the biography, called "the extreme obscurity which surrounds the whole of Collins's private life."[8]

In the United States, there are similar kinds of records to be searched, including census returns, voters' lists, local directories and newspaper files, and property records such as are found in county courthouses. It was a combination of these that enabled the director of the Yale University black studies research center to identify the Harriet E. Wilson who in 1859 had privately printed a purportedly autobiographical novel entitled *Our Nig; or, Sketches from the Life of a Free Black, In a Two-Story White House, North, Showing That Slavery's Shadows Fall Even There*. Who was Wilson: was she really a black writing from her own experience, or a white abolitionist, writing in the vein of Harriet Beecher Stowe? The fact that the book had been entered for copyright in the District Court of Massachusetts suggested that the author was a New Englander, and patient search through the census returns, local histories, and town clerks' records of that region enabled the investigator to trace the Harriet Wilson in question. But only one document, the death certificate of her seven-year-old son, who died in Milford, New Hampshire, the year after her book was printed, contained the crucial piece of evidence. There she was identified as a black woman, and thus she has acquired the distinction of being "probably the first Afro-American to publish a novel in the United States."[9]

[8]See William M. Clarke, *The Secret Life of Wilkie Collins* (London, 1988) preface.

[9]See Henry Louis Gates, Jr.'s introduction to the facsimile reprint of *Our Nig* (New York, 1983). The "Notes to the Text" and "Chronology" ap-

Many repositories that are, quantitatively speaking, pygmies among the celebrated giants are nevertheless of prime importance in particular fields of research. There are, for example, the various houses that have become memorial shrines to their former occupants. The Dove Cottage Library at Grasmere, now owned by the Wordsworth Trust, has an increasingly rich collection of Wordsworthiana, including the thirty-one love letters exchanged between the poet and his wife that a stamp dealer in Carlisle happened upon in the 1970s, in a bundle of old documents he had bought for five pounds. The Haworth Parsonage Museum in Yorkshire, which is said to attract as many sightseers as Stratford-on-Avon, contains, in addition to many physical memorabilia of the Brontës, including their dresses and bonnets, a major collection of their letters and related documents. The Burns Birthplace Museum at Alloway, Scotland, has the largest single group (131) of the poet's letters.

Local libraries sometimes have valuable collections associated with writers who have had ties to the region. At the City Library in the English cathedral town of Lincoln, there is the Tennyson Research Center, with an extensive archive relating to the Lincolnshire-born poet, including part of his library and personal effects. Occasionally, too, a single valuable literary item is found in an extremely out-of-the-way place that is unassociated with its author. The manuscript of *Great Expectations,* for instance, is owned by the library at Wisbech, a tiny town in Cambridgeshire.

The papers and memorabilia of some American authors are similarly distributed and housed. Many of John Steinbeck's are at the house he occupied in Salinas, California, and Vachel Lindsay's are at his home in Springfield, Illinois. The papers of Thomas Merton are preserved at the Trappist abbey of Gethsemane in Kentucky, and in a warehouse in Tarzania, California, are stored fifty-two book manuscripts by Tarzan's creator, Edgar Rice Burroughs, as well as 200,000 [*sic*] letters by him and

---

pended to the text cite all the local documents that made it possible to reconstruct the outlines of Wilson's life in New England.

an equal number to him, and 30,000 books containing his marginalia. The manuscript of *Tom Sawyer* is at the Clemens Birthplace House in Florida, Missouri, and the (partial) one of *Huckleberry Finn* can be studied at the Buffalo and Erie County Public Library in upstate New York.[10]

Recent social and political movements, which have expanded the scope of literary scholarship into areas that previously were almost totally neglected, have resulted in the founding or enlargement of libraries concentrating in those fields. The Radcliffe College Library has become a focus of studies in women's history, including, of course, women as authors, and the Schomburg Center for Research in Black Culture, a branch of the New York Public Library founded many years ago, is now equally a focus of studies in black literature and history.

The research libraries mentioned throughout this chapter differ considerably in their admission policies. Some, such as the Library of Congress, the New York Public (reference collection), and the Newberry, are freely open to all serious students, from undergraduates on up. Others, like the Berg and the Ransom Humanities Research Center in Austin, are more restrictive. Some will admit graduate students equipped with good credentials, and the Folger, Newberry, and Huntington, for example, make a special point of welcoming such readers, who are, after all, the mature scholars of the next generation. At the British Library, admission to the reading room is only by "ticket," a card that can be obtained without trouble by presenting a letter of introduction, accompanied by a more or less *pro forma* assurance that the work one proposes to accomplish there cannot be done in any other, less crowded, library in the city. The Bodleian is less restrictive than the Cambridge University Library, which requires an introduction from a don or other university dignitary. When in doubt whether you would be allowed to work in a certain American or British library, it is always advisable to write ahead or

---

[10]In 1991, it was revealed that the rest of the *Huckleberry Finn* manuscript—the first 665 pages, containing lengthy passages not in the printed text—had been found in a trunk in a Los Angeles attic. It had been missing from the Buffalo library for over a century.

to consult a scholar who knows the ropes. It is well to remember, also, that several major research libraries, among them again the Folger, Huntington, and Newberry, offer fellowships to postdoctoral scholars (and in some cases dissertation writers as well) whose projects require extensive use of those libraries' specialized collections. The chief sources of research subsidies are listed in the annual Directory Number of *PMLA*.

Researchers leave every library they visit with more than a sheaf of notes. For libraries, in addition to the wealth they possess on vellum, paper, and film, are physical and personal presences, and each has an atmosphere of its own. The papery redolence of an old library's stacks; the air-conditioned immaculateness and ease of the Houghton and Folger and Huntington reading rooms, where scholarship is made to seem not only a dignified but almost a luxurious way of life; the somnolent attendants in soiled jackets who bring you your books at one library, and the extraordinary courtesy and helpfulness of the staff at another; the noble dimensions of the King's Library in the British Museum, its walls lined with folios in the richest of bindings; the tourists peering into the display cases containing great documents of history in the exhibition room at the Public Record Office.... These general sensations of place mingle, in retrospect, with closer, more personal ones: the comeliness of a well-printed book, its type still black, its margins still ample, its rag-content pages still crisp, strong, and white after the passage of three centuries; your own expectancy as you open a cardboard file-box and undo, for the first time since his widow tied it very long ago, the ribbon that binds a stout bundle of a famous author's private letters. These are elements of the scholarly experience that do not ordinarily suffuse the books and articles one writes, but they leave ineffaceable traces in the memory, and they are not the least of the personal satisfactions afforded by the profession of literary research.[11]

[11]An appreciative account of the English libraries visited in the course of one research project can be found in Richard D. Altick, *Writers, Readers, and Occasions* (Columbus, OH, 1989) ch. 19.

CHAPTER SIX

Making Notes

He walked much and contemplated, and he had in the head of his Staffe a pen and inke-horne, carried always a Note-Book in his pocket, and as soon as a notion darted, he presently entred it into his Booke, or els he should perhaps have lost it. He had drawne the Designe of the Booke [Leviathan] into Chapters, etc. so he knew whereabout it would come in. Thus that booke was made.
— John Aubrey, "Thomas Hobbes" (*Brief Lives*, 1813)

N o two persons make research notes in exactly the same way, and there is, in fact, no absolutely "right" or "wrong" way to do so. The two goals are efficiency and accuracy, and whatever methods achieve them for the individual scholar are wholly legitimate. The prescriptive portions of what follows will be clear enough. The rest we offer simply as the fruit of our own experience: these are the techniques that have served us best. The following discussion assumes that one is making notes for a large project, such as a monograph, and that the method chosen is the manual (data recorded on slips) rather than the mechanical, where the material is directly entered in a computer and electronically organized, stored, and made ready for instant retrieval. But our suggestions can easily be scaled down to be useful in collecting data for a term paper or an article, and the recommended form of the notes applies in any case.

Unless circumstances require that you take notes by hand (see n. 2 below), always type. You save an incalculable amount of time, and your notes will always be legible. No matter if your handwriting is itself utterly clear, at least to you; machine-assisted note-taking is faster and more efficient.

Slips are preferable to cards: they take up less space, making them both more convenient and more portable if the amount of information you accumulate is considerable. Furthermore, slips on high quality bond paper (no other kind of paper is satisfactory) are just as durable as cards. Most chapters of advice on note-taking stress that cards or slips should be of uniform size, but we recommend two sizes, each for a specific purpose: three-by-fives for bibliographical references *only*, five-by-eights for the notes themselves. The former are as large as necessary for the amount of information they will have to contain, but they are not large enough for comfortable recording of facts, ideas, and quotations, especially when you do not know how many more related notes you will eventually want to enter, for convenience, on the same slip. In addition, they are easily distinguishable and can be filed separately.

For every book and article you consult, make out a bibliographical (three-by-five) slip. If your project is a fairly modest one, to be finished in one or two months' time, before your memory starts to fail, this point is less important; in such a case, modify the rule to read "for every book and article in which you find information." But if you are working on a dissertation or a book, it is extremely useful to keep a record of every source you examine, whether or not you take anything from it. A few months later, running across a reference to a certain article that sounds as if it might be valuable, you may forget whether or not you looked at it. Quick recourse to your file of bibliographical slips may save you, at the very least, the labor of hunting it down again in the library and, often, the trouble of rereading it.

On the face of the bibliographical slip, copy the author, title, edition (if any is specified), place and date of publication, and (if it is a fairly recent book) the publisher. Or, if it is an article you are recording, note the author, title, periodical, volume number, year, and pagination. *Always take this information*

from the source itself as it lies before you, never from any
reference in a bibliography or someone else's footnote. Authors'
initials and the exact spelling of their names, the titles of books
and articles, and dates have a way of getting twisted in secondary sources. Play safe by getting your data from the original, and
doubly safe by rechecking once you have copied down the
information. On the face of the same slip record the call number
of the book or periodical, and if it is shelved anywhere but in
the main stacks of the library, add its location. If you have used
the item at a library other than your headquarters, record that
fact too ("Folger," "Newberry," "Huntington"). These are small
devices, seemingly unimportant, but in the aggregate they are
great time-savers if you are dealing with scores of sources and
the storage space in your brain is reserved, as it should be, for
more vital matters.

On the back of the bibliographical slip (or attached to the
computer entry), write a phrase or even a short paragraph of
description and evaluation. This precaution against fading
memory should be taken even if you expect that the source's
usefulness to you will end with the completion of the current
project. There is always the chance that a future project will
involve the same source, and such a statement, recorded when
the book is fresh in your mind, will save the labor of reacquaint-
ance at that time. Since nobody else sees these slips, you can be
as candid, peevish, scornful, or downright slanderous as you
wish; if a book is bad, record exactly what its defects are, so that
you will not refer to it again or, if you must do so, in order that
you will remember to use it with extreme caution. If, on the
other hand, it is a valuable book, note its outstanding features.
And also record just what, if anything, it has contributed to your
present study. Perhaps leave a memo to yourself to reread or
recheck certain portions of it at a later stage of research, when
conceivably it will provide further data that at this point you do
not anticipate needing. Finally—and this is particularly recommended to students whose research requires them to scan large
quantities of dull material, such as books of garrulous Victorian
literary reminiscences in four disorderly volumes—note the degree of exhaustiveness with which you inspected the item by

some such phrase as "read page by page" or "thoroughly checked index." (Bear in mind, though, that indexes in many books, even the most scholarly looking, are not to be trusted, particularly if the name or subject in which you are interested occurs only incidentally in the text. Few indexes are absolutely exhaustive, and the unindexed reference may be the very one you need.)

We recommend also that you make a slip for every bibliography you have consulted, so that you can later be sure that you have not inadvertently overlooked it. If it is one of the serial bibliographies of literary scholarship, such as the annual bibliography of studies in romanticism, record the precise span of years you've covered. If it is a subject bibliography, such as *Poole's Index,* list the individual entries under which you have looked ("Education," "Literature," "Reading") in case other possibilities occur to you later on. Similarly, if you have done an electronic search, record the particular key words you used. You may later want to try others to ensure thorough coverage. Once again, the whole idea is to save wasteful duplication of effort. Three or four minutes spent in making such a slip can save a whole day's work a month or two later.

So much for the three-by-five slips. Now for the larger ones, which can accommodate enough material to minimize the nuisance of riffling through a whole sheaf in search of one elusive piece of information. Every slip should be devoted to a single topic, perhaps a very small subtopic; you must be the judge of that. It should therefore bear, at the top, a readily intelligible caption. And it should be strictly confined to that single topic. That means that when you have finished with a certain book or article—and don't take any notes until you have finished; simply jot down page references on a piece of paper until you have come to the very end—the data it contains may have to be distributed among a dozen or more slips. That may take a bit more work, but in the end it's worth it, because you will have all related material where it should be—in the same place. As your slips on the same topic multiply, use the same heading and add consecutive numbers.

A definite skill is attached to note-taking. Most novices write far too much. There is no inherent advantage in putting down whole sentences when compressed phrases are just as meaningful ("Percy Bysshe Shelley was born on August 4, 1792, at Field Place, near Horsham, Sussex": why not "PBS b. Aug. 4, 1792, Field Place, nr. Horsham, Sussex"?). Definite and indefinite articles and other such amenities can be dispensed with. And if you can devise a consistent personal system of abbreviations, which will be absolutely clear and incapable of later misinterpretation, you will save more time and space than you can easily conceive. In note-taking type *shd* and *wd* for *should* and *would, bg* for *biography* and *bgr* for *biographer, edn* for *education* or *edition, pbd* for *published, ptr* for *printer,* and so on. In addition, you can create a stock of abbreviations for the names of authors you are making notes on: RB, MA, ACS, DGR, CD, WMT, HWL, WW (William Wordsworth or Walt Whitman?), STC, TC, MT, RWE.

It follows that in note-taking, verbatim quotations should be kept to a minimum. If you are simply extracting facts or ideas from your source, reproduce them in as small a compass as accuracy permits; it is substance, not wordage, that you want for your slips. Thus, you can boil down a *DNB* sketch of a minor eighteenth-century writer just by eliminating all the prose in which it is embodied and confining yourself to the hard facts— names, places, dates; and you can handily summarize a critic's four-page interpretation of *The Turn of the Screw* in a paragraph, by disregarding both the complete sentences and (if it is not essential for your purposes) the step-by-step construction of the argument.

There are many occasions, of course, when direct quotations must be copied into your notes. Any hitherto unpublished documentary material, such as a record of marriage or a holograph letter, should be transcribed word for word. Even if only the substance is desired, it is useful, and what is more, a valuable safeguard, to have the exact reading, rather than a summary, in your possession. Later developments may make desirable its literal reproduction. Again, when dealing with crucial points of biographical or critical opinion, you should have at your fingertips the author's exact words, so that you can re-examine them. Often after a lapse of months, and with the advantage of further knowledge and longer thought, a writer's position proves not to be what you first assumed, or has implications of which you were earlier unaware. Word-for-word copying un-questionably is a weariness of the flesh (the author of Ecclesias-tes may have had it especially in mind when he [or they] com-plained of study and the making of books), but it often cannot be avoided.

In transcribing anyone else's actual words, one precaution is absolutely requisite: enclose every phrase or sentence you copy in quotation marks, to remind you that you have borrowed it and thus must retain the quotes if it appears, unaltered, in your finished product. Failure to do so often results in embarrass-ment, if nothing worse. To a reader who detects the unacknowl-edged "borrowing," the offense is known, less charitably but accurately, as plagiarism. The plea that the identifying quotation marks were absent from the original research note by reason of momentary carelessness, or that they were lost somewhere be-tween the original note and the merciless daylight of print, is no defense. It has been used unsuccessfully in several well-publi-cized recent cases (not involving literary scholars), and the pro-fessional careers of the careless transcribers have been seriously impaired if not actually destroyed.[1]

When occasion requires you to transcribe verbatim, do so with clear head, patience, and devotion to absolute accuracy: not a comma omitted, not a phrase accidentally skipped. Recog-nizing the vicissitudes a quotation can undergo in successive drafts of a manuscript, most scholars as a matter of routine compare the version in their final draft with the original source. This is good practice, but it is time-consuming, and in any event some of the originals may not again be accessible, having been seen at other libraries or having in the interim mysteriously disappeared from the shelves of one's own. An even better practice, therefore, is to certify the accuracy of your initial tran-

[1]See Thomas Mallon, *Stolen Words: Forays into the Origins and Ravages of Plagiarism* (New York, 1989).

scription on the noteslip itself. Having copied a paragraph from Mikhail Bakhtin, take the time—even though it is a nuisance, the hour is late, and your eyes are tired—to collate your slip, word by word, with the page before you. When you have corrected your transcription (and the odds are that you will have to—the capacity for faithful copying is one of human-kind's rarest talents), put along the margin some private sign of approval, such as "Text√d", which will bear eternal, unequivo-cal witness to the fact that the passage as copied is, *is*, IS accurate. Five minutes spent rechecking in January are an hour in the pocket in necessitous May.[2]

The importance of such a precaution is better appreciated when we realize that in the history of literary studies many an exciting "discovery" has proved to rest on the false premise of a quotation that is incomplete, misread, or separated from its context. As Geoffrey Tillotson once wrote (*Criticism and the Nineteenth Century* [1952] ix), it is a sobering but prudent practice to recheck one's quotations against their source before using them in any argument:

> There are occasions when the checker finds his transcript so badly wrong that it could only serve the present occasion if kept wrong. . . . To check the transcript of a quotation is sometimes to discard the quotation. Further, even if the tran-script is accurate, turning it up may lead the checker to find that he has so far forgotten its context as to have come to misunderstand what the writer of the quotation intended it to mean. To re-examine the context of a quotation is sometimes to discard the quotation.

[2]The copying machine has unquestionably made it easier to accumulate the documentary data one needs, even to the extent that the reckless feeding of coins into a slot sometimes becomes a means by which students postpone having to discriminate among the raw materials they unearth. But photocopying is not always available or practicable—some materials cannot be photocopied because of the nature or age of their bindings, and some may not because of copyright restrictions—and at such times the necessity for manual transcription with mechanical fidelity remains undi-minished.

One more word about quotations, again having to do with the changes that affect them as they pass from one writer to another. A cardinal rule of scholarship requires that quotations be made from the source that is closest to the author—the book in which the passage first appeared or, in the case of manuscripts that are themselves unavailable, the most authoritative printed text. If for any reason you are unable to use these original sources, and must rely instead on the passage *as quoted by* someone else, always state that fact in your footnote reference. This is a means of self-protection. If the quotation is inaccurate in the source you have used, you show that the fault lies there, and not with you. Nevertheless, quote secondhand only when absolutely necessary. It is worth much trouble to get the words precisely as originally recorded. The same caution applies to facts derived from a secondary source. No matter how reputable the book, it is always advisable to go back to the place where its author or compiler got the information; a typographical error, a careless transcription, or an omission of important qualifications may make the account in some respect inaccurate or misleading. And the bibliographical reference may itself turn out to be wrong.

To return to the actual process of note-taking: after every statement of fact, every condensed or paraphrased generalization, and every direct quotation, write the source. Here is where the system of separate bibliographical slips comes in especially handy, for it enables you to use the shortest reference form possible. If you are borrowing from an author represented in your file by only one slip, you need to write after your note only "Lewalski, 133"; the bibliographical slip will provide you with all the further information you need for your documentary footnote and for rechecking if that is necessary. And if you have consulted more than one book or article by the same author, or anticipate doing so before you are finished, you still can abbreviate without any danger of misunderstanding: "Lewalski, *Major Poets,*" or "Lewalski in *Introduction to Scholarship*"— each of which is clue enough to the full bibliographical information on your three-by-five slip. It thus becomes unnecessary to repeat the full reference after every substantive note; all you need do is specify the page. If, in a single note, you take material from several successive pages of your source, the best practice is to put page references along the lefthand margin, indicating by a slash or two (//) in the body of the note exactly where your use of one page ends and the next begins.

In addition to being a repository of factual data and ideas drawn from your sources, content (substantive) slips provide a way of storing your own ideas, fresh from the mint. Often, as you read, your mind may go a step or two beyond what is on the page, extending an argument the author left incomplete or generalizing from the data presented; or, on the other hand, you may disagree with the statement before you. In order that these quick flashes of inspiration be not lost, record them as they come, no matter how fragmentary or tentative they may be. You can organize, criticize, and amplify them later on; the important thing at the moment is to preserve them while they are fresh in your mind. But to keep them entirely separate from ideas that are present in your source, make plain to your future self that they are genuinely your own by initialing them. In the course of most scholarly projects, as opinions and interpretations churn around inside a scholar's mind, there is eventually bound to be some confusion as to which were acquired from preceding authorities and which were self-generated. A scholar can guard against this (and appease his or her conscience) by maintaining this simple record of ideas independently arrived at.

Write on only one side of each slip—at the outset. Save the other side for incidental addenda, corrections, and queries directly relating to the notes contained on the face of the slip. To ensure that these later accretions are not overlooked, write a big red "OVER" in the margin alongside each item to which they refer.

Fresh notes, as distinct from brief commentary and added details on previous points, call for fresh slips. And these, in any major program of research, mount up at a surprising rate. To keep them well classified and accessible with the least trouble, use dividers in your file and arrange them in some logical order; roughly, perhaps, in the succession in which you anticipate dealing with them in the prospective book. When, as is inevitable, a fact or remark on one slip has a bearing on a fact or remark on a slip farther down the line, enter some sort of cross-reference on the margin of both, so that you will know where each is. At a fairly late point in your research, after your major ideas have fallen into a reasonable sequence and you consequently have a set of principles for arranging your various groups of slips (and you are working without computer assistance), it is worthwhile to number them. First, divide the notes into major topics and give each slip the number of the category to which it belongs. Then subdivide them, and if necessary sub-subdivide them; to each division give numbers. Just as each book in a library has its own unduplicated call number, every slip should receive a distinctive designation (12.3.6), which means that it has its own inalienable—and fairly logical—place in the file. Furthermore, such a system facilitates cross-referencing; later slips can be interfiled and given a higher terminal number (12.3.6.1, 12.3.6.2, *et seq.*).

All the recommendations we have so far made for the manual mode of note-taking are directly applicable to the creation of computer databases. A variety of software programs for PCs— the best are *Nota Bene* and Wordperfect, with their respective supplements; the former is the more comprehensive—enable researchers to conveniently and accurately record, organize, and store the totality of their formal notes and informal jottings.

The number of entries or individual records that can be created on the computer is virtually unlimited, and each may be searched for or called up variously—e.g., by bibliographical particulars (author, title, date), by subjects or other topical subsets, by particular key words or phrases. These entries or records may be retrieved at any point, even from multiple files, and added to or edited.

Certain of the more sophisticated of the computer's many functions, such as organizing materials on more than one principle at a time, are great boons for scholars. Yet many writers will say that neither these nor the more common indispensable functions—e.g., footnoting, indexing—constitute in themselves the chief forte of these programs. Most impressive, some argue, is their ability to reproduce bibliographical and footnote material correctly (capitalization, punctuation, abbreviation, underlining, margins, italics, superscripts), in the principal scholarly styles or formats (MLA, APA, Chicago), and as often as desired—from *an entry typed only once.*[3]

While there is no question that personal computer technology enables researchers to organize, file, and retrieve data with an efficiency and speed hitherto unattainable, it does entail (to some people, at any rate) a certain loss. The physical act of handling and rehandling one's notes, as the traditional method makes necessary, has its own value, in that it means that the facts and quotations they contain come repeatedly to one's attention rather than being sequestered in an electronic storehouse. A seasoned scholar, the biographer of Robert Browning, Matthew Arnold, and Jane Austen, reports his personal experience: "I have not found a computer that can match my filing methods or analyze incoming data well enough to be of use; I may tomorrow. But I am primitive in this way; I want to contend with the fuss of sorting, so that something may rub off in the process and lodge in my mind."[4] So intimate and subtle a mental process is not easily described, and it cannot be measured, but it is nonetheless real and potentially profitable.

It remains only to say a little about the habits that mark responsible researchers when they are in libraries. For one thing, they *never* bring bottles of ink anywhere near books or manuscripts; and many rare-book libraries, bearing traumatic

[3]While speaking of scholarly formats, we should observe that most professional journals welcome manuscripts submitted on disk. Because of the variety of software programs, however, editors may ask for one hard copy (printed) of the text and a disk with the text in one or more of the common programs and also converted to ASCII (the American Standard Code for Information Interchange, a generic set of 255 characters representing letters and most other typographical symbols, which produces a generally accurate, though not faultless, text). For valuable suggestions for preparing an electronic manuscript, see the *Chicago Guide to Preparing Electronic Manuscripts for Authors and Publishers* (Chicago, 1987).

[4]Park Honan, *Authors' Lives: On Literary Biography and the Arts of Language* (New York, 1990) xvii.

memories of awful accidents, forbid even the use of fountain pens. Scholars come to work with a good supply of well-sharpened pencils, which are the safest tools to use if typewriters or laptops are unavailable. But they *never* place the paper on which they are writing on top of the manuscript or opened book; pencil points or ballpoint pens leave embossings on the receptively soft paper beneath the note slip. Scholars *always* keep the manuscript or book from which they are taking notes safely away from any possible source of damage, and if they prop a heavy book up for easier reading, they make sure it can't fall. (Most libraries have stout book racks to help prevent this.) And scholars *always* handle their materials with the utmost care; they turn pages carefully; they treat manuscripts, which are often extremely frail, with the delicacy connoisseurs always accord to fragile *objets d'art,* opening folds slowly and cautiously, lifting their leaves—depending on their form and condition—either by the margins or in the flattened hand. Although perspiration mingled with the dust acquired from old books may coat their fingers with a species of mud, scholars *never* leave a trace of smudging, even the faintest thumbprint, on a document or book they have been using.

Another caution relates to the inexorably deteriorating condition of many of the books and periodicals used by literary researchers. From the middle of the nineteenth century down to our own time, many printers used a kind of cheap paper with high acid content, with the result that the pages have become increasingly fragile and indeed are quietly crumbling to dust. In such collections as those of the Library of Congress, the New York Public Library, and the British Library literally millions of volumes are in an advanced state of decay, and proportionate loss is being sustained in all other research collections, large and small. Recent estimates suggest that in excess of "80 million volumes" in American research libraries, "about one quarter of our libraries' holdings, and more than 2.5 billion pages in the nation's archives are in danger of being lost through oxidation." Techniques of restoration and conservation have been developed, but they are expensive to apply and will save only a tiny fraction of the volumes affected by chemical instability. In addition, the bindings of many frequently used books and periodicals are coming apart, and because their paper is so brittle, they cannot be rebound. Another of the scholar's professional obligations is to treat such materials with the utmost care, so as to avoid additional damage.

A further risk is incurred every time one uses a copying machine. Placing a book face down on the machine strains the binding, no matter how stout it may seem. Since photocopying has now become a way of life and limitations can scarcely be placed on its use, all that can be asked of users is that they be careful not to exert any more pressure on the opened, flattened book than is necessary to obtain a reasonably legible rather than a perfect copy.

Even with the best precautions, library materials unavoidably suffer from these unanticipated consequences of modern technology. But one kind of injury, the oldest, possibly the most serious and certainly the most avoidable, is the wanton defacement of books. When some guides to "better study habits" encourage the lavish use of colored marking pens on the pages of an undergraduate student's textbooks, it is perhaps only to be expected that another form of this practice, a dubious one at best, carries over to books that are for public, not merely private, use. Call it by its proper name: the defacement of a book, by whatever means, is sheer vandalism.

The best deterrent to one's temptation to mark a library book is to consider one's own reaction to a book already marked. How many times have you been annoyed by the marginalia left by some idiot—huge and redoubled exclamation points, uncomplimentary expressions ("absurd," "oh, come now," "for God's sake!!!!"), and long, scrawled explanations of what seems perfectly clear in the printed text? The critical points may be well taken, but the margin is no place to utter them. Pencilings of this sort—including compulsive underlining, a sophomoric affliction if there ever was one—are bad enough; even worse is marking with ink. And worst of all is that indefensible sin, outright mutilation: the removal of whole pages or sequences of pages. Every library has penalties for such misdemeanors, which, in many cities and states, is what they are in the eyes of the law, but the penalties are not severe enough. At least they do not discourage either the vandal-by-momentary-impulse or the vandal-by-habit. The result is that everybody else suffers; for who can read with comfort an ink-glossed book, or contemplate with equanimity a volume from which some essential pages have been rudely sliced out? Our indignation can be all the freer, our execrations the more profane, if our own consciences are perfectly at ease.

CHAPTER SEVEN

The Philosophy of Composition

The idea that histories which are delightful to read must be the work of superficial temperaments, and that a crabbed style betokens a deep thinker or conscientious worker, is the reverse of the truth. What is easy to read has been difficult to write. The labour of writing and rewriting, correcting and recorrecting, is the due exacted by every good book from its author, even if he know from the beginning exactly what he wants to say. A limpid style is invariably the result of hard labour, and the easily flowing connection of sentence with sentence and paragraph with paragraph has always been won by the sweat of the brow.

—G. M. Trevelyan, "Clio, A Muse" (1930)

I n the early days when literary scholarship was establishing itself as an academic discipline, the chief reproach laid against it was that it was sterile, unimaginative, divorced from both life and literature, and preoccupied with absurd trivialities—"the date of Hegetor, swan maidens, Celtic cauldrons of plenty, the priority of the A or B versions of the prologue to the *Legend of Good Women,* medieval lives of Judas

219

Iscariot, Vegetius in English, or Caiaphas as a Palm Sunday prophet."[1] Although a glance through the tables of contents of some current issues of scholarly periodicals would suggest that things have not improved much since then, on the whole the tendency of present-day literary research has been, if anything, toward the opposite extreme—a kind of scholarship, often brilliantly imaginative, that sweeps on the pinions of hard facts toward broad and credible generalizations.

But oftener heard today, and with good reason, is the complaint that more than a few literary researchers, working in the very medium of their subject, cannot write intelligible English. The hallmark of good scholarly prose is lucidity. The single, simple requirement, as incumbent on scholars as it is on journalists, who write for a larger public, is that *the meaning of every sentence should be unmistakably clear on first reading.* If your reader has to pause and read a second time to try to discover your meaning, there is something wrong with your choice of words or your phrasing. Such an ideal is never easy to achieve, and it has become less so at a time when much of the critical writing on which the beginning scholar is nurtured, is laden with the ugly and impenetrable jargon and clumsy constructions that are notorious characteristics of the various postmodern schools, leading to the oft-heard charge that its practitioners form small, isolated coteries talking and writing among themselves in a form of discourse only they understand. There cannot, however, be any absolute *cordon sanitaire* between the two communities, because every scholar needs to know what is going on among the critics of the day and when desirable borrow their insights for the enrichment of his or her own work.

What the scholar is obligated *not* to borrow is their "critspeak," drawn from the ponderous special vocabularies of epistemology, sociology, psychology, psychoanalysis, neo-Marx-

[1]This particular indictment dates from as long ago as 1913 (Stuart Pratt Sherman in *The Nation,* September 11; reprinted in his *Shaping Men and Women* [Garden City, NY, 1928] 66).

ism, semiotics, structural anthropology, communication theory, and linguistics. Such a diversity of sources reflects the spread of the major intellectual influences that have shaped recent thinking about the nature and processes of literary art, and while this thinking unquestionably involves subtle concepts and modes of interpretation that can be expressed only with the aid of specialized terminology, every writer on a literary subject has a professional responsibility to avoid pretentious language that needs to be translated into plain English, as in these examples:

> To get the proper "mix" of factors in the instance of *Kaddish* (Ginsberg's lament on the death of his mother), we need an addresser-context ratio, for the biographies of Allen (addresser) and his mother (context) determine the message to a great extent—which is not to say that other factors do not influence the message.
>   What I am saying, in effect,[2] is that once the framework has been exhausted as a series of compartmentalized factors used to generate information (although the model is necessarily simplified for heuristic purposes), then the factors can be combined in ratios, and the investigator can begin to work back toward the holistic view that was so unmanageable originally.
>
> *   *   *
>
> Eve [in *Paradise Lost*] is the pure lyric principle, in a presympathetic and almost premodal form. . . . She is fluidity and pure space, undefined and circumscribed by poles and forces as in the lyric paradigm. It is as if magnetism were freed from its field. She is not the imagination, because she cannot maintain the center necessary to stay in modality and then move into the revitalizing modes.
>
> *   *   *

[2]Reliance on such a phrase (even worse: "What I am trying to say is . . .") is a sign of an author's failure to make his or her argument clear at the outset. Writers who feel they should simplify and clarify late in the game should go back and consider what has been wrong with the initial exposition that requires subsequent simplification and clarification. The reader may reasonably ask, "Why didn't you say so in the first place?" In the present example, however, the purported clarification never occurs.

On the one hand, Arthur [in Tennyson's *Idylls of the King*] assumes words can be used with a morally redemptive precision that will make possible a final stabilization of personality. Thus, he affirms logocentrically "Man's word is God in man" and trusts that solemn linguistic structures imposed predictively ("vows") can effect an erotic transformation, sufficient to save his knights from sensual entrapment in randomness, assuming "the maiden passion for a maid" will stifle "the base in man." On the other hand, Merlin, hermetic source of the "sacred mount" and "dim rich city" of Camelot, the very externalizations of Arthur's assumptions, distrusts these assumptions and perceives only "Confusion, and illusion, and relation, / Elusion, and occasion, and evasion." Merlin's pessimism is manifested tropologically and validated literally in the *Idylls* by the mist and water that overwhelm and negate all human endeavor (Arthur's allies and enemies alike), and that thereby distort traditional Christian rhetorical devices which repeatedly describe only vulnerable maleficence by means of a vocabulary that connotes liquid fluctuation.

* * *

The problematic of proto-professional ideological production denied autonomous political weight in a society struggling to preserve the hegemony of an aristocratic class-ideology is here displayed in order to be ridiculed.

* * *

Although the metacategories imply a reading by retroaction, in the essays themselves I trace the fictions in their linear continuity, and deliberately follow the sentences of the heroine's plot as it unfolds. This step-by-step reading derives both from my lingering attachment to the early structuralist preoccupation with narrative sequence—the grammar of the *consecutive*—and from the persistent sense of sexual *consequence* I feel to be at work in these novels which follow either the logic of seduction, or the logic of a female curriculum vitae—or both.

* * *

There is only one major order of being, that of common natural and human reality, but within that order there arise tensional relations that recall, without reproducing, something of the tensions that had formerly arisen from the yoking of ontologically heterogeneous objects. While both terms are drawn from a single order of being, the sphere of common experience, in their tension they mimic the ontological tension of paradoxes like those that lie at the heart of dyadic ontologies.

* * *

. . . the psychology of transgression projected by the utopian intersection of the subgenres of romance and pastoral, in which romance desire strives for what it is forbidden, for what is constitutively absent from the pastoral world, is the final symbolic form taken by the counterplot. Predestination is thus figured as an ethical psychology of work in creation, and this logic provides the dominant generic explanation of the fall, hence of the failure of political desire in the revolution.[3]

Indulgence in a style that is the antithesis of clear, accurate communication is a form of pretentiousness. Another is what might be called pseudoerudition—learned name-dropping, or the superstitious veneration of authority. Novices in the profession, troubled by a sense of inadequacy, often seek to add weight to their arguments by making calculatedly offhand references to whoever happen to be the big names in critical fashion at the moment—Barthes, Derrida, Foucault, Kristeva, Lacan. But, unless a reason for quoting an authority exists apart from reiterating a point already made, such a device smacks of ostentation.

Even if historically oriented scholars resist the temptation to write trendy gobbledygook, striving instead to adjust the focusing lens of their prose so as to project a sharp image before their readers, there are other enemies of clear writing to be guarded against. Such vigilance has its practical reward. Those who write clear, efficient English have a greater chance of success in their competitive profession than those who do not. Command of an easy prose style is an undoubted advantage when it comes to

[3]The contributor to *The Year's Work in English Studies* for 1986 who quoted this gem remarked, "If this book finds a fit audience, they will be few." See n. 17 below.

publishing the fruits of research. Printed books and articles are not necessarily reliable models to follow; one must not assume that because a scholarly manuscript has found its way into print, it is by that very token well written. All the cautionary examples we have just cited have been taken from books issued by reputable university presses and articles published in equally reputable journals. These showcases of the scholarly world, which among them publish the great bulk of today's production, have elementary safeguards in the form of consultants who are depended upon to screen out the worst-written books and articles that are submitted. But these advisors have varying standards of acceptable style, and all too many submissions make the cut on the ground that they have something significant to say despite the deficiencies of their prose. The fact remains that a manuscript which is a pleasure to read has a decided initial advantage over one that is painful to struggle through.

The editors and consultants who decide whether or not a novice scholar's manuscript should be published often summarize its flaws of presentation by the single term "dissertation style," by which they mean that it is too stiff, self-conscious, possibly too tolerant of jargon, and with the bare bones of structure too much in evidence. There is no reason why even the earliest work of a master's or doctoral candidate should (in the pejorative sense) "read like a thesis." No one expects a person reporting on his or her research to be a brilliant stylist. Writers with so pronounced a gift for language and form that they can make a twenty-page paper or a two-hundred-page dissertation into a work of art are as rare inside the profession as they are outside. But though scholarly writing is not meant to offer the reader an esthetic experience, it does not have to be dull or unnecessarily complicated. Its form should be so lucid as to do justice to the content.[4]

---

[4]For sage and urgent counsel on this important aspect of scholarly practice, see Jacques Barzun and Henry F. Graff, *The Modern Researcher* (3rd ed., New York, 1977). Part 3 ("Writing") should be read in conjunction with the present chapter, as should Louis Budd's essay, "On Writing Scholarly Articles," in DeNeef et al., *The Academic's Handbook* (see For Further Reading, p. 259) 201–15.

One inviolable rule of good scholarly writing is: Say what you have to say, and when you have said it, quit. Longwindedness, repetitions, digressions are as out of place in a research article or book as they are anywhere else. Rare is the paper that cannot be cut by at least 15 percent by deleting verbose locutions and substituting single words that are just as accurate and often more emphatic. So long as neither clarity nor *necessary* substance is sacrificed, the shorter the article the better.

Undergraduate theme writers tend to add weight by loading their pages with quotations. Serious researchers seldom deliberately do so, but sheer indolence—copying being, on the whole, easier than original composition—sometimes tempts them to "lard their lean books," as Robert Burton put it, "with the fat of others' works." The truth is that another writer's exact words are not sacrosanct if you can convey the same point more succinctly in your own language. You can do it oftener than you may think. When you are about to quote more than a sentence or two from a secondary source, pause a moment. Couldn't you adequately summarize the idea in half the space? If you can, why burden the page with the superfluous wordage that direct quotation would entail?

On the other hand (to return to a point made in the preceding chapter), if by condensing or paraphrasing your author's statements you risk distorting his or her position, then you have no choice but to quote the writer verbatim. Nuances of meaning can be as important in learned writing as they are in poetry, and no scholar wants to appear to misrepresent someone else's assertion or position. To ensure that its author's intention is faithfully conveyed, the quotation not only must be absolutely accurate, as has been stressed in chapter 6, but must incorporate all pertinent qualifications and details. It may not make much difference, perhaps, that Katharine Anthony (*The Lambs* [1945] 136) writes, "The celebrated painter Benjamin Hayden [*sic*] complained that Hazlitt's infant 'put his fingers into the gravy,' " whereas what Haydon really recorded (*Life of Benjamin Robert Haydon . . . from His Autobiography and Journals,* ed. Tom Taylor [1853] 1: 264–65) was that "the boy, half clean and obstinate, kept squalling to put his fingers into the gravy." The effect on the onlookers no doubt would have been the same in either case. But careless or

inadequate quoting can seriously distort meaning, as this example shows:[5]

> The next paragraph, indeed, calmly begins by saying that
> what this news caused at the time was "a melancholy slack-
> ening." But they hurry on down the gorge and see

>   The immeasurable height
> Of woods decaying, never to be decayed . . .
> Winds thwarting winds, bewildered and forlorn . . .
> The rocks that muttered close upon our ears,
> Black drizzling crags that spake by the way-side
> As if a voice were in them; the sick sight
> And giddy prospect of the raving stream . . .

> Nature is a ghastly threat in this fine description; he might
> well, as in his childhood, have clasped a tree to see if it was
> real. But what all this is *like,* when the long sentence arrives
> at its peroration, is "workings of one mind" (presumably
> God's or Nature's, so it is not merely *like*),

>   Characters of the great Apocalypse,
>   The types and symbols of Eternity,
>   Of first, and last, and midst, and without end.

> The actual horror and the eventual exultation are quite
> blankly identified by this form of grammar. . . . No doubt
> some kind of pantheism is implied, because Wordsworth
> feels that Eternity is turbulent like the Alps and not calm like
> the Christian God. But the last line of the passage contradicts
> this idea by putting the calm back, and in any case the meta-
> physics would be a deduction only; what he sets out to do is

---

[5]We owe the example to Professor M. H. Abrams. Another instance of
distortion through selective quotation, pointed out by Gordon S. Haight in
his Riverside edition of *Middlemarch* (xii–xiii), is F. R. Leavis's treatment
of that novel in *The Great Tradition.* Compare Leavis's quotations (61–79)
with George Eliot's full text.

to describe the whole development of his feelings about crossing the Alps, and he asserts it as a unity.
(William Empson, *The Structure of Complex Words* [London, 1951] 303)

Compare, now, Wordsworth's actual lines (*The Prelude* [1850 text] 6: 624–40; the passages omitted by Empson are italicized).

> The immeasurable height
> Of woods decaying, never to be decayed,
> *The stationary blasts of waterfalls,*
> *And in the narrow rent at every turn*
> Winds thwarting winds, bewildered and forlorn,
> *The torrents shooting from the clear blue sky,*
> The rocks that muttered close upon our ears,
> Black drizzling crags that spake by the way-side
> As if a voice were in them, the sick sight
> And giddy prospect of the raving stream,
> *The unfettered clouds and region of the Heavens,*
> *Tumult and peace, the darkness and the light—*
> *Were all like* workings of one mind, *the features*
> *Of the same face, blossoms upon one tree;*
> Characters of the great Apocalypse,
> The types and symbols of Eternity,
> Of first, and last, and midst, and without end.

(How would inclusion of the omitted lines affect Empson's argument?)

Next: organize, organize, organize—but without ever seeming to do so. Construct your paper as coherently as your resources of thought and language allow. Never leave readers uncertain as to your—and their—destination or the relevance of each statement to your purpose. Keep your direction sure and steady and the pace as brisk as the amount of pertinent material and the complexity of the argument permit. The sentences and paragraphs should fit as tightly as the teeth of a zipper. The familiar cohesive fragments of language—*thus, therefore, again, on the other hand,* and the rest—may be used, but sparingly. And the finished structure should contain no trace of the rough scaffolding that went into its erection. Such self-conscious locutions, so redolent of a high-school classroom "presentation," as "Up to this point, my intention has been . . ." or "Now let us turn to . . ." merely distract the reader. Your chief dependence should be upon the forward thrust and clarity of the argument: upon the tenon and mortise of rigorous thinking, not the easily available hot glue of methodical rhetoric.

While the pains we take to increase logical coherence are amply justified by their service to our intended reader, they are still more valuable as stimulus and safeguard to our own thought. By the time most of us sit down at our typewriter or personal computer (the latter's revising and rearranging capability is among the most welcome advantages the electronic age has bestowed on painstaking writers), we bask in the illusion that we have our material and our ideas well under control: all we have to do now is let flow on paper the close-knit sequence of our argument—or so we regard it—that we have already formed in our mind. Ordinarily, things just do not work out that way. We need first to outline and then to write; and after that, we rewrite.

An outline, including abbreviated cues to all the data and logical relationships to be covered in the proposed paper, may be as informal and scrawled as we like. Nobody else will ever see it. But the simple act of making it forces us to collect, review, and systematize our thoughts before starting the first paragraph and provides at least a tentative itinerary for the whole trip. A preliminary chart in black and white affords an invaluable overview of everything that is to be said and often, by exposing gaps or non-sequiturs, may forestall time-wasting digressions that prove to lead either nowhere or in the wrong direction. It is much more economical to discover weaknesses at this stage than after a first (freehand) draft has been toiled over, read and groaned over, and thrown into the wastebasket.

But even the most conscientious preliminary outlining and sentence-by-sentence writing seldom results in a first draft that can also stand as the final one. Some writers, in fact, confess that their hardest and most profitable thinking is done in the very act of composition. Only when they are compelled to lay out their argument in sentences and paragraphs, scrupulously designed to lead the prospective reader from point to point, do they finally see it as a logical whole, and only then do remaining deficiencies of evidence and reasoning become apparent. Rethinking calls for rearrangement, and rearrangement means rewriting; perhaps a paragraph here, a whole page there—or the whole article or chapter. But one can find a positive gain in necessity. For if the process of writing is in part destructive, exposing as it does the flaws of one's thinking, it can also be creative, because by forcing reconsideration of what has been said, it sharpens insight into the meaning of one's material, suggests new sources of data, perhaps makes it possible to extend the argument a further step.

Completion of an outline and the ceremonious insertion into the typewriter of a clean sheet of paper or the conjuring-up of the blank PC screen, a tabula rasa radiant with expectancy, is far, then, from marking the end of thought and the beginning of art. The two will proceed simultaneously, each nourishing the other. But that very first page may remain immaculate (or else hideously besmirched with x-ed out sentences) for some time; for a well-known neurotic symptom, called First Paragraph Block, often attends the beginning of composition. Its causes, amateur psychiatrists say, are a subconscious awareness of one's incomplete state of preparation and fear of what lies ahead. Under these circumstances, the introductory page or two that you manage to squeeze out may well represent the stalling action of a writer still unsure of the direction to be taken. Browning caught the essence of the difficulty in lines he once addressed to a fictive poet, in the poem "Transcendentalism":

> . . . why such long prolusion and display,
> Such turning and adjustment of the harp,
> And taking it upon the breast, at length,
> Only to speak dry words across its strings?

As you fumble for an opener, you may justifiably hear at your back the impatient prospective reader exclaiming, "Get on with it!"

The best way to get on with it is to let the first page stand for the time being, even though you know in your heart of hearts that it is not merely provisional but will, in fact, never do. Go on to the second page, or wherever you get down to the brass tacks of concrete detail, and you will begin to pick up momentum; following your preliminary outline of I, II (a), (b), (c), and so forth, sentences and paragraphs will naturally fall into place. Eventually, you will have said all you planned to say. Then, still despising the first page, put the completed paper away for a time, and when you take it up for revision, rewrite Paragraph One in the light of what follows. The very fact that it no longer stands alone but serves as an introduction to the whole argument, which now lies before you in print, will help you improve it.

In any event, don't discourage your reader with the point-blank announcement in Sentence One that "The purpose of the following article is to . . ." This is as feeble a gambit as that favorite among freshman theme writers, the quoting of a dictionary definition. Nor is much to be said for a plodding initial Review of Previous Knowledge (or Opinion) on the Subject at the gateway of an article that promises either to add to the knowledge or reverse the opinion. Some better way can be found of enlisting the reader's attention, such as a terse, question-raising statement of the problem, a pertinent anecdote, or an apt quotation from the literary text under discussion that will serve as a springboard into the paper itself. (The previous history of the topic, if it needs to be reviewed, may be summarized unobtrusively in a footnote or the relevant material recalled as you go along.)

We consider these, in their respective ways, attractive openings:

> Comedy deals in stereotypes rather than fully rounded, three-dimensional, living characters, just as much of social life is conducted by stereotypes rather than by fresh, objective appraisal of each situation as it arises. It is possible for those who habitually deal in stereotypes to break loose from their moorings and to engage in fresh appraisals, but the latter is

counterpointed against the former. That is, we are conscious of making a special effort for a special case, different from the customary ebb and flow of daily existence. These rules (or rules of thumb) also apply in comedy, where there is continual skirmishing between originality and convention, between the demands of live persons and the easy familiarity of stock types. Great comic characters like Falstaff are both highly original and highly traditional, depending upon what aspect of the character we choose to consider, but the originality is especially striking because of (and not in spite of) the basis in convention.[6]

* * *

A seldom discussed resource for literary and cultural studies of colonial America is the genre that I shall comprehensively label "early American gallows literature." Included under this label are sermons, moral discourses, narratives, last words and dying sayings, and poems written for, by, and about persons executed for criminal activity in America before 1800. Although the genre accounts for only a very small percent of the 50,424 titles listed in Charles Evans's *American Bibliography* and Roger Bristol's *Supplement* to that work, the genre clearly had a hold on the American imagination from the earliest days of New England's Puritan settlements through the last decades of the eighteenth century. Unlike some of the literary types introduced to the colonies by Puritan settlers, this genre, with its several forms, survived the disintegration of Puritan faith during the mid-eighteenth century, and during the period from 1750 to 1800, the genre actually continued to develop and to exceed in numbers and variety the forms of gallows literature initially developed by New England Puritans.[7]

* * *

The nineteenth-century bourgeois experience of love was both stylized and spontaneous. Efficient middle-class institutions all the way from the adroitly orchestrated dinner party

---

[6]Maurice Charney, *Comedy High and Low: An Introduction to the Experience of Comedy* (New York, 1978) 50–51.

[7]Ronald A. Bosco, "Early American Gallows Literature: An Annotated Checklist," *Resources for American Literary Study* 8 (1978): 81.

to the cool treaty between mercantile clans fostered suitable unions. They could not keep the impressionable from falling in love, but they could make sure that young men and women encountered few except eligible partners. If one refused to marry for money or good family, it became proverbial that one might be persuaded to go where money or good family could be predicted. Acceptable paths to love were plainly marked and heavily guarded; the penalties annexed to misalliances threatened or consummated—social ostracism, transfer to remote posts, legacies withheld—were extremely harsh. But their very severity speaks to the urgency of the temptations. The clashes of social styles, pressures of temperament, neurotic inhibitions or proclivities, the anarchic charm of infatuation, made for variety in patterns of respectable love, sometimes for surprises. They provided generous space for amorous motives less calculating than material advantage or social ascent. Impulse increasingly won out over defense.[8]

*   *   *

During the antebellum era, when black narrative in the United States developed into a highly self-conscious and rhetorically sophisticated tradition, black writers who aimed at a serious hearing knew that the authority they aspired to was predicated on the authenticity that they could project into and through a text. As new, quintessentially "other" faces on the literary scene, and in the antebellum period further estranged from the white reader by a slave past, black narrators knew that they would have to *win* the literary authority they desired for themselves and their stories. The slave narrator who described an escape from cruel bondage in the South would have to prove worthy of the trust and deference that whites almost automatically awarded one of their own race who recounted an escape from cruel Indian captivity. By the early nineteenth century black narrators realized that to assume the privileged status of author in the literary discourse of white America, they would have to write self-authorizing, that is, self-authenticating, narratives. First of all, the raw

[8]Peter Gay, *The Bourgeois Experience: Victoria to Freud.* Vol. 2, *The Tender Passion* (New York, 1986) 3.

material of their stories, the who-what-where-when information that constituted the "fable" of their narratives, would
have to sound factual. Second, the narrative statements, the
structure in which the facts take meaningful shape in what
many now call the "sujet" of narrative, would also have to be
credible. And finally, the narrative itself, the voice that embodies the "producing narrative action," the storytelling,
would have to sound truthful or risk suspicion about its
sincerity.[9]

* * *

Among the critical issues that have been debated over the
past decade and a half, none is more urgent than how we are
to write historical criticism. Much the greater part of the
material we work on is literature written in the past. Yet,
since literature became a discrete subject of academic study,
most of the prestigious fashions or critical New Waves, ever
since romanticism, have been modernist, formalist, esthetic,
ahistorical—in a word, have declined to address themselves
to, or even to acknowledge, the intellectual problems facing
those who have to read outside their own culture and sphere
of intuitive understanding. The past, the historical point at
which a particular book was produced, is *different* from the
present, in which it is being read. How fully should our
theory or (for my purposes, more urgent) our critical practice
allow for that fact?[10]

The final paragraph offers a cognate problem, which, however, can be solved more easily. Conventionally the last paragraph should summarize all that has preceded it and point up
the ultimate significance of the discovery or argument. This is
good sense. But the writer cannot say, in so many words, that
"the purpose of the foregoing article has been . . .": that is a
privilege reserved for scientists. Instead, it should sum up with-

[9]William L. Andrews, "The Novelization of Voice in Early African American
Narrative," *PMLA* 105 (1990): 23.

[10]Marilyn Butler, "Against Tradition: The Case for a Particularized Historical Method," *Historical Studies and Literary Criticism,* ed. Jerome J.
McGann (Madison, WI, 1985) 25.

out seeming to do so; it should be a coda, not an abstract, and it should leave the reader with a satisfying sense of gain—new information acquired, an enlarged historical apprehension, a stimulating critical perception:

> For four decades or so, Milton himself spoke to his nation in the figure of the recollective mediator and spoke to teach his people. If we learn anything to our own advantage now from Milton's poetry of the past, we learn how a poet put himself both in success and in failure at the service of a public program. He himself would deny that a long dead poet can say only sublime and timeless things to his readers, having so wholeheartedly affirmed the intentionality of every political gesture and having so faithfully registered each self-correction in later works. If the poet's process of shaping experience is ideally matched by the readers' collaborative effort to reconstitute that experience, then some very great works of literature are not best studied impersonally. And finally, since the interlinked examination of a poet's life and works is the least narcissistic reading possible, it may be that the greatest literary pleasure open to us is the pleasure not of reading between the lines of a poet, but reading between the poems, following the arc of his growth, responding to the presence of his program. The pleasure of reading between works in an oeuvre is the most intense where that space is bracingly occupied by the artist's own educative self-characterizations.[11]

                              *   *   *

If ultimately Glasgow revised rather than revolutionized the southern pastoral and her social satires are perhaps more successful than her agrarian fiction in criticizing southern mores, her use of land imagery and visualization of new kinds of rural communities in these novels represent an integral part of her artistic vision. They provide the setting for the development of more active and self-aware women protagonists. As Glasgow's pastorals demonstrate, changing the im-

[11]Mary Ann Radzinowicz, " 'To Make the People Fittest to Chuse': How Milton Personified His Program for Poetry," *CEA Critic* 48/49 (1986): 20–21.

agery of the southern garden not only dispels a prevailing literary and social myth, but also imagines the possibility of a new society based on more equal relationships among its members. Finally, the author's contribution to an evolving *female* pastoral tradition places her in company with her contemporaries Willa Cather and Zora Neal Hurston and confirms her importance as a major influence on later southern women writers.[12]

* * *

It is in the break between the Wedding Guest's stunned question and the mariner's resumption of his tale that the pedagogical moment is represented as inherently and constitutively missed—represented by the dash that marks the place where what is not known is evoked as the blank that makes the story go on forever. That blank is precisely what must—and cannot—be taught. And literature is the means by which such a blank—the very agony of teaching—can somehow, nevertheless, be captured.[13]

* * *

Ulysses was her trial, her torture, and finally her triumph. It brought Shakespeare and Company a second celebrity, a living bard, who turned the shop into a literary shrine. It burdened our literature with a work of extraordinary versatility. It canonized Sylvia Beach. To those fitfully wondering whether to try and follow in her footsteps she was the object of envious glances and acclaim. What she had accomplished they had only dreamed of doing and, remarkably, she had done it despite a shaky budget and with little knowledge of what the effort would entail. She succeeded partly because she did not know what she could not or should not do. To contend, however, that success was practically guaranteed, given the prepublication publicity *Ulysses* received, is to suggest that the publisher was endowed with a degree of prescience she could not have had prior to February 1922. Even Joyce gloomily predicted dismal sales for his book. Sylvia

---

[12]Beth Harrison, "Ellen Glasgow's Revision of the Southern Pastoral," *South Atlantic Review* 55 (1990): 66.

[13]Barbara Johnson, "Teaching as a Literary Genre," *Yale French Studies* 63 (1982): vii.

Beach had what every publisher needs—intuition—and on
that quality rested her lasting belief in Joyce and in the great-
ness of *Ulysses*.[14]

All the paragraphs between the opening and closing ones
offer an equally healthy challenge to the scholar's shaping and
stylistic powers. The construction and phrasing of a research
paper demand as much care, in their own way, as do those of
a work of imaginative literature. Not only must transitions be
managed, relationships clarified, emphases developed, proportions adjusted, meanings expounded: the right tone must
be achieved. The gray stylistic mien worn by the authors of so
much of "the literature on the subject"—any subject—certainly gives substance to the old charge that the greatest success of scholarship has been its relieving literature of its connection with life. Nothing can devitalize a topic more
effectively than the manner in which it is discussed, and how
remote those grave files of journals on the library shelves
seem from the dreams and impulses and triumphs of the
human spirit! One is inescapably reminded of Yeats's lines in
"The Scholars":

> Bald heads forgetful of their sins,
> Old, learned, respectable bald heads
> Edit and annotate the lines
> That young men, tossing on their beds,
> Rhymed out in love's despair
> To flatter beauty's ignorant ear.

Literature is a record of life, and it has its abundant portion
of gaiety. In writing about it, we do not have to don suits of
solemn black and assume a dejected 'haviour of the visage. We
can talk about literature with the seriousness it deserves and yet
not be grim or heavy-footed. There is no harm, for instance, in
disclosing that a human being has written your article. The

[14]Hugh Ford, *Published in Paris: American and British Writers, Printers,
and Publishers in Paris, 1920–1939* (New York, 1975) 33.

notion that the first-person singular should not be used in scholarly writing is nothing more than a superstition lingering from the days when literary researchers, being regarded as a breed of scientists, were expected to be as impersonal in their prose as in their procedure. Scientific writing to this day abhors the "I"; but in writing about literature no virtue resides in self-effacement per se, and if you think that the first-person singular is appropriate at a given place, use it without apology, though sparingly. A scholarly or critical article is no place for an ego trip.

A cognate superstition maintains that scholarly writing cannot accommodate humor. A touch of wit in a serious article is no more reprehensible than a bon mot in a lecture, yet it is a hundred times less common. Fortunately, there have been and there are a few scholars and critics who are unashamed to lighten their discourses. Everyone who has read Douglas Bush's books remembers with gratitude the unaffected wit that flickers here and there in those learned pages:

The sound and prosaic wisdom of the goddess [in Tennyson's "Oenone"] is so very Victorian that we become embarrassingly aware that she is undressed, apart from a spear, and it seems to violate chronology and propriety, as if the Queen herself had started up in her bath and begun to address the Duke of Argyll.[15]

* * *

Mr. Eliot has even complained of Milton's obscurity. One may have, as I have, a great admiration for Mr. Eliot's writing in both verse and prose and still find a certain pleasure in visualizing the author of *The Waste Land* as he struggles with the meaning of *Paradise Lost*. Milton is too big, too sternly strenuous, to allow us to feel at ease in his presence. . . . Like Dante, Milton is not what P.G. Wodehouse would call a "matey" person.[16]

[15]*Mythology and the Romantic Tradition in English Poetry* (Cambridge, MA, 1937) 205–6.

[16]*The Renaissance and English Humanism* (Toronto, 1939) 102–3.

Readers of the annotative footnotes in Cecil Y. Lang and Edgar F. Shannon, Jr.'s exemplary new edition of Tennyson's letters come upon such touches of humor as these:

[The problem of identifying the "Geschwister" mentioned in a letter from Tennyson to his friend Lushington] Sister or brother, or brother or sister, or brothers or sisters. Lushington having eight sisters and three brothers, the total number of identifications possible could be 68,588,312. . . .

* * *

Samuel Rogers (1763–1855) was an institution, his house, at 22 St. James Place, an academy and museum, and he had everything to declare but genius, though his life showed an infinite capacity for taking pains.

* * *

[Letter] dated by circular reasoning and leap of faith.

* * *

The evidence for the date [of another letter] is persuasive primarily because there is none against it.

* * *

Harriet Martineau (1802–76), a remarkable writer (on nearly all subjects), and a formidable woman (with an intimidating ear-trumpet).

* * *

John Reuben Thompson (1823–73). Born in Richmond, Va., he was well educated, having attended the University of Virginia [where this edition was produced], and, for better or worse, became a southern gentleman.

Even bibliographical articles, under the right auspices, can delight as well as inform. From 1976 to 1984 a British scholar, David Daniell, contributed the Shakespeare section to *The Year's Work in English Studies*. His judgments on the annual crop of books and articles were always forthright, and often wittily expressed in the case of publications that for one reason or another fell short of his standards:

The footnotes astonish when they do not offend, as they often do; he provides, moreover, a glossary of about eighty words which provide him, and I am sure, him alone, with the ripest hidden sexual meanings for the play [*The Two Gentle-men of Verona*]. It is not often that I carry a book between thumb and finger to the dust bin.

* * *

[On momentarily fashionable subjects in Shakespeare criticism] Last year it was Shakespeare and alcoholism; this year Shakespeare and swearing. No doubt next year it will be Shakespeare and little green men.

* * *

Quite the most peculiar book to come my way for some time seems to be about [*Antony and Cleopatra*]. . . . The wild typography, the fringe "thought," and the frequent references, made this the Shakespearean equivalent of those grubby sub-religious tracts pressed into one's hands at street-corners by sad, demented people.

* * *

The sight of the title of René E. Fortin's essay in *Shakespeare Studies* makes me want to slam the book shut and weep. It is "Hermeneutical Circularity and Christian Interpretation." "I wish," he says, "to suggest to consider the secular reading as exclusively valid is as much an act of dogmatic assertion as is the comforting vision offered by the Christian interpreters, since the assertion in question in either case is based on a selection of evidence as well as a selective interpretation of the evidence." Quite so.

* * *

[Of a book on Shakespeare's Rome] It is library work, useful, of course, and to be commended for its determination to conquer everything Shakespeare-Roman that there is, even if that comes to feel a touch arrogant. At the end, Shakespeare's Roman plays do still, I find, run from his hand and, relieved of the weight of such correct academic accumulation, scamper away to a vulgar playhouse, there to enact Julius Caesar in the Capitol to the rabblement, who have never even heard of a footnote.[17]

---

[17]Still, footnotes, including this and the following one, are useful for making incidental points, if not necessarily to the rabblement. Familiar phrases that most readers can be relied upon to recognize will, if appropriate, add a bit of literary polish to your prose. To call attention to them by quotation

But what about us less gifted mortals, who nevertheless are once in a while visited with humorous inspiration that we are tempted to preserve in our pages? The only possible answer is, Put it up to your conscience—and your taste. If, in the course of writing, an epigram or pun comes unbidden, it may, after a preliminary scrutiny, be allowed to stay—until our more sober judgment and our friends have a chance to review it.[18]

---

marks, however, as the author might have done in the present allusion to Polonius's speech in *Hamlet* (3.2.99–100) and the use of "rabblement," a word found only once in Shakespeare (*Julius Caesar,* 1.2.244), would imply an unwarranted and certainly tactless condescension to your readers' presumably inferior knowledge. In like fashion, Bertrand Evans trusted his readers to spot, and appreciate, the echo of the first sentence of *Pride and Prejudice* in the first sentence of his own book, *Shakespeare's Comedies:* "It is a truth universally acknowledged as unfortunate that a commentator who would study Shakespeare's tragedies chronologically is obliged to begin with *Titus Andronicus.*" In the note identifying Samuel Rogers, quoted above from the edition of Tennyson's letters, there is an unannounced fusion of well-known remarks by Oscar Wilde and Thomas Carlyle. On rereading the two sentences following the lines from Browning (p. 229), we find that we have unconsciously echoed a lyric by Andrew Marvell, a speech of Hamlet to Horatio (3.2.70), and the first words of a notorious review, by Francis Jeffrey, of Wordsworth's *Excursion* (1814). We have let the sentences stand—without quotation marks—for the sake of additionally illustrating our present point.

[18]This footnote is the proper locale for a subsidiary plea: avoid cryptic titles. For too many years there has been a vogue among scholars and critics for picturesque, esoterically allusive, and studiedly uninformative titles. In column 166 of the *NCBEL,* vol. 3, *The Broken Cistern* flows, nine entries later, into *The Sacred River,* and in the next column *The Visionary Company* is quickly metamorphosed into *The Lost Travellers,* who have a possibly significant proximity to *The Drunken Boat.* Most such titles, admittedly, are followed by subtitles that more or less explain what the book is about ("Studien und Interpretationen zur Dichtung der englischen Romantik"; "A Reading of English Romantic Poetry"; "A Romantic Theme with Variations"; "The Revolutionary Element in Romanticism"), but it would seem advisable to give this explanation, so far as possible, in the beginning; the subtitle should provide, not a key to the mystery, but a

Which brings us to a point on which we are admittedly a bit fanatical. To undergraduate and graduate students, we are aware that what we are about to say will sound like a ukase from Utopia. We know that there are inexorable deadlines to be met; we know that academic terms rush by, and the concurrent requirements of two or three courses, with term papers and all the trimmings, drive students frantic. Nevertheless, we will say it, for the sake of that later day when the heat is off and what has been written in haste can be revised at leisure. Or, rather, we will let Dr. Johnson say it for us, in his "Life of Pope":

> His publications were . . . never hasty. He is said to have sent nothing to the press till it had lain two years under his inspection: it is at least certain, that he ventured nothing without nice examination. He suffered the tumult of imagination to subside, and the novelties of invention to grow familiar. He knew that the mind is always enamoured of its own productions, and did not trust his first fondness. He consulted his friends, and listened with great willingness to criticism; and, what was of more importance, he consulted himself, and let nothing pass against his own judgment.

In this respect, at least, Pope was a wise man (and the wiser Johnson implies his own approval). No piece of scholarly writing can be the worse for mellowing; most books and articles, in fact, improve if they are allowed to age before bottling. A cardinal rule of scholarship, as of criticism, is to be wary of one's first enthusiasm. Indulge it, to be sure; let it run its course in the composition of the first draft. But then let time do its slow work.

---

further explanation. There may be no grace in such titles as "Is Oxford the Original of Jefferson in William Faulkner's Novels?" or "The Dashes in Hemingway's *A Farewell to Arms*," but at least there is no concealment for the sake of a recondite reference. Fancy titles are especially troublesome when fed into computerized bibliographies and subject indexes, since their constituent elements automatically become key words (*cistern, river, company, travellers, boat*) that, by their very nature, lead the searcher in a false direction—or nowhere.

Put the manuscript away for as long as you can—weeks, months, years. When you finally take it out again, you will have a new perspective. You will see where love-at-first-sight infatuation with your discovery or line of argument led you to exaggerate or confuse relationships, neglect contrary evidence, even draw wrong conclusions. But you will also see new implications in your material, and perhaps you will find yourself going to hitherto unthought-of sources to clarify and substantiate facts. "It is certain," Gamaliel Bradford wrote in his journal (February 7, 1920), "that even in investigating what seems to be the smallest and most limited subject there are always nooks and crannies that slip by one, facts of greater or less interest and importance that turn up afterwards and tend at least, or appear to tend, to modify one's judgment—too late." One of the reasons why manuscripts should be put aside for a reasonable time is to provide for that contingency.

Restraining the impulse to publish one's brainchild as soon as it is bathed and breeched has also this advantage: it encourages a second look at the style as well as the substance. The successive revisions we have spoken of above are best undertaken at fairly wide intervals, so that each time we return to the manuscript, our critical eye is as fresh as possible and the remedial measures more immediately apparent.

It is good to be your severest critic, but there are limits to the detachment with which you can view your own work. When you have done the best you can, ask people for whose judgment you have respect to read your manuscript. Don't pick yes persons; turn, rather, to readers on whom you can depend to wield the blue pencil and ask the pointed question in utter candor, for they are the writer's best friends. Ask for, and receive in good and thankful spirit, the sternest criticism of which they are capable. Two or three such readers may represent a cross-section of the public that will eventually read your work in print, and they can alert you, before publication, to flaws that would otherwise be irrevocably preserved in type.

Now a word about documentation. A superstition akin to the one about avoiding the first-person singular holds that the scholarly quality of a paper is directly proportional to the number of footnotes, as if the heavy ballast at the bottom of each page insures against the balloon's soaring errantly into Cloud-Cuckoo-Land. No such thing. Footnotes, it is said, are for use, not ostentation.[19] They have two purposes. "Documentary" footnotes provide readers with the sources of all the facts, as well as of the opinions that are not original with the writer, so that if they are at all skeptical, they can check for themselves. Moreover, notes are an indispensable courtesy to later scholars who may wish to utilize some of the material and need clear directions as to where to find it. "Substantive" footnotes allow the writer a place to put incidental but relevant comment that would interrupt the flow of discourse in the text proper. The recent tendency has been toward absorbing some documentation into the text—a practice we have sometimes followed in this volume to illustrate the kinds of occasions on which it is appropriate.

In our field, the traditional guide on all matters of form, including footnotes, is the *MLA Style Manual,* obtainable at small cost at campus bookstores. Its rules have been adopted by the English departments of most American colleges and universities and, sometimes with minor differences, by many university presses and learned journals in the humanities. No matter what your intended audience is, master the *Manual* so thoroughly that its prescriptions become second nature to you. On questions outside its scope, probably the most widely used guide is the University of Chicago Press's *Manual of Style.* These two works of scripture should be on every scholarly writer's desk, next to a good dictionary and H. W. Fowler's classic (and sometimes delightfully cranky) *Modern English Usage.* They, like footnotes, are for use; for it is remarkable how often we are content to play our typewriter by ear.[20]

---

[19]Cf. the Roman emperor in Gibbon's *Decline and Fall of the Roman Empire* (ch. 7): "Twenty-two acknowledged concubines, and a library of sixty-two thousand volumes, attested the variety of his inclinations; and from the productions which he left behind him, it appears that the former as well as the latter were designed for use rather than ostentation."

[20]An excellent practical guide for entry-level scholars who aim to publish is Beth Luey, *Handbook for Academic Authors* (Cambridge, 1987). Luey

Once we have verified all dubious spellings, corrected false idioms, ironed out faulty parallel constructions, and made sure that all documentation is in prescribed and consistent form, there remains the indispensable task of scanning the final copy for typographical errors. No matter how time presses, nor to whom the paper is addressed—a teacher or an editor of a journal—every line must be proofread. Courtesy and self-interest both require it, for a reader cannot be expected to do full justice to the argument of a paper if his attention is recurrently distracted, and his patience tried, by careless errors of typing.

Nearly every practicing scholar has experienced at one time or another the sinking feeling induced when a cherished article bounces from a journal, or a publisher rejects a book. If the manuscript comes back with merely a printed slip, or what is obviously a form letter from the editor, there is nothing to do but look up Browning on welcoming each rebuff—and then, after having cast a cold and critical eye over the neatly typed pages and perhaps rewritten an inferior paragraph here and there, send it out again. As often as not, however, the editor of the journal or press sends along specific comment, which may embody also the criticisms of consultants to whom the manuscript was referred. For whatever comfort it may be, remember that editors and their readers are not infallible. George Meredith, who for many years read manuscripts for the firm of Chapman and Hall, declined an imposingly long list of books that subsequently became famous. Sometimes readers are just plain obtuse (though the writer may be at fault, for not making his ideas sufficiently clear); sometimes they really don't know as much about the subject as the writer does. Every editor of a

distills ten years' experience as an editor of scholarly books and textbooks in chapters dealing with, among other topics, preparing manuscripts, revising dissertations for possible publication, preparing journal articles and choosing the most likely places to submit them, and finding publishers for scholarly books and textbooks and working with them once a contract has been signed. See also the shrewd advice offered in Terence Martin, "Meditations on Writing an Article," *AL* 55 (1983): 72–76.

scholarly journal and every director of a university press can testify how often a proffered manuscript can evoke bluntly opposite reactions from consultants to whom it is sent for their expert opinion. And most scholars have had an experience similar to that of a well-known member of the profession who once had an article returned to him from a leading journal accompanied by a reader's comment: "This is not an article. It's an example of how an article should not be written. Mr. X knows how to use the language. But he has nothing to say. The paper is a useless collection of unstructured information—useless because unstructured." The article was accepted and printed by the next journal to which it was submitted, and immediately after it appeared its author received a note from another scholar, also well known in the profession though not to him personally. "My congratulations upon a very fine study," she wrote. "I have assigned it to my graduate seminar as a paradigm of the just and the lively."

Discrepant though the reactions of critics often may be, most manuscripts are rejected with good cause, and the criticisms should be weighed with all the detachment at one's command. If the editor says the article is too long, probably it could be cut without grievous loss. If he says it does not make its case, probably it doesn't. If he notes that you have failed to take into account certain items of previously published scholarship that affect your argument—well, haven't you? In any event, apply to your colleagues, not for commiseration but for further criticism. Maybe it would be best to shelve the whole business for a while to gain additional perspective. But if you still have faith in what you have written (and never abandon faith too readily), let it resume its rounds.

Eventually, if the article or book really deserves to be published, it will be, for there are now enough periodicals and university presses to assure every scholar a hearing. Then comes that "one far-off divine event / To which the whole [of scholarly] creation moves"—the arrival of galley proofs. Now (if you are like most writers) your doubts are resolved, your sagging morale receives a boost; for how authoritative, how convincing your hard-wrought sentences look in black type! Rejoice, and, apart from correcting whatever typographical errors there are, and verifying your quotations and references once again, make no changes. Corrections in proof are expensive, and it is standard practice to charge an author for any that increase the printer's bill by more than 10 or 15 percent of the cost of original composition. Many authors are prone to detect in galley or even page proof deficiencies they failed to notice before, no matter how often they re-examined and revised their manuscript—ambiguities, awkward phraseology, false emphases, repetitions, overloaded paragraphs, outright errors. Somehow one's writing looks quite different when it appears in printer's type. But the price to be paid in "author's alteration" charges is steep, and only a Winston Churchill or a William Faulkner could afford the luxury of rewriting a book in galleys.[21]

And now, after a suitable rest, to the next project—the one for which you've been accumulating notes over the past several years. Other topics, other materials, other methods of approach, but the four great requisites of good scholarly writing never change:

1. Accuracy of facts
2. Soundness of reasoning
3. Clear explanation of the topic's significance
4. Unaffected, terse, LUCID prose

[21]Complicated and intractable though the histories of some English and American literary texts may be, *Ulysses* among them, they are editorial child's play compared with those of Balzac, who rewrote his books so many times in proof that an edition recording the development of the text is almost a practical impossibility. See Bernard Weinberg, "Editing Balzac: A Problem in Infinite Variation," in *Editing Nineteenth-Century Texts,* ed. John M. Robson (Toronto, 1967) 60–76.

CHAPTER EIGHT

The Scholar's Life

That academical honours, or any others should be conferred with exact proportion to merit, is more than human judgment or human integrity have given reason to expect.
  —Samuel Johnson, *A Journey to the Western Isles* (London, 1774)

L iterary scholars never cease being scholars. Today the great majority of them earn their living as members of teaching faculties in colleges and universities throughout the world. As such, they have responsibilities quite remote from the pursuit of knowledge. But in the midst of alien affairs that necessarily command their talents and energies as teachers, administrators, and academic committee members, and in their private roles as spouses, parents, and participants in community activities and other good works, scholars cannot suppress, even if they wished to do so, that portion of their consciousness that insists on asking questions about literary matters and seeking answers. Their literary awareness keeps twenty-four-hour days: the bookish excitement that has attracted them to the profession in the first place permeates their lives.

It is now almost a century since literary studies began to be professionalized—that is, transformed from an avocation pursued by persons who made their living as cultural journalists, British civil servants, or in other occupations, into what has become a highly organized and sophisticated intellectual discipline centering in the academy.[1] Professionalized literary scholarship is now old enough to possess its own pantheon of revered figures, most (but not all) of whom were teachers in American institutions of higher learning or were their counterparts in British universities: Douglas Bush, E. K. Chambers, R. W. Chapman, Helen Gardner, W. W. Greg, Howard Mumford Jones, George Lyman Kittredge, Roger Sherman Loomis, A. O. Lovejoy, John Livingston Lowes, Kemp Malone, F. O. Matthiessen, Marjorie Hope Nicolson, Perry Miller, Frederick Pottle, F. N. Robinson, Hyder Rollins, Robert K. Root, George Sherburn, Henry Nash Smith, Rosamond Tuve, Helen White, Karl Young . . . We have met many such names, and those of many of their students and successors (now the third or fourth generation), in the pages of this book.

Those groundbreakers in the profession, the commanding figures during the "golden age" when research dominated English studies from the 1920s through the 1960s, thought of themselves as being first and foremost explorers of literary history and biography whose great design was to add to the world's store of literary knowledge—to provide the factual materials by which they, and ideally the reading public at large, might better understand and evaluate a work of art. Alternative systems for reading and interpreting literature developed from the late 1940s onward: the "New Criticism" exemplified by the work of Cleanth Brooks, John Crowe Ransom, and Allen Tate, and then, successively, the work of Northrop Frye with its revised concepts of irony and myth, and the first manifestations of what were to become the multiple strains of structuralism.

Some historians and critics of our profession claim for the early formative decades a now lost breadth of learning and intellectual rigor. Wayne Booth, for instance, has regretted the proliferation of dissertation topics that concentrate on the formal aspects of literary texts "isolated from the influences of

---

[1]See the items listed in the first section of For Further Reading, "The Profession: Then, Now, and to Come" (pp. 259–60).

ethics, politics, history, logic, dialectic, and even grammar." Others, like Robert Scholes, consider the narrowing of focus to have occurred in another way, "bracketing out certain domains of textuality in order to concentrate on others," first excluding "all those uses of the English language that were utilitarian or speculative, retaining only those that could be covered by such designations as 'oratory' or 'belles lettres' " and then deleting "oratory" so that all that remained was " 'belles lettres' alone, which we learned to call by the now focussed honorific title of 'literature.' "[2]

Opposing this constriction of interest, and perhaps more influential in the long run, has been the expanding tendency of structuralist and poststructuralist theories that have, among other effects, broadened the traditional canon to embrace numerous kinds of writing, gender- and ethnic-oriented works, for example, that previously were considered to lie outside the pale of "literature." The scope of English studies now also includes writing theory and pedagogy. At the same time, the meanings of that eternally slippery word "meaning" have been drastically redefined. It is quite likely that some of the "immortals" mentioned above would today scarcely recognize the profession of English studies they helped found and develop.

Precise figures on the present size of the profession are hard to come by, but because it constitutes the largest component of the umbrella organization, the Modern Language Association, some indication of the latter's size can suggest the magnitude of the former. Today the MLA has some thirty thousand members, as many as ten thousand of whom attend the annual convention, bearing thick programs that list as many as eight hundred meetings on a range of topics that regularly, and with good reason, inspire humorous feature stories in the press.

These figures, impressive in themselves, do not reflect another form of communal scholarly activity, the scores of confer-

[2]Booth's and Scholes's comments were delivered at the Conference on the Future of Doctoral Studies in English held at Wayzata, MN, in 1987. On the outlook for "literature" and thus for literary studies, see Kernan's *The Death of Literature*, cited in For Further Reading, p. 260.

ences of special-interest groups that are held each year, with their own array of prepared papers and discussions. Yet, despite all this elaborate programming and, in the case of the MLA, bureaucratic infrastructure, the study of literature remains at base an intensely private pursuit. No one ever entered the profession burning with a single-minded ambition to read papers before an audience of peers or to see his or her original ideas on a literary topic printed in a learned journal. These forms of scholarly communication, however indispensable to a curriculum vitae, are the spinoffs of a higher ambition, the same strong impulse that presumably motivates every reader of this book: the simple fact that some men and women like to read and are drawn to a profession in which they are actually paid to do so. They may not earn as much or enjoy as much social status as do their contemporaries in other lines of work, but they have the sharper satisfaction of having a vocation that enables them to do what they most want to do in life.

Hence, though time is always short, we have the lifelong company of books; and what is more, we have good human companionship. Literary scholars probably are no more gregarious than those in other lines of work. Nonetheless, our bond of common interest, of commitment to the humanistic ideal in general and in particular to literature as queen of the arts, is a peculiarly strong one. Love of books and a consuming interest in the intellectual and esthetic questions they pose unite persons with amazingly different backgrounds and tastes. In scholarship there is no prejudice born of national origin, creed, color, or social class; we live in the truest democracy of all, the democracy of the intellect. One of the unofficial but highly compelling functions of the year-end meetings of the Modern Language Association is to provide an occasion for the reunion of men and women who toiled together as graduate students, or later as colleagues in the same department; or who, one sabbatical spring, drank ale together at the Museum pub, the lunchtime annex of the British Library.

We are no cloistered order. Though our closest professional associations outside the circle of fellow-scholars are, of course, with librarians and other booklovers-by-profession, our investigations often lead us to meet all sorts of men and women far removed from the library stacks. Some of us have had the good fortune to contract lasting friendships with people who have provided us with our documents or their personal memories of a great writer: people who sometimes have had initially to be approached with tact and deference, cultivated, discreetly flattered, indulged in their caprices and crotchets until the field was ours.[3]

In research, then, there are numerous perquisites: the constant company of books, the pleasures of travel, the unlooked-for adventure, the frequent encounter with delightful and helpful people. But we earn our perquisites with obligations. Like all professions, ours has its code of manners and ethics, the heart of which is the proposition that we are working together for the benefit of society, not for private aggrandizement. Scientists and inventors have their patents, but in humane learning all knowledge is in the public domain. To be sure, there are legitimate property rights that must be respected.[4] Various libraries, moreover, have their own regulations about the use of unpublished documents in their possession. But there is no room in scholarship for the person who, having discovered or gained access to a body of documents or other as yet undistributed information, claims squatter's rights. Although no professional statute governs the matter, it is generally agreed that the possessors are entitled to exclusive rights to the use of their material only so

[3]For shrewd, sound advice on how scholars should deal with collectors (and, by extension, owners of family archives), see Gordon N. Ray, "The Private Collector and the Literary Scholar," in Louis B. Wright and G. N. Ray, *The Private Collector and the Support of Scholarship* (Los Angeles, 1969) 27–84. Another valuable guide is an MLA brochure (1974) by James Thorpe, *The Use of Manuscripts in Literary Research: Problems of Access and Literary Property Rights*. See also a number of the books and articles cited in "A Scholar's Miscellany" (pp. 272–79).

[4]Every trade publisher has its own policy regarding the amount of material that may be quoted without payment from books it controls. The American university presses, however, have adopted a uniform, and liberal, policy in respect to quotations from their books; see *PMLA* 77 (1962): iv–v.

long as they are actively working toward publication. But if they simply sit on their claim indefinitely, meanwhile refusing to let any other, more energetic, scholar mine it, such action contravenes the very spirit of scholarship.

This plea is not as altruistic as it might seem. The same treasury of wisdom that deplores a dog's growling over his bone also urges one to cast one's bread upon the waters, and the Golden Rule is apropos here, too. Put bluntly, the idea is this: one who cooperates, gets cooperated with. For every close-fisted researcher, happily, there are a hundred others who readily share what they have with whoever needs it. The lists of acknowledgments found in many books are proof enough of most scholars' generosity in providing extra information and in reading other people's manuscripts with an expert eye for errors of fact or interpretation. All of us, even the most learned, repeatedly need the help not only of our fellow-specialists but of colleagues in areas far removed from our own.

Thus, two principles emerge. First, let others know what you are working on. Don't worry about boring them; if you are genuinely excited, your excitement is bound to be contagious. Time after time, as a result, you'll receive valuable tips: "Have you seen this article in the new *Speculum?* I know you don't usually expect anything related to your book to turn up there, but . . ." or, "I was thinking over what you were talking about the other day at lunch, and I seem to remember that in the Berg Collection . . ." The second principle is corollary to the first: Keep up with what other people are doing, not only in your own field but in others as well. Maintain the same interest in their research that you hope they have in yours. If you run across something that might have escaped their attention, drop them a note. If they already possess the information, no harm done; if it's new to them, they will be grateful.[5]

---

[5]For an interesting example of informal scholarly collaboration, "the coöperative pursuit and recapture of an escaped Coleridge 'sonnet' of 72 lines," see David V. Erdman, "Lost Poem Found," *BNYPL* 55 (1961): 249–68. Even though no copy of the London newspaper in which the poem appeared is known to exist, the various clues contributed by five researchers resulted in locating its printed text.

Our profession has no room for intemperate criticism of any kind, least of all in print. Differences of opinion there will always be, and scholarly competence not being a gift distributed equally among all practitioners, lapses of judgment and imperfections of knowledge will sometimes call for comment. Otherwise literary study would stagnate, complacent in its intellectual lethargy and spotted with uncorrected errors. But the necessary process of debate and correction can, and should, be conducted with dignity and courtesy. Name-calling, personalities, aspersions on one's professional ability, and similar below-the-belt tactics are not to be condoned. Controversial points can be made, effectively and adequately, without betraying the ancient association of scholarship with civility.[6]

Thus our profession has ethical standards that, while unwritten, are as binding as the Hippocratic Oath and the Bar Association's canons. They are sustained by the desirability of fair play, self-respect, and professional morale. But these are obligations that relate primarily to ourselves, and an even more pressing one is to the society that—however reluctantly, insufficiently, and bemusedly—supports us in our mysterious pursuits. In the midst of a culture that is often said to be more determinedly

---

[6]A notorious display of bad manners is found in the editorial material of Randolph Hughes's edition of Swinburne's *Lesbia Brandon* (1952) and Hughes's letters to the *TLS* beginning with the issue of October 17, 1952: 677. Cecil Y. Lang's reply (*TLS*, October 31, 1952: 716) is a model of restraint. The chief occasion for the utterance of critical strictures on somebody else's work is, of course, a scholarly review. The caustic wit A.E. Housman used against other editors of classical authors (see *A. E. Housman: Selected Prose,* ed. John Carter [Cambridge, 1961]) can be relished by all of us, since we luckily are not among the number whose incompetence he excoriated. (Furthermore, much can be learned from Housman's exposition of the highest ideals of textual criticism. His was the dictum, "Accuracy is not a virtue; it is a duty.") But the furious tone of these prefaces, reviews, and "adversaria"—the Shropshire lad's *Dunciad*—would hardly be acceptable in present-day scholarly controversy. It is perhaps noteworthy that the sour polemics of Dr. and Mrs. F. R. Leavis (see, for example, their *Dickens: The Novelist* [1970]) were seldom returned in kind by their adversaries, sore though the temptation may have been.

materialistic and anti-intellectual than any other in history (though our scholarly insistence on seeing our age in historical perspective may persuade us to query the pervasive assumption), we sometimes are discouraged and may share the belief, so prevalent in the world outside, that our achievements have an unreal quality, or, if they are real, at least they are futile: that they add nothing to the sum of human wisdom or happiness.

Yet if we are unappreciated and undervalued, the fault is partly ours. We gladly learn, but outside the classroom many of us are curiously uninterested in teaching. Many modern critics and scholars have developed the habit of talking only to each other, neglecting the broader audience of educated people. Perhaps the sustained indifference, even at times open hostility,[7] of the world has driven us to do so, but regardless of the provocation, we have much to answer for if we accept the notion that we are doomed to be forever talking to a virtually empty house. If the humanities, including the study of literature, are in perennial crisis—more so at the present moment, perhaps, than ever before—and the outlook for their survival grim, blame must lie as heavily on us, their appointed agents, for our lack of enterprise, as on the supposed unreceptiveness of the prospective consumers.

It is our responsibility to seize every opportunity to communicate with the lay audience, as in book reviews or in articles and essays in the popular press on history, biography, and culture (and to make such opportunities where they do not exist). Our contribution as scholars in this regard is only a slight modification of our essentially two-fold task in the classroom:[8] to educate students at all levels to read, write, and think, developing in them the intellectually curious habit of mind that casts

[7]For a recent survey of hostility in the press regarding various changes in our field, particularly to the revision of the traditional canon, see Donald Lazere, "Literary Revisionism, Partisan Politics, and the Press," *Profession 89* (1989): 49–54.

[8]The following description originally appeared in John J. Fenstermaker, "Imagined Victorians, Real Victorians, and the Literary Canon," *Teaching English in the Two-Year College* 16 (1989): 260.

a disinterested eye over all important issues, appreciating their complexities; and to lead students by extensive reading and critical analysis of recognized writers and thinkers, ancient and contemporary, inside and outside the mainstream, to seek, in Matthew Arnold's words, "the best that is known and thought in the world" for the purpose of creating in their own lives a "current of new and fresh ideas" appropriate in this, our time.

ANTI-EPIGRAPHS

Suche faultes as have paste in Printyng, as ther in dede bee many, and everywhere aboundante, so of thy courtesie excuse us, whether they bee but letters, whole wordes, or otherwise, and as the sense shall leade thee, so amende what so thou findeste, or lackyng, or superfluous, assuryng thyself that it sometymes paste us in more perfecte wise than thou in these receivest them.

> —T. Fortescue's translation of P. Mexia, *The Foreste* (1571), quoted by H. S. Bennett, *English Books & Readers 1558 to 1603* (Cambridge, 1965) 283–84

* * *

More errors have crept in than I could have wished. In some cases, in deference to some accepted authority, I have altered names and dates and other particulars which I had in my notes, and have found when too late that my original note was right and that my trusted guide was wrong. In other cases the mistakes are slips or oversights. In dealing with such a multitude of particulars, and with entries in many languages, it is difficult to avoid inaccuracy. The bibliography has been written on the margins and backs of a long series of proof sheets, so that occasionally some things have got out of joint and transcription has been at fault. What has been done I have done myself without assistance of any kind.

> —David Murray, *Museums: Their History and Their Use* (Glasgow, 1904) 1: xii

* * *

. . . These kind friends—by researches through old newspapers and periodicals—unearthed correct dates for many of the earlier letters of E. D. to his brother John Dowden, which were either undated or bore dates which proved to be astray—often by several years. The erroneous figures were due to the fact that at a later period the Bishop of Edinburgh [John Dowden] wrote, from imperfect recollection, conjectural dates on the letters. In arranging the MS. for the printers we, the Editors, accepted unquestioned the dates thus written on these letters, and thereby determined their sequence.

With the correction of the errors in dates, came of course a disturbance of the order as previously arranged. But it was not possible to attempt a redistribution, the book being far advanced through the press when the discovery was made of what was amiss.

We can only ask the readers' indulgence, whenever they find themselves obliged to trace the sequence up and down through scattered pages.

A few other misplacements have occurred in consequence of our making, at the eleventh hour, an entire change in the structure of our book.

Yielding to the wise advice of our publisher, we adopted then the plan of chronological order, instead of that at first chosen—the grouping of all letters under the names respectively of each correspondent, regarding chronology only within each group.

In making this alteration, with the haste required, it chanced that some pages escaped their rightful sequence, and the mishap was not perceived until too late to remedy it.

These defects are obvious—and—regrettable.

> —Edward Dowden's widow and daughter, in *Letters of Edward Dowden* (London, 1914) Editors' Note

*   *   *

I have not thought it necessary to put in asterisks on the few occasions when I have either omitted words or phrases in a paragraph [of quoted matter], or placed together sentences from different letters relating to the same subject.

> —Lady Anne Hill, *Trelawny's Strange Relations* (Stanford Dingley, 1956) Foreword

For Further Reading

The Profession: Then, Now, and to Come

Benstock, Shari, ed. *Feminist Issues in Literary Scholarship*. Bloomington, IN, 1987.

Booth, Wayne C. "The Scholar in Society." *Introduction to Scholarship in the Modern Languages and Literature*, ed. Joseph Gibaldi. New York, 1980. See also, in the same volume, G. Thomas Tanselle, "Textual Scholarship," and Barbara Kiefer Lewalski, "Historical Scholarship."

Centennial Issue. *PMLA* 99 (1984). See especially Karl Kroeber, "The Evolution of Literary Study"; Phyllis Franklin, "English Studies: The World of Scholarship in 1983"; Carolyn Heilbrun, "The Profession and Society, 1958–83"; and Paul Lauter, "Society and the Profession, 1958–83."

DeNeef, A. Leigh, Craufurd D. Goodwin, and Ellen Stern McCrate, eds. *The Academic's Handbook*. Durham, NC, 1988.

A valuable collection of essays on such topics as the nuts and bolts of academic employment, teaching and advising, and funding research. See especially part 5, "Publishing Research."

Graff, Gerald. *Professing Literature: An Institutional History*. Chicago, 1987.

An account of how English literary studies in American academia came to be what they are, with particular attention to the effect successive trends in criticism had on the teaching of literature in the classroom.

Kernan, Alvin. *The Death of Literature*. New Haven, 1990.
A survey of the numerous developments in present-day culture, including deconstructionism and the "electronic revolution," which are conspiring to destroy the authority of a language- and print-based institution. "We are now seeing, all of us today, the gradual end of the classical age of reading" (George Steiner). The implications for the future of the scholarly profession are dire.

Lehman, David. *Signs of the Times: Deconstruction and the Fall of Paul de Man*. New York, 1991.
Part 1 describes the impact of deconstructionism on literary studies. Part 2 is a polemical history of the "scandal in Academe" that erupted in 1987 when the *New York Times*, headlining "Yale Scholar's Articles Found in Nazi Paper," revealed that a leading deconstructionist had been a Belgian collaborator during the Second World War.

Lunsford, Andrea, Helene Moglen, and James F. Sleven, eds. *The Future of Doctoral Studies in English*. New York, 1989.

McMurtry, Jo. *English Language, English Literature: The Creation of an Academic Discipline*. Hamden, CT, 1985.
An informal history of English studies as they developed a century ago. Miniature biographies of four pioneers—the American Francis J. Child and the British Henry Morley, David Masson, and Walter Skeat—show what it was like to be a scholar-teacher in those days.

Rosovsky, Henry. *The University: An Owner's Manual*. New York, 1990. See chapters 8 ("Graduate Students: Welcome to the Ancient and Universal Company of Scholars"), 9 ("Academic Life: Some Virtues, Some Vices"), and 19 ("Tenure").

Vanderbilt, Kermit. *American Literature and the Academy: The Roots, Growth, and Maturity of a Profession*. Philadelphia, 1986.
A detailed history of the emergence of scholarship in American literature since about the time of the First World War and the inclusion of American masterpieces in the educational curriculum.

For discussions of the most important current issues concerning college teachers and the practice of literary scholarship, see the quarterly *ADE Bulletin* and the annual *Profession* series published by the Modern Language Association.

Illustrations of the Usefulness of Textual and Historical Data in Literary Criticism

Boehrer, Bruce Thomas. "Renaissance Overeating: The Sad Case of Ben Jonson." *PMLA* 105 (1990): 1071–82.
  Details how Jonson's propensity for excess and certain social realities of the Stuart ruling class made it possible that this "famous fat man and legendary drunkard" has (paradoxically) "survived as the preeminent Jacobean poet of moderation."

Landry, Donna. "The Resignation of Mary Collier: Some Problems in Feminist Literary History." *The New Eighteenth Century: Theory, Politics, English Literature,* ed. Felicity Nussbaum and Laura Brown. New York, 1987.
  Uses the literary success of the poet Mary Collier—laundress, housekeeper, sometime fieldhand—to warn feminist historians and literary critics not to judge too quickly writings by eighteenth-century working-class women as "unproblematically liberating."

Lang, Cecil Y. "Narcissus Jilted: Byron, 'Don Juan,' and the Biographical Imperative." *Historical Studies and Literary Criticism,* ed. Jerome J. McGann. Madison, WI, 1985.
  A brilliant demonstration of the way the close study of a poem—here, an episode in *Don Juan,* canto 9—involves a host of small, but illuminating, biographical facts.

McGann, Jerome J. "Tennyson and the Histories of Criticism." In his *The Beauty of Inflections: Literary Investigations in Historical Method and Theory.* Oxford, 1985. See pages 191–202: a "historical reading" of Tennyson's "The Charge of the Light Brigade." "Its achievement as a poem can only appear now through a critical elucidation of the work's historical aspects."

Shannon, Edgar, and Christopher Ricks. " 'The Charge of the Light Brigade': The Creation of a Poem." *SB* 38 (1985): 1–44.

Examination of the twenty states through which the text of the poem went "make[s] it possible to trace in considerable detail the skill and tact . . . with which the artist perfected his work." Interestingly, there is virtually no overlap between this article and McGann's, cited above: proof of how various are the scholarly techniques that can contribute to the understanding of a literary work.

Cultivating and Applying the Critical Spirit

On the Critical Examination of Evidence and Allied Matters

Barzun, Jacques, and Henry F. Graff. *The Modern Researcher.* 3rd ed. New York, 1977.
   Full of excellent practical advice. Part 2 has useful chapters on the critical spirit in research; see especially chapter 4 ("Finding the Facts") and chapter 5 ("Verification").
Elton, G. R. *The Practice of History.* New York, 1967.
   A skillfully written description of the spirit of the true historian—a combination of hard thinking, skepticism, and imagination—and of the intellectual rewards of the craft.

Books, Chapters, and Articles That Illustrate Some of the Points Made in Chapter 2

Adams, Percy G. *Travelers and Travel Liars, 1660–1800.* Berkeley, 1962.
   On fraudulent travel narratives set in eighteenth-century America; a good demonstration of the methods used to expose literary fakery.
Adams, Ramon F. *Burs Under the Saddle: A Second Look at Books and Histories of the West.* Norman, OK, 1964.
   A large bibliographical catalogue in which 424 books about the Old West are analyzed for their rich assay of misinformation and sheer invention.
Allott, Miriam. "Arnold and 'Marguerite'—Continued." *Victorian Poetry* 23 (1985): 125–43.
   A vigorous criticism of Park Honan's purported identification of the elusive "Marguerite" addressed in Matthew Arnold's love poems and his estimate of her effect on the poet's imagi-

nation. Honan's response is printed in the following pages (145–59). An instructive exercise in the delicate handling of documentary evidence and using the facts to throw biographical light on literary texts.

Blanck, Jacob. "A Calendar of Bibliographical Difficulties." *PBSA* 49 (1955): 1–18.

On some of the anomalies and perplexities the author encountered in compiling his *Bibliography of American Literature;* replete with examples and written with a light touch.

Cross, Wilbur L. *The History of Henry Fielding.* 3 vols. New Haven, 1918.

See 3: 140–50: a dissection of the anecdotes (mostly unauthentic) contained in early biographies of Fielding. Additional materials in Frederic T. Blanchard, *Fielding the Novelist: A Study in Historical Criticism* (New Haven, 1926), *passim:* a noteworthy case history of biographical misinterpretation

Fruman, Norman. *Coleridge, the Damaged Archangel.* New York, 1971.

A devastating attack upon the poet as a compulsive and calculating plagiarist, in the form of a large-scale critical revaluation and interpretation of evidence, much of which was long available to scholars who failed to recognize its significance. Fruman possibly overstates his case against the received image of Coleridge as "the da Vinci of literature," but his analytic method, as well as hostile reviews of the book, should be studied by every aspiring scholar.

Furnas, J. C. *Voyage to Windward: The Life of Robert Louis Stevenson.* New York, 1951.

Appendix (456–71) has much material on the growth of the Stevenson myth. See also G. Miallon, "La critique Stevensonienne du centenaire (13 Novembre 1950)," *Études anglaises* 7 (1954): 165–84.

Levin, David. "The Hazing of Cotton Mather: The Creation of a Biographical Personality." In his *In Defense of Historical Literature* (New York, 1967), chapter 2.

A case history of modern biographical interpretation and assertion that far exceeds the documented facts. See also the next chapter, on Franklin's *Autobiography.*

Lounsbury, Thomas R. *Studies in Chaucer.* 3 vols. New York, 1892.
   See volume 1, chapters 1 and 2: a peppery, though perhaps a shade overindignant, narrative of the manifold myths and corruptions that flourished in Chaucer biography until a century ago.

Lovell, Ernest J., Jr. *His Very Self and Voice: Collected Conversations of Lord Byron.* New York, 1954.
   The introduction contains an excellent discussion of the credibility of witnesses, as illustrated from the scores of books and articles that contemporaries wrote about Byron.

Nowell-Smith, Simon. *The Legend of the Master.* London, 1948.
   The introduction is an absorbing account of the development of the "legend" of Henry James.

Schoenbaum, S. *Shakespeare's Lives.* New ed. Oxford, 1991.
   A massive but highly readable narrative of the way in which many biographers, sane and insane, have elaborated the few grains of solid information about Shakespeare the man into imposing, usually fragile structures of speculation and myth.

Sutherland, James R. "The Progress of Error: Mrs. Centlivre and the Biographers." *RES* 18 (1942): 167–82.
   The title is sufficiently descriptive.

Viljoen, Helen Gill. *Ruskin's Scottish Heritage: A Prelude.* Urbana, IL, 1956.
   The introduction, in addition to describing the destruction, withholding, and dispersal of Ruskin's papers, reveals the wholesale undependability of E. T. Cook and Alexander Wedderburn as Ruskin's editors and biographers.

Weber, Carl J. "The 'Discovery' of FitzGerald's *Rubáiyát.*" *Library Chronicle of the University of Texas* 7 (1963): 3–11.
   Was it Rossetti or Swinburne whose discovery of a copy of the *Rubáiyát* in a bookseller's cheap box led to the poem's fame? Neither, as an examination of the old story and the invocation of other, neglected evidence demonstrates.

White, Newman I., Frederick L. Jones, and Kenneth N. Cameron. *An Examination of the Shelley Legend.* Philadelphia, 1951.
   Reprints three long reviews of R. M. Smith et al., *The Shelley*

Legend (1945): a demonstration of the many ways in which evidence, assumptions, and conclusions are subjected to critical scrutiny.

Wilson, John Harold. *The Court Wits of the Restoration*. Princeton, 1948.

See especially "The Wits in Private Life" (25–46): a chapter rich in examples of how spicy facts have been embellished into scandalous fiction.

Winks, Robin W., ed. *The Historian as Detective: Essays on Evidence*. New York, 1968.

A lively anthology of excerpts from historical works and biographies illustrating the application of the rules of evidence, with a running accompaniment of references to detective stories involving the same points.

Winnifrith, Tom. *The Brontës and Their Background: Romance and Reality*. London, 1973.

In part, a feisty survey of the manifold errors that have poisoned the well of Brontë scholarship, such as faulty texts and biographical myths. "The unreliability of the primary evidence is . . . equalled only by the fallibility of secondary authorities." See also Edward Chitham and Tom Winnifrith, *Brontë Facts and Brontë Problems* (London, 1983), especially chapter 2 ("Texts and Transmission").

The Several Branches of Scholarship

A representative selection, supplementing the titles in the notes to chapter 3.

GENERAL

Beaurline, Lester A., ed. *A Mirror for Modern Scholars: Essays in Methods of Research in Literature*. New York, 1966.

A collection of exemplary and in some instances "classic" articles in the various fields of literary scholarship.

Thorpe, James, ed. *The Aims and Methods of Scholarship in Modern Languages and Literatures*. 2nd ed. New York, 1970.

Discussions of basic problems and opportunities awaiting

scholars in four fields: linguistics, textual criticism, literary history, and literary criticism.

————. *Relations of Literary Study: Essays on Interdisciplinary Contributions.* 2nd ed. New York, 1970.

Brief essays by several authorities on the literary relations of myth, biography, psychology, sociology, religion, and music.

Wellek, René, and Alvaro Ribeiro, eds. *Evidence in Literary Scholarship: Essays in Memory of James Marshall Osborn.* Oxford, 1979.

Twenty-three essays exemplifying a wide variety of present-day scholarly procedures. Wellek's introduction is an interesting account of the career of a wealthy former banker who devoted most of his life and fortune to scholarly research.

Zitner, Sheldon P., ed. *The Practice of Modern Literary Scholarship.* Glenview, IL, 1966.

An anthology similar to Beaurline's, but with wider scope.

ANALYTICAL BIBLIOGRAPHY AND THE EDITING OF TEXTS

Battestin, Martin C. "A Rationale of Literary Annotation: The Example of Fielding's Novels." *SB* 34 (1981): 1–22.

On "the general principles governing the purpose of literary illustration" (i.e., annotation) and "more practical matters of procedure." Updates Arthur Friedman's "Principles of Historical Annotation in Critical Editions of Modern Texts" (*English Studies Annual 1941* [New York, 1942]).

Davison, Peter. "Editing Orwell: Eight Problems." *The Library* 6th series 6 (1984): 217–28.

The editor of the complete edition of Orwell's works comments on the various "tricky" problems presented by the writer's nine books and his large output of essays and journalism: determining priority of texts and their exact wording, evidence of his intentions when revising, and the textual significance of French translations.

Gaskell, Philip. *From Writer to Reader: Studies in Editorial Method.* Oxford, 1978.

Discussions of editorial difficulties presented by the progress of twelve authors' works from manuscript through various printed editions. The writers considered range from Milton to Tom Stoppard; the editorial principle growing out of the issues examined is that "the editor should not base his work on *any* predetermined role or theory."

Gill, Stephen. "Wordsworth's Poems: The Question of Text." *RES* ns 34 (1983): 172–90.
  Three concerns: problems relating to the received texts (editions published in Wordsworth's lifetime and the apparatus in the DeSelincourt edition), to the poet's working habits and the evidence of these in his manuscripts, and to recent textual activity.

Heine, Elizabeth. "Annotating the Imagination." *E. M. Forster: Centenary Revaluations,* ed. Judith Scherer Herz and Robert K. Martin. Toronto, 1982.
  On lessons learned when the author was assisting Oliver Stallybrass in preparing the Abinger edition of *The Manuscripts of "A Passage to India."*

Laird, J. T. *The Shaping of "Tess of the D'Urbervilles."* Oxford, 1975.
  Documents, from the manuscript and the various printed editions, the extensive revisions of the novel over nearly a quarter-century. Disposes of many half-truths and outright errors, most of which resulted from Hardy's own misleading statements.

Latham, Robert. "Pepys and His Editors." *Journal of the Royal Society of Arts* 132 (1983/84): 390–400.
  An informal, anecdotal supplement to the introduction to the Latham-Matthews *Pepys* (see above, p. 34, n. 10).

Mackenzie, Norman H. "On Editing Gerard Manley Hopkins." *Queen's Quarterly* 78 (1971): 487–502.
  One of the best articles of its kind. Editing Hopkins's poems requires "the logic of a detective, the patience of a medieval monk, . . . the sensitivity of an artist," the laboratory at Scotland Yard, and a command of Victorian books on philology and the nature of lightning.

Menikoff, Barry. *Robert Louis Stevenson and "The Beach of Falesà": A Study in Victorian Publishing.* Stanford, 1984.
  On the hapless history of the text of Stevenson's novella. "A

comparison of the manuscript with the printed texts enables us to see precisely how a finished and artistically sophisticated novel was reduced [by editors and publishers] to a vulgar and meretricious shadow of itself."

Patrides, C. A. "John Donne Methodized; or, How to Improve Donne's Impossible Texts with the Assistance of His Several Editors." *MP* 82 (1985): 365–73.

Critical comments on the shortcomings of several editions of Donne, from Grierson to A. J. Smith. "A text of Donne's poetry should aspire, not to reduce his 'roughness' into harmony, but to allow readings, however 'clumsy' or 'defective' in appearance, to reflect his remarkable sense of reality."

Reiman, Donald H., ed. "Some Recent Romantic Texts: Review." *Studies in Romanticism* 21 (1982): 476–546.

An excellent survey of recent editions of the Romantic poets, important for its discussion of various principles and practices of textual editing. See also, in the same volume (553–71), the reminiscences of a number of prominent scholars who participated in the "coming of age of Romantic scholarship."

Sanders, Charles Richard. "A Brief History of the Duke-Edinburgh Edition of the Carlyle Letters." *Studies in Scottish Literature* 17 (1982): 1–12.

Includes a description of the editorial procedures adopted in preparing this edition.

Thorpe, James. *Principles of Textual Criticism*. San Marino, CA, 1972.

A somewhat more conservative exposition of the uses of textual criticism than that of Bowers and his followers.

———, and Claude Simpson, Jr. *The Task of the Editor*. Los Angeles, 1969.

Simpson's lecture is a lively and informative description of some of the problems confronting the editor of Hawthorne's *American Notebooks*.

Wilson, F. P. *Shakespeare and the New Bibliography*. Revised by Helen Gardner. Oxford, 1970.

A readable and authoritative summary of the contributions "the new bibliography" made toward the establishment of Shakespeare's text.

An important series dealing with issues of textual editing in various fields is that drawn from the annual University of Toronto Conference on Editorial Problems. Titles in this series published thus far:

Editing Sixteenth-Century Texts, ed. R. J. Schoeck (1966)
Editing Nineteenth-Century Texts, ed. John M. Robson (1967)
Editing Eighteenth-Century Texts, ed. D. I. B. Smith (1968)
Editor, Author, and Publisher, ed. William J. Howard (1969)
Editing Twentieth-Century Texts, ed. Francess G. Halpenny (1972)
Editing Seventeenth-Century Prose, ed. D. I. B. Smith (1972)
Editing Texts of the Romantic Period, ed. John D. Baird (1972)
Editing Canadian Texts, ed. Francess G. Halpenny (1975)
Editing Eighteenth-Century Novels, ed. G. E. Bentley, Jr. (1975)
Editing British and American Literature, 1880–1920, ed. Eric W. Domville (1976)
Editing Renaissance Dramatic Texts: English, Italian, and Spanish, ed. Anne Lancashire (1976)
Editing Medieval Texts: English, French, and Latin Written in England, ed. A. G. Rigg (1977)
Editing Nineteenth-Century Fiction, ed. Jane Millgate (1978)
Editing Correspondence, ed. J. A. Dainard (1979)
Editing Illustrated Books, ed. William Blissett (1980)
Editing Poetry from Spenser to Dryden, ed. A. H. de Quehen (1981)
Editing Texts in the History of Science and Medicine, ed. Trevor H. Levere (1982)
Editing Polymaths: Erasmus to Russell, ed. H. J. Jackson (1983)
Editing Early English Drama: Special Problems and New Directions, ed. A. F. Johnston (1987)
Editing, Publishing and Computer Technology, ed. Sharon Butler and William P. Stoneman (1988)

QUESTIONS OF AUTHORSHIP

Basker, James G. *Tobias Smollett: Critic and Journalist.* Newark, DE, 1988.

New attributions, based on a marked set of some volumes of the *Critical Review,* now at the University of Oregon. Valuable for application of various kinds of internal and external evidence to each item that is possibly Smollett's.

Erdman, David M., and Ephim G. Fogel, eds. *Evidence for Authorship: Essays on Problems of Attribution.* Ithaca, NY, 1966.

A large collection of scholarly articles discussing and illustrating the usefulness and pitfalls of applying internal and external evidence to questions of authorship. The bibliography lists many other such treatments.

Hoy, Cyrus. "Studies in Attribution: What Can They Prove?" *Literary Research* 12 (1987): 5–12.

The latest thinking on this debatable subject.

Lemay, J. A. Leo. *The Canon of Benjamin Franklin: 1722–1776: New Attributions and Reconsiderations.* Newark, DE, 1986.

Presents the scholarly basis for attributing to Benjamin Franklin seventy-seven of ninety-six pieces examined here but not included in *The Papers of Benjamin Franklin* (Yale University Press).

McElrath, Joseph R., Jr. *Frank Norris and "The Wave": A Bibliography.* New York, 1988.

Introduction explains the removal (deattribution) of 519 pieces from the canon of Frank Norris's contributions to the San Francisco periodical *The Wave* (1891–98), attributed to the novelist by biographers and bibliographers from 1903 to 1985.

Schoenbaum, S. *Internal Evidence and Elizabethan Dramatic Authorship: An Essay in Literary History and Method.* Evanston, IL, 1966.

A sensible, often witty account of what internal evidence can and cannot contribute to determining the true authorship of anonymous, multi-authored, and falsely attributed plays.

Vieth, David M. *Attribution in Restoration Poetry: A Study of Rochester's "Poems" of 1680.* New Haven, 1963.
Applies the various tools of evidence to "the many problems of the Rochester text and canon."

ON SOURCE STUDY

Dent, R. W. *John Webster's Borrowing.* Berkeley, 1960.
The introduction, on the problems posed by the "most impressive borrower" of the Elizabethan age, contains many sound observations applicable to all source study.

Georgianne, Linda. "Carlyle and Jocelin of Brakelond: A Chronicle Rechronicled." *Browning Institute Studies* 8 (1980): 103–27.
On Carlyle's creative use of the medieval chronicle that serves as the background for *Past and Present*.

Sanders, Andrew. " 'Cartloads of Books': Some Sources for *A Tale of Two Cities*." *Dickens and Other Victorians: Essays in Honour of Philip Collins,* ed. Joanne Shattock. London, 1988.

Walsh, John. *Poe the Detective: The Curious Circumstances Behind "The Mystery of Marie Roget."* New Brunswick, NJ, 1968.
Poe's tale was based on the mysterious murder of Mary Rogers in New York in 1841. Walsh compares the documented facts with Poe's treatment, especially Dupin's "solution" of the mystery.

STUDY OF REPUTATION AND INFLUENCE

Buckingham, Willis J., ed. *Emily Dickinson's Reception in the 1890s: A Documentary History.* Pittsburgh, 1989.
A collection of 591 "reviews and notices" of Dickinson's poetry in the earliest phase of her fame.

Primeau, Ronald, ed. *Influx: Essays on Literary Influence.* Port Washington, NY, 1977.
Ten essays and a selected bibliography illustrating some aspects of current thought on the nature of literary influence. Particularly stimulating sections consider intellectual history and tradition as essentially revisionist readings or misread-

ings, and the role of the reader as a shaper of his own influences.

Sattelmeyer, Robert, and J. Donald Crowley, eds. *One Hundred
Years of "Huckleberry Finn": The Boy, His Book, and American Culture.* Columbia, MO, 1985.

A large collection of essays that reflect and summarize both
the popular and the critical fame of the book. See especially
John C. Gerber's "Introduction: The Continuing Adventures
of *Huckleberry Finn."*

West, James L. W. III. "The Second Serials of *This Side of Paradise* and *The Beautiful and Damned." PBSA* 73 (1979):
63–74.

Describes how "many readers . . . gained their first or only
impression of Fitzgerald" from the "butchered or botched"
texts of these novels as they were serialized by newspapers in
Chicago, Atlanta, Washington, and New York.

Wittreich, Joseph. *Feminist Milton.* Ithaca, NY, 1987.

Demonstrates Milton's importance for female readers of the
period 1700–1830, revealing not only how, "in unpredictable
ways, women were reading Milton but also how their readings of his poetry affected—and in some instances determined—interpretation."

A Scholar's Miscellany

Some books, or portions thereof, which in their various ways
reflect the excitement, comedy, exasperation, and rewards of
literary scholarship and book collecting—addenda, in effect, to
the longer list of such writings contained in the Bibliographical
Notes to *The Scholar Adventurers.*

Alpers, Antony. "Biography—The 'Scarlet Experiment.' " *TLS,*
March 28, 1980: 369–70.

Episodes incidental to the revision and expansion of the author's biography of Katherine Mansfield.

Altick, Richard D. *The Scholar Adventurers.* New York, 1950.

A collection of case histories and anecdotes that depict literary research as a form of learned detective work.

————. *Writers, Readers, and Occasions.* Columbus, OH, 1989.

See especially the chapters on "Four Victorian Poets and an Exploding Island," "The Volcano and a Coral Reef," and "Adventures of an Annotator." The final chapter reviews the history of the professional study of Victorian literature from the 1940s to the present time.

Baring-Gould, William S., ed. *The Annotated Sherlock Holmes.* 2 vols. New York, 1967.

". . . a beautifully presented, and never tedious, exercise in parody of scholasticism. No man who is incapable of seeing the ludicrousness of the excess should be allowed to edit, or write for, a 'serious' literary journal" (*The Year's Work in English Studies* 49 [1968]: 320).

Bennett, Betty T. *Mary Diana Dods, A Gentleman and a Scholar.* New York, 1991.

Dissatisfied with the inadequacy of a footnote in her three-volume edition of Mary Wollstonecraft Shelley's letters, the author embarked on a course of pertinacious documentary research that led to the discovery that the "husband" of a supposedly married couple in Mary Shelley's circle, the pseudonymous contributor of essays, stories, and poems to *Blackwood's Edinburgh Magazine* and literary gift books, was a female transvestite. An exemplary demonstration of how a scholar, fitting together scattered fragments of biographical minutiae, can uncover unsuspected facts of literary history—in this case, a deception that went undetected for a century and a half.

Buchanan, David. *The Treasure of Auchinleck: The Story of the Boswell Papers.* New York, 1974.

An engaging and authoritative narrative beginning with Boswell's ambiguous will and including such matters as the momentous consequences of an erroneous footnote, the five-year conspiracy of silence on the materials at Fettercairn House, three decades of legal maneuverings, in-fighting among scholars and publishers, and finally the arrival of the whole collection at Yale. See also below, under Pottle.

Burnett, T. A. J. *The Rise and Fall of a Regency Dandy: The Life and Times of Scrope Berdmore Davies.* Boston, 1981.
See especially the introduction by Bevis Hillier, describing the discovery in 1976, in a London bank, of a large cache of papers relating to Byron and his friends, and the aftermath of that headline event.

Byatt, A. S. *Possession: A Romance.* New York, 1990.
A rich, expertly crafted novel (winner of Britain's prestigious Booker Prize) about the discovery of a bundle of poignant letters that revealed a hitherto unsuspected love affair between a great Victorian poet and a woman who was a poet in her own right, the problems the find presented to half a dozen American and British scholars, and their subsequent machinations, part cooperative and part adversarial.

Clifford, James L. *From Puzzles to Portraits: Problems of a Literary Biographer.* Chapel Hill, NC, 1970.
Part 1, "Finding the Evidence," abounds in anecdotes of the author's search for material on Mrs. Thrale and Dr. Johnson; part 2, "Putting the Pieces Together," discusses questions of biographical evidence and its presentation. See also Clifford's "Some Problems of Johnson's Obscure Middle Years," in *Johnson, Boswell, and Their Circle: Essays Presented to Lawrence Fitzroy Powell in Honour of His Eighty-Fourth Birthday* (Oxford, 1965).

Coburn, Kathleen. *In Pursuit of Coleridge.* Oxford, 1978.
Charmingly details the author's lifelong search for Coleridge material, particularly marginalia and notebooks.

Foxon, David F. *Thomas J. Wise and the Pre-Restoration Drama: A Study in Theft and Sophistication.* London, 1959. (Supplement to the Bibliographical Society's Publications, no. 19.)
An additional chapter in the criminal career of Thomas J. Wise: discoveries made after the classic exposé by Carter and Pollard (see p. 60, n. 35).

Ganzel, Dewey. *Fortune and Men's Eyes.* Oxford, 1982.
A biography of John Payne Collier, the pre-eminent scholar-forger of Elizabethan literary documents in Victorian times, when "enthusiasm and credulity were as yet uncurbed by the rigorous standards of modern bibliographical study."

Guthke, Karl S. *B. Traven: The Life Behind the Legends*, trans. by Robert C. Sprung. Brooklyn, NY, 1991.

"B. Traven" was the best-known pseudonym—actually, alias—used by an obsessively secretive, myth-enshrouded novelist (*The Treasure of the Sierra Madre*) who claimed to be an American but was actually a German anarchist. It has been asserted that his life and work constitute "the greatest literary mystery of this century." The narrative of this, the fullest biography, takes the form of the methodical presentation and weighing of all the evidence known to exist.

Hamilton, Ian. *In Search of J. D. Salinger*. New York, 1988.

"I had it in mind to attempt not a conventional biography— that would have been impossible—but a kind of *Quest for Corvo* [see below, under Symons], with Salinger as quarry" (introduction). This particular literary quest ended up in the United States Supreme Court.

Holmes, Richard. *Footsteps: Adventures of a Romantic Biographer*. London, 1985.

Backpack research: the reflections and speculations of a poet-biographer as he visits scenes associated with particular passages in the lives of three writers: Stevenson, Mary Wollstonecraft Godwin, and Shelley.

Lane, Margaret. "The Ghost of Beatrix Potter" and "Beatrix Potter: The Missing Years." In her *Purely for Pleasure*. New York, 1967.

Two formidable obstacles to the writing of biography: an uncooperative subject and then her equally obstructive widower. (For the story of how an engineer cracked Beatrix Potter's cipher, see Leslie Linder's edition of *The Journal of Beatrix Potter, 1881–1897* [London, 1966].)

Lindenberger, Herbert. *Saul's Fall: A Critical Fiction*. Baltimore, 1979.

A dense, unclassifiable tour de force centering on the text of a play, at once fictitious and not fictitious, that a Stanford professor allegedly found in a suitcase left by its reclusive author. The elaborate editorial apparatus is a rich brew of "background materials" and the application of various types of critical theory. The resemblance to an overblown, eccentric Norton Critical Edition is unmistakable.

Lodge, David. *The British Museum Is Falling Down.* New York, 1967.

A moderately bawdy comic novel, with authentic Reading Room atmosphere; the anti-hero and his cronies are trying, not very hard, to write their dissertations. Several of Lodge's later novels—*Changing Places* (1975), *Small World* (1984), and *Nice Work* (1988)—portray, with a satirical edge, faculty life in present-day English and American universities and the international world of literary scholarship.

Maddox, Brenda. *Nora: A Biography of Nora Joyce.* London, 1988. The appendix describes the migration of "the largest collection of Joyce material in private hands, the richest source of material in the world on the life of Joyce until 1920" from Trieste to Cornell, and the controversy aroused by the publication of some of the obscene letters included in the purchase.

Malone, Michael. *Foolscap.* Boston, 1991.

An entertaining and well written serio-comic novel involving members of the English Department at a rich university in North Carolina, a hard-drinking, foul-mouthed genius revered as the greatest living American playwright, his scholarly biographer, and the discovery of the manuscript of a drama attributed to Sir Walter Raleigh.

Merton, Robert K. *On the Shoulders of Giants: A Shandean Postscript.* New York, 1965.

The avocational romp of an eminent sociologist: a digressive, discursive narrative, in the manner of a Sterne or a Burton, of the author's search for occurrences of the epigram "If I have seen farther, it is by standing on the shoulders of giants" (this particular phrasing is Sir Isaac Newton's). Merton eventually found no fewer than forty-seven instances, beginning with Bernard of Chartres (ca. A.D. 1126) and including uses by Coleridge, John Stuart Mill, and Friedrich Engels. The very definition of "serious fun," which pervades not only the text but the footnotes and the concluding "Onomasticon or a Sort of Index."

Munby, A. N. L. *Portrait of an Obsession: The Life of Sir Thomas Phillipps, the World's Greatest Book Collector,* adapted by Nicolas Barker. London, 1967.

Phillipps was a megalomaniac of appalling character and behavior. The book is based on Munby's more detailed *Phillipps Studies* (5 vols., Cambridge, 1951–60).

Murray, K. M. Elizabeth. *Caught in the Web of Words: James A. H. Murray and the Oxford English Dictionary.* New Haven, 1977.

Based on family and business correspondence, an account, by Murray's granddaughter, of his heroic thirty-eight-year struggle to produce the *OED*.

Phelan, James. *Beyond the Tenure Track.* Columbus, OH, 1991.

An intimate record of fifteen months in the professional and private life of a self-styled "aging jock" (basketball Academic All-American at Boston College) who is also a dedicated teacher and scholar. Of special interest: his running account of the delights and occasional distresses of teaching and advising graduate students.

Pottle, Frederick A. *Pride and Negligence: The History of the Boswell Papers.* New York, 1984.

The famous, complicated story told from a perspective different from that of Buchanan (see above).

Rampersad, Arnold. "Too Honest for His Own Time." *New York Times Book Review*, December 29, 1991: 3, 17–18.

Reviews the history of the censorship that publishers and book clubs applied to the books that made Richard Wright famous, to explain why the Library of America volumes devoted to his major works represent them, for the first time, "as he had wanted them to be read."

Reid, B. L. *The Man from New York: John Quinn and His Friends.* New York, 1968.

Prize-winning biography of a New York lawyer who collected the MSS and first editions of numerous modern writers, among them Eliot and Joyce, and often subsidized them as well.

Robbins, Rossell Hope. "Mirth in Manuscripts." *Essays and Studies* (English Association) ns 21 (1968): 1–28.

The pleasure and profit to be had from studying medieval manuscripts, including the acquisition of many kinds of curious information.

Rollins, Hyder E., and Stephen M. Parrish. *Keats and the Bostonians*. Cambridge, MA, 1951.

The story of Tantalus re-enacted in twentieth-century Boston: the redoubtable Amy Lowell at the sadistic mercy of a Keats collector who told her what he had but refused to let her see his prizes.

Sadleir, Michael. *XIX Century Fiction: A Bibliographical Record Based on His Own Collection*. 2 vols. Cambridge, 1951.

"Passages from the Autobiography of a Bibliomaniac" (1: xi–xxvi): the frustrations and triumphs of a collector of popular Victorian literature. The collection described in these volumes is now at UCLA.

Seelye, John. *The True Adventures of Huckleberry Finn*. Evanston, IL, 1970.

Mark Twain's book rewritten to conform to what a number of critics in the 1960s thought it should be like, not what it is. "Now that they've got *their* book, maybe they'll leave the other one alone" (introduction). A second version might be written to accommodate the approaches of post-1970 criticism.

Skom, Edith. *The Mark Twain Murders*. New York, 1989.

Investigation of a suspected case of plagiarism, set mainly in the library of "Midwestern University" in a Chicago suburb and involving the faculty of the Department of English there. Among the better of the numerous detective stories with American academic settings. Another is "Robert Bernard," *Deadly Meeting* (New York, 1970); the meeting in question is the MLA convention.

Stewart, George R. *Doctor's Oral*. New York, 1939.

An entertaining novel of graduate student life as it was fifty years ago. In essentials it was not all that different from the life doctoral candidates lead today.

Summers, Joseph H. " 'George Herbert: His Religion and Art': Its Making and Early Reception." *George Herbert Journal* 5 (1981): 1–18.

A personal account of the author's life as a Herbert scholar, from English 1 at Harvard to the publication of his influential book on the poet in 1954.

Symons, A. J. A. *The Quest for Corvo: An Experiment in Biography.* New York, 1934.
   The classic biography in the form of a research narrative: the author's piece-by-piece reconstruction of the eccentric character and murky career of the turn-of-the-century novelist Frederick William Rolfe ("Baron Corvo").

Wolf, Edwin, 2nd, with John F. Fleming. *Rosenbach: A Biography.* Cleveland, 1960.
   An ample, unexpurgated narrative of the life and transactions of America's most famous rare-book dealer, a shrewd, tireless, profane, hard-drinking, and not ungenerous Philadelphian who had a Ph.D. in English literature.

Wolff, Robert Lee. *Nineteenth-Century Fiction: A Bibliographical Catalogue.* 5 vols. New York, 1981–85.
   "Introduction: Some Pleasures of the Chase" (1:xi–xxxii): an essay obviously inspired by Sadleir's "Passages from the Autobiography of a Bibliomaniac" (above). Wolff's collection of almost eight thousand minor novels is now at the Harry Ransom Humanities Research Center, University of Texas at Austin.

Young, Philip. "Author and Critic: A Rather Long Story." In his *Ernest Hemingway: A Reconsideration.* University Park, PA, 1966.
   A lively, sometimes farcical tale of how Young and his publishers had to contend with Hemingway's opposition to the publication of this book, of whose thesis he disapproved.

Exercises

The exercises in the following pages are intended to encourage acquaintance with the printed materials of research and to afford practical experience in collecting material, weighing evidence, reaching conclusions, and writing scholarly notes and articles. Some of the questions can be answered briefly; others can serve as subjects for term papers. Some require original investigation in primary sources, but the majority utilize, in various ways, the published results of scholarly study.

I. The Tools of the Trade

The following questions are designed to illustrate the scope and usefulness of the chief bibliographies and reference works used by literary investigators, and to provide practice in one important and constantly recurring phase of research, the establishing of individual facts. The books containing the answers, or guidance to books that do, are listed in the most up-to-date bibliographical manuals for the study of English and American literature. In each instance, the answer should be accompanied by a statement of the means by which it was found, including missteps.

1. How many works are currently ascribed to John Lydgate? How many of these are in prose?

2. On p. 242 above, a quotation is given from Gamaliel Bradford's journal. Who was Bradford, and what was his peculiar
literary specialty?

3. Volume 1 of the *MLA International Bibliography* arranges its
contents by major national or regional area—British Isles,
British Commonwealth, English Caribbean, American Literatures—and then by subregion—Australian, Welsh, Canadian, and so forth. Where exactly will one find Margaret
Atwood, Derek Walcott, Patrick White, and Raymond Williams?

4. Identify the bibliography published in 1979 about which the
following claim has been made: "This book will now be the
starting point for every critic, scholar, and student who sets
out to write on a work of Old English literature or on the
Anglo-Saxon period in general, and for every teacher preparing a course in Old English literature."

5. What important books were published and what noteworthy
public events occurred in the year of Aphra Behn's birth?

6. After it appeared in 1928, Herbert R. Mayes's *Alger: A Biography Without a Hero* was relied upon—by subsequent
biographers as well as by such standard authorities as the
Dictionary of American Biography—as a source of authentic information on the life of that popular nineteenth-century
American author of rags-to-riches stories. It is now totally
discredited. What, according to the author when he admitted
his "fraud" in the early 1970s, was his purpose in writing it?

7. Look up synopses of a novel you know well in three standard reference sources. Are they inaccurate in any significant
respect? How do they differ in emphasis? Is there any evidence of derivativeness?

8. At what point in the poem's publication history were the
marginal glosses added to Coleridge's "The Rime of the Ancient Mariner"?

9. In 1847–50 a series of sensational murders in England pro-
voked much public discussion. Make a list of at least a half-

dozen periodical articles published at that time which dealt with the supposed crime wave and its social implications.

10. What is the name of a series of fifty-one reprinted autobiographies of American women? Who published it? What is its announced scope?

11. Where is the nearest complete file of *The Englishwoman's Domestic Magazine* (1852–79)?

12. Much attention is now focusing upon the novelist Susan Warner (1819–85), one major critic referring to her first novel, *The Wide, Wide World* (1850), as the "Ur-text of nineteenth-century America." List at least five articles assessing her work. What exactly is the case being advanced for her importance?

13 Make a reasonably full list of scientific books published in 1693 that would have been of interest to a member of the Royal Society.

14. Quote the entry for Hooker's *Laws of Ecclesiastical Polity* in the Stationers' Register, find its *STC* number, and, without reference to the *NUC*, locate a copy of the first edition (1593) in America.

15. In what important ways does the second edition of the *Oxford English Dictionary* differ from the first edition?

16. Locate three or four articles that discuss rhetorical features characteristic of the critical essay. Be certain to include recent developments in feminist criticism as they bear upon this subject.

17. In the winter of 1849–50, Margaret Fuller (Ossoli), the New England critic and feminist, was working on a history of the Roman revolution, which had occurred the preceding year. What happened to it?

18. Prepare a checklist of articles discussing the significant similarities among and differences between women "local colorists" and "domestic sentimentalists" in late nineteenth-century and early twentieth-century America.

19. Aleksandr Solzhenitsyn was awarded the Nobel Prize in 1970 but for political reasons was unable to receive it. In what year did he take possession of the prize?

20. Where on the East coast of the United States is a good collection of Henry James first editions and manuscripts?

21. After reading four or five articles on the subject, summarize the most important issues in the debate about the existence of a "black women's literary tradition."

22. Describe, from a secondary source, the contents of Thomas Foxcroft's *Lessons of Caution to Young Sinners* (Boston, 1733). What is the library closest to your campus that possesses a copy of this book?

23. In England between 1700 and 1710 only two women published collections of their own verse. Who were they?

24. What is the current state of the argument over the dating of Shakespeare's *Merry Wives of Windsor?* Is 1597 still generally accepted?

25. How many editions of Virginia Woolf's *To the Lighthouse* were published in England down to 1990?

26. Mark Twain's *Roughing It* contains the popular long-winded anecdote "The Story of the Old Ram." What version of this story did Twain use on his lecture tours, and why?

27. In how many European countries were editions or translations of Byron's *Childe Harold* published down to 1850?

28. How many dissertations on Phillis Wheatley (perhaps in conjunction with other figures) have been accepted at American universities in the past five years?

29. Using at least three sources, compile a list of all books and articles published on Blake in 1990. Why is it necessary to refer to more than one source?

30. Name the more important texts and the standard modern works dealing with rogues and vagabonds in the Elizabethan era.

31. Locate at least three articles that discuss the parallels between the notorious marital difficulties of Lady Caroline Norton and her fictional counterpart, Diana Warwick in Meredith's *Diana of the Crossways*.

32. Two major British writers died the same day that President John F. Kennedy was assassinated. Identify them.

33. Compile a preliminary bibliography of recent theoretical books and articles that examine the ways readers apprehend and respond to literary works.

34. In a letter written by a young Victorian girl you find a reference to a mechanical chamber organ called the Apollonicon. Write a footnote explaining what it was and where she probably saw and heard it.

35. *Godey's Ladies Book* appeared under seven different titles over its sixty-eight-year history (1830–98). For forty years (1837–77), the journal had a single "editress," who is credited with wielding a major influence over the "reading, learning, and even the political consciousness of women across the American continent." Who was this person and what have recent scholars said of the place of *Godey's Ladies Book* in nineteenth-century American literature and culture?

36. Approximately how many versions are known of the medieval "Debate Between the Body and the Soul"? How many manuscripts are there of what is said to be "the best-known Middle English piece," "Als I lay in a winteris nyt / in a droukening bifore the day"? Where are they, and have they all been printed?

37. After more than fifty years in a cottage attic, the G. K. Chesterton archive of some thirty thousand items, including two hundred unpublished poems, plays, and short stories, found a permanent home in 1990. Where is this archive housed and what is its history?

38. Your study of the popular reception of the novels of Raymond Chandler and Dashiell Hammett necessitates consid-

eration of motion picture adaptations of their stories. How can you identify these films and find sufficient details about them for your needs?

39. Copy, from an authoritative modern source, the exact wording on the title page of *Every Man in His Humour* (1601).

40. Make a list of the explications so far offered of specific passages in Marvell's "The Garden."

41. At what London theaters and on what dates were Wilkie Collins's dramatizations of his novels *No Name, Armadale, The Woman in White,* and *The Moonstone* first performed?

42. Using more than one reliable source, identify to whom Gertrude Stein was speaking in her famous remark "You are all a lost generation." What were the circumstances?

43. How many pre-1700 editions of Bunyan's *Grace Abounding* are known to exist?

44. How many stories by the science fiction writer Robert Silverberg have been anthologized in English-language publications?

45. What are the present retail prices of the complete *NCBEL,* Baugh's *Literary History of England,* the *Concise DNB,* and the compact edition of the *Oxford English Dictionary?*

46. You have found a hitherto unknown letter by Thoreau that internal evidence proves was written between 1849 and 1856. It is dated simply "Friday, May 5." What was the year?

47. Compile a list, including publishers and prices, of Robertson Davies's works published in Canada and still in print.

48. What bibliographical aids exist for a study of the English poet laureate Ted Hughes?

49. What is the distinction between the heresy of Molinism (Miguel de Molinos, 1627–96) and the Molinism associated with Luis de Molina (1535–1600)?

50. In what year and under what circumstances was Henry Miller's *Tropic of Cancer* permitted to be published in the United States for the first time?

51. Twelve presentation copies of Mrs. Henry Wood's Victorian best-seller, *East Lynne,* were specially bound. What was the color of that binding? How was Michael Sadleir's imaginative reconstruction of the circumstances behind the choice of binding proved to be a mistake?

52. What is the relative value, for research, of the several twentieth-century editions of the *Encyclopaedia Britannica,* and which current encyclopedias have the best reputation for accuracy?

53. Is the manuscript of James Jones's *From Here to Eternity* available for scholarly scrutiny?

54. Sometime in the 1960s a book was published in England under the title of *Search Your Soul, Eustace.* What was its American title, and what was it about?

55. You are examining a rare book that you have reason to believe was part of the library of Richard Heber (1773–1833). What identifying mark should you look for?

56. In recent years, the appearance of previously unpublished fiction, autobiography, and letters by Bloomsbury figures has increased interest in that group. Cite at least ten recent book-length biographical and critical studies relating to the Bloomsbury group.

57. *Songes and Sonettes,* by Sir Thomas Wyatt, the earl of Surrey, and others (1557), is familiarly known as "Tottel's Miscellany" because it was printed by Richard Tottel. Name four other books he printed in the same year. What was his London address?

58. What was the first full-length critical study of Langston Hughes?

59. You have written a paper on Elizabeth Gaskell's novel *North and South* that your instructor thinks may well be

publishable. Your citations, however, are to the Penguin edition, which the class used, and scholarly practice requires that, whenever possible, a published paper cite the most reliable text. What text of the novel is best?

60. Where is the manuscript of Thomas Shadwell's play *The Humorists?* What company first performed it? When?

61. What was the association between T. S. Eliot and the *Boston Daily Evening Transcript?*

62. Books with the following titles have been written about a major English poet: *Some Graver Subject, From Shadowy Types to Truth, The Celestial Cycle, The Club of Hercules, The Harmonious Vision, Heroic Knowledge.* Who is the poet? What is the source of each title?

63. What were the nineteenth-century British and American antecedents of the modern paperback?

64. Joseph Conrad embellished his actual achievements when he referred to his career as a ship's captain. Identify two or three authoritative discussions of Conrad's demonstrated competence in that role. What is the truth about his seagoing career?

65. In 1770 there was printed at New York a broadside entitled *The Dying Speech of the Effigy of a Wretched Importer.* . . . Whom did the effigy represent, and what was the occasion of its being burned? Where can one find a copy of the broadside?

66. Make a list of the materials published in the past three years on the mythic and folklore elements in *Beowulf.*

67. How were the opening scenes of *Hamlet* altered for the 1990 Zeffirelli film?

68. What is the collation of the first edition of Jack London's *The Call of the Wild?* What is the evidence for its date of publication?

69. After examining the six or eight latest issues of the *TLS,* make a list of a half-dozen distinct and important services its various editorial features supply to literary scholars.

70. You are studying the significance of metaphors relating to time in the work of a modern novelist and need to broaden your philosophical orientation. Find a source that discusses the various conceptions of time entertained by modern philosophers as well as by such figures as St. Augustine, St. Thomas Aquinas, Bergson, Proust, and Sartre.

71. How many different productions of Dryden's *All for Love* appeared in London theaters in the eighteenth century?

72. Where would one find information about the imprint "Clarendon Press," first used by Oxford University Press in 1713?

73. English travelers to America in the 1840s, including Dickens, praised the working and living conditions in the textile factories at Lowell, Massachusetts. Among the amenities was a magazine, the *Lowell Offering*, written, edited, and published by the factory girls. Has any book been published about this periodical?

74. In what kind of literary work, and from what period, might an allusion to each of the following be found? the Gorham case, the Quoin, Robert the Devil, Mohocks, Grace Darling, Anacharsis Clootz, Babu, Martin Marprelate.

75. What public figures made statements to the English press on the occasion of the death of Graham Greene in 1991?

76. On May 15 (25), 1696, in a letter preserved among the manuscripts at Longleat, seat of the marquis of Bath, Sir William Trumbull paid a handsome compliment to his correspondent, the poet Matthew Prior. What was it? (And why, incidentally, is the double date given?)

77. How many of the novels of Edna Ferber are currently in print?

78. Limiting yourself to one source, identify the single work in which all of the following words appear: *inaccessibleness, decays* (noun), *misappear, miswrite, divineness, dwarfishly.*

79. You need to refresh your memory concerning the essential nature of Freud's theories of sexuality, the unconscious, repression, and regression. Where can you find succinct summaries of these topics, along with a selected bibliography?

80. What single source provides a complete list of the publications of the Cambridge University Press 1700–1750?

81. Establish a checklist of materials for a paper on the history of copyright, centering upon but not limited to the first Berne convention in 1885.

82. The novelist Walker Percy died in 1990. In what university library are his manuscripts and other papers?

83. It is well known that Longfellow derived some of the materials for *Hiawatha* from the ethnological writings of Henry R. Schoolcraft. Why is it highly unlikely, however, that he used Schoolcraft's *Cyclopedia Indianensis: or a General Description of the Indian Tribes of North and South America* (New York, 1842)?

84. In 1980 an English television comedian, Terry Jones *(Monty Python's Flying Circus),* published a book that radically challenged the customary view of Chaucer's Knight. What was his argument, upon what kinds of evidence was it based, and how was the book received by Chaucer scholars?

85. What was Samuel Johnson's involvement in *The Harleian Miscellany* (8 vols., 1744–46)?

86. In reviews that compare Stanley Kubrick's film of *Barry Lyndon* with Thackeray's novel, are any of the differences between the versions regarded merely as necessary results of the differences between print and film?

87. Would the Franklin J. Meine collection of material on various aspects of American social history housed at the University of Illinois—Chicago Circle library be of any value to a student of nineteenth-century American humor?

88. Compile a list of at least five articles in the past decade discussing the place of science fiction in American literature.

89. Identify: *Le Diable Boiteux,* Julius Caesar Scaliger, Gongorism, Skidbladner, epicedium, Jean Crapaud, Dismas, Flavius Josephus.

90. The British Museum acquired the first autograph draft of Carlyle's *Past and Present* in 1928. Of how many leaves does it consist, who presented it, and what is its number among the Additional Manuscripts?

91. What clues led investigators to discover a dozen early stories by George Gissing buried in the files of Chicago newspapers? Where were two additional ones found in 1980, and what was the clue this time?

92. Of how many printed items does the canon of Cotton Mather consist?

93. In some anthologized versions of Joel Chandler Harris's "The Wonderful Tar-Baby Story" only half of the complete episode involving Br'er Rabbit and his sticky adversary is printed. What are the title and content of the second part of the tale? Where were both parts first published? Why, do you think, have anthology editors often ignored this second part?

94. In his important introduction to the *Portable Faulkner,* written in 1945, Malcolm Cowley helped initiate serious consideration of Faulkner's fiction. How many of the novelist's works were then in print?

95. Identify five articles detailing Thomas Pynchon's use in *Gravity's Rainbow* of popular movies, songs, comic book characters, and radio melodramas from the 1930s and 1940s.

96. Where would one find a list of the successive editors of the *Quarterly Review* from 1851 to the death of Thomas Carlyle in 1881?

97. A study you are making of the English popular novel in the 1830s and 1840s requires that you focus particular attention on the publishing house of Richard Bentley & Son. Where are the firm's archives, and how can you gain access to them?

98. With the aid of the appropriate reference tools, explain the biblical allusions in this passage (*Paradise Lost* 6: 750–59):

> . . . forth rush'd with whirl-wind sound
> The Chariot of Paternal Deity,
> Flashing thick flames, Wheel within Wheel, undrawn,
> Itself instinct with Spirit, but convoy'd
> By Four Cherubic shapes, four Faces each
> Had wondrous, as with Stars thir bodies all
> And Wings were set with Eyes, with Eyes the Wheels
> Of Beryl, and careering Fires between;
> Over thir heads a crystal Firmament,
> Whereon a Sapphire Throne, inlaid with pure
> Amber, and colors of the show'ry Arch.

99. Here is a list of words, found in sixteenth- and seventeenth-century English poems, whose meanings in those contexts are no longer current. Assuming that each suggested synonym fits the context, what reason is there to believe that it represents a current meaning of the italicized word at the date shown?

> *disease* (Howard, 1557): "discomfort"
> *read* (Spenser, 1589): "advised"
> *freakes* (Spenser, 1590): "unpredictable tricks"
> *inward touch* (Sidney, 1591): "true imagination"
> *engaged* (Shakespeare, 1598): "held as hostage"
> *triumphs* (Marlowe, 1604): "parades"
> *adulteries* (Jonson, 1609): "adulterations"
> *determinate* (Shakespeare, 1609): "expired"
> *tells* (Jonson, 1616): "counts"
> *slack* (Crashaw, 1633): "backward"
> *sped* (Herbert, 1633): "supplied, satisfied"

approve (Donne, 1633): "put to proof, find by experience"
bestead (Milton, 1645): "help, avail"
pale (Milton, 1645): "enclosure"
quaintest (Vaughan, 1650): "most elaborate"
perspective (Vaughan, 1655): "telescope"
close (Marvell, 1681): "unite"
dishonest (Dryden, 1681): "disgraceful"

100. What does each of the following words, used by American
writers, mean, and when and where was it apparently first
used?

smallage (Hawthorne, 1835)
a face of country (Emerson, 1836)
unhandselled (Emerson, 1837)
a Norway mile (Poe, 1841)
a virgin-zone (Hawthorne, 1844)
scoriac (Poe, 1847)
Bose (Thoreau, 1854)
crook-necks (Lowell, 1867)
pungle (Twain, 1884)
Jonah's loss (Melville, 1888)
crawfished (Twain, 1895)
Vega-cura (Dreiser, 1900)
Snow Bird (Fitzgerald, 1931)

II. Bibliographical Listing and Identification

1. Two older guides to the printed works of English Renaissance authors are Lowndes's Bibliographer's Manual of English Literature (new ed., 1857–64) and the various volumes
of "collections and notes" by W. Carew Hazlitt (1867–1903;
most of these are conveniently indexed by G. J. Gray, 1893).
Choose a relatively minor sixteenth- or seventeenth-century
author and, using the most authoritative modern bibliographical tools, including the STC and Wing, establish how
trustworthy and complete Lowndes's and Hazlitt's information is.

2. A similar older guide is Allibone's *Critical Dictionary of English Literature and British and American Authors* (1858–71, 1891). Select a nineteenth-century English or American author in whom you are interested, and as in the preceding exercise, determine what value, if any, Allibone has to a scholar wishing to do intensive work on that author.

3. How up to date, thorough, and accurate are the existing bibliographical guides to the writings by and about the following authors?

Sean O'Faolain	Doris Lessing
Philip Roth	Jean Toomer
Gwendolyn Brooks	Leroi Jones
Tom Stoppard	Robert Lowell
Lillian Hellman	Maya Angelou
Anthony Burgess	Alice Walker
John Cheever	Aldous Huxley
John Berryman	Iris Murdoch
Toni Morrison	Denise Levertov
John Osborne	Carson McCullers
Joyce Carol Oates	Robert Penn Warren

4. Describe the means by which one can compile a full bibliography of the publications of a present-day literary scholar.

5. (a)* The library of the poet Edmund Waller, to which his descendants added after his death in 1687, was sold in 1832. The sale catalogue includes the following items. Establish the correct title and date of each and identify by *STC* or Wing number. Are there any that the poet could not have known?
   Bacon's Natural History, and The Sovereign's Prerogative
   Palmerin of England, 2 Parts
   Josephus's Works, by L'Estrange, 3 vols.
   Turner's Military Essays, and Knox's History of the Island of Ceylon

---

*Materials for parts a–d of this exercise are drawn from A. N. L. Munby's series of facsimile *Sale Catalogues of Libraries of Eminent Persons* (London, 1971–75).

Memoirs of the Sieur de Pontis, and Bentivoglio's History of the Wars in Flanders

Weever's Funeral Monuments, and Richardson's State of Europe

Spriggs's Anglia Rediviva, and Wotton's State of Christendom

Swinburne's Travels through Spain—Buck's Life of Richard III. and Wilson's History of King James

General Ludlow's Memoirs, 3 vols.—Perrault's Characters of Illustrious Men, 2 vols.—Life of Robert Earl of Leicester, and Hayward's Lives of the Three Norman Kings

(b) Try to locate a copy of each of the following works represented in Swift's library, sold in 1745:

[Berkeley, Geo. Bishop] His Discourse address'd to Magistrates. Dub. 1738

A new Miscellany of original Poems. [London] 1701

Buchanan Rerum Scotiarum Historia. Elzev. Amst. 1643

Fontenelles Nouveaux Dialogues des Morts. Par. 1683

Wilkes on the Existence of God. Belf. 1730

Doctor Gibb's Translation of David's Psalms in Verse; with Doctor Swift's Jests upon it. Lond. 1701

The Barrier-Treaty vindicated. Lond. 1712

Vossius, de Sybillinis [n. d.]

Ludlow's Memoirs 3d. vol. Switz 1699

(c) Give the full and correct title of each of these works, included in the sale of Laurence Sterne's library in 1768. Can you find a contemporary notice (in book trade sources, periodicals, etc.) of the publication of each work?

Tarsis and Zelie, a famous Romance. 1685

Koehoorn's new Method of Fortification, with Cuts. 1705

Cleopatra, or Love's Master-piece, a Romance. [n.d.]

Fuller's Pisgah-Sight of Palestine, with Cuts. 1662

Chaucer's Works, "a very old Copy, black Letter, wants Title, imprinted at London by Kele." [n.d.]

Fraser's History of Kuli Khan, Emperor of Persia. 1742

Marriott's Female Conduct. 1759

Young's Centaur not fabulous. 1755

King's Art of Love, in Imitation of Ovid de Arte Amandi.
   [n.d.]
Trapp on the Trinity. 1731
Young on Opium. 1753
Cadiere's Case, wherein Father Girard is accused of seduc-
   ing her.—Father Girard's Defence, 3 parts. 1732

(d) Identify the following books owned by the self-taught
poet Robert Bloomfield (1766–1823). Can you also identify
Blackets, Freeman, Flowerdew, Hitchcock, and Evans?
   Loder's History of Framlingham
   Mason's English Garden
   Kentish Poets. 2 vols.
   Guthrie's Grammar
   Antiquarian Cabinet. 4 vols.
   The Remains of Joseph Blackets
   Dayes' Essays on Painting. 8vo
   Freeman's Regulbium (presented by the Author)
   Flowerdew's Poems (presented by the Author)
   Poems, by David Hitchcock (the self-taught American
      Poet) sent by the Author to Mr. Bloomfield
   Evans' Seasons (presented by the Author)
   Memoirs of the Peers of England
   North Georgia Gazette

(e) The following items are drawn from a list made by Rich-
ard Woodhouse of books owned by John Keats. Printing the
list in his *Keats* (1917), Sidney Colvin remarked, ". . . it
would be an attractive bibliographical exercise . . . to
identify particular editions." How far can this be done? Are
any of Keats's copies known to exist today?
   Aikin's History of the year   12mo
   Davies' Celtic Researches   8vo
   Lady Russell's Letters   12mo   2 vols.
   Erasmus' Moriae Encomium   36mo
   Ariosto da Boschino   18mo   2 vols.
   Coleridge, Lamb and Lloyd   8vo
   Auctores Mythographi Latini   4to
   Lemprière's Class. Dict.   8vo

Z. Jackson's Illus. of Shakespeare   8vo
Bailey's Dictionary   8vo
Fencing familiarized   8vo
Conducteur à Paris   12mo
Mickle's Lusiad   18mo

(f) In the passages in his *Autobiography* describing the reading he accomplished as a youth, Benjamin Franklin mentions the following:

"Dr. Mather's . . . Essays to do Good"
"a Book, written by one Tryon, recommending a Vegetable Diet"
The New England Courant
—Using Evans, Sabin, Brigham, and whatever other standard guides to early American printing may be needed, identify these items, give fuller bibliographical information, and locate copies in American libraries.

Defoe's *Essays on Projects*
"Cocker's Book of Arithmetick"
"an odd Volume of the Spectator"
"Locke on Human Understanding"
"Xenophon's Memorable Things of Socrates"
—Were there American editions of these works at the time mentioned (ca. 1720–25)? In lack of American editions, what English edition may Franklin have known?

Franklin also mentions a "Dr. Brown" who "wickedly undertook some Years after to travesty the Bible in doggrel Verse as Cotton had done Virgil." Identify Brown's and Cotton's books by title and date of publication.

6. Compile a working bibliography of materials discussing British periodicals in the last third of the nineteenth century designed specifically for girls or for boys.

7. From its inception in 1902 (originally as the Dun Emer Press) into the 1940s, the Cuala Press was one of the most successful private presses of its time. List ten or twelve of its most important publications.

8. Compile a secondary bibliography of works about Celia Thaxter, "probably the best known female poet in late nineteenth century America." What is this poet's principal subject?

III. Computers, Machine-readable Texts, and Databases

1. The Oxford Text Archive is currently the largest collection of machine-readable texts. Describe this collection and list four or five uses for the literary scholar of this technology, discussing in detail one of these applications.

2. Review four or five computer analyses of Chaucer's style in the *Canterbury Tales*. What new stylistic discoveries, if any, do these articles describe? Are you persuaded? Why or why not?

3. Describe the "Century of Prose Corpus," a database of British prose texts from the period 1680–1780. What are three or four important uses of this collection for scholars working in the eighteenth century?

4. The Eighteenth-Century British Biography project (EBB) will constitute "the most complete and authoritative listing of the British people of the 18th century." Give a full description of this machine-readable scholarly resource, and describe its progress to date.

5. Describe the electronic hypertext system being developed for Charles Dickens's *Little Dorrit* at the Oxford Centre for Humanities Computing. What is hypertext? What is the role in literary research of such electronic systems?

6. Personal computer communication systems such as BitNet and InterNet make possible direct information sharing among scholars from around the world via electronic mail and bulletin boards and other forms of electronic exchange. Available to individuals as well as institutions, these informal scholarly tools promote "calls for papers, notes and queries,

arguments, friendly backchat" and the like. Investigate one such electronic exchange system for literary scholars and record the topics and types of commentary that occur over the period of your brief examination.

7. The Text Encoding Initiative is an international project to establish "guidelines for the transfer of computer-readable texts." What are the project's sponsoring organizations? Discuss several of the more serious issues for scholars interested in transmitting texts via computer networks that are behind this work.

8. The advent of the personal computer has eased the life of the scholar in many ways, but not in all. Desk-top publishing, for example, may create a situation where, in the case of an inveterate reviser, every copy of a specific work differs from every other and only the last version is retained in the computer file. Find and summarize discussions of this and other problems created for textual bibliographers and critics by the microcomputer.

9. Describe the current and prospective developments for the collation of texts offered by optical scanners and the process of digital imaging.

10. Identify important differences between the *Oxford English Dictionary* and the *OED on CD*. Is the latter an effective substitute for the former? Compare costs.

11. Describe specific software advances over traditional concordances that organize the words at multiple levels, encouraging the scholar "to view the text as texture rather than as words strung together linearly."

12. List several commercial magazines or other technical publications that feature articles about and reviews of computers and software packages that are of value to literary scholars.

IV. The Detection and Correction of Error; Conflict of Authorities

1. In the *TLS* for April 20, 1973, a reviewer listed some of the mistakes in Felix Felton's book on Thomas Love Peacock:

   > Thomas Taylor, the Platonist, is described as of Norwich, which seems to summon up the ghost of William Taylor; Shelley and Harriet depart for Tanyrallt with a mysterious and hitherto unknown Helen Tinsley, presumably Miss Hitchener, the Brown Demon; the Bentley's Standard Novels volume which contains the first collection of Peacock's novels is not No LXII but No LVII. Far more serious, one of the best of Peacock's shorter poems, "I dug, beneath the cypress shade", is irretrievably ruined by the inclusion (twice) of the word "they" when it ought to be "thy".

   In like manner, correct all the errors alleged by the same reviewer in the passage just preceding the one quoted:

   > Shelley and Hogg were sent down from Cambridge; Mary Wollstonecraft had an affair with Ismay; Fair Rosamund was a martyred nun; Thomas Avory was a novelist, the author, presumably, of "John Bancle"; Rabelais was responsible for a character called Frère Jean Entanmeures; Blake's "Island in the Moon" caricatures statesmen; Meredith wrote a novel called *The Angry Marriage*.

2. Choose a certain number of pages in J. W. Saunders's *The Profession of English Letters* (1964), and attempt to verify each factual statement in a dependable source. How many errors can you find?

3. The late Winifred Gérin acquired a considerable reputation for her biographies of the Brontë sisters, especially for her study of Charlotte (*Charlotte Brontë: The Evolution of Genius* [Oxford, 1967]). At least two critics, however, have questioned her reliability as a scholar. (See Tom Winnifrith, *The Brontës and Their Background: Romance and Reality* [London, 1973] 5–6, 221, and Valentine Cunningham, *Everywhere Spoken Against: Dissent in the Victorian Novel* [Oxford, 1975] 291.) Compare the charges of Winnifrith and

Cunningham with the evidence cited for praise (and blame) in the popular and scholarly reviews, and formulate your own assessment of Gérin's accomplishment in *Charlotte Brontë*.

4. In a review of James Baldwin's *Another Country*, Trevor Blount noted an important inconsistency in the opening scene of chapter 4. What is the inconsistency and what interruption in tone and mood is the result?

5. Describe the controversy over the acknowledgment of sources in John Gardner's *The Life and Times of Chaucer* (New York, 1977). What was Gardner's response?

6. The son of the prolific novelist Mary Elizabeth Braddon (*Lady Audley's Secret*, etc.), writing late in life, said that "all records" of her early career as an actress had disappeared. Her stage name, he thought, was "Mary Seaton." Describe how a recent biographer's correction of this error enabled him to reconstruct Braddon's acting career. What were the main sources of his information?

7. Find five or six reviews of William Styron's *The Confessions of Nat Turner* and as many interviews as you can with Styron and others on the subject of this book. Then summarize in a short paper the controversy that surrounded Styron and his novel.

8. *Hanta Yo*, a novel by Ruth Beebe Hill depicting Sioux Indian life on the plains in the period from roughly 1750 to 1835, became in 1980 a center of controversy and litigation. Explain the major points of the dispute. Were any of the charges, defenses, or explanations made on artistic grounds?

9. Correct the following entries appearing in the *NCBEL*, volume 3 (the numbers in parentheses refer to columns, not pages):

> Hartmann, J. E. The mess of Gareth and Lynette. Harvard
>   Lib Bull 13 1959   (431)
> DeVane, W. C. A. Browning handbook. Ithaca 1935, New
>   York 1955 (rev). The standard handbook.   (440)

[three successive entries:]

Wallace, S. A. Browning in London society. MLN 66 1951.

———— Curious annals: new documents on Browning's murder case. SP 49 1952.

———— New documents relating to Browning's Roman murder story. Toronto 1956.   (456)

Tanzy, C. E. Browning, Emerson and Bishop Blougram's apology. MP 58 1960.   (458)

Cazamian, L. L'influence de la science 1860–90. Strasbourg 1923.   (659)

Rogers, W. H. Portraits of romantic poets in contemporary minor fiction. Western Research Univ Bull 34 1931.

(661)

Haycroft, H. Murder for pleasure: the life and times of the detective story. 1942.   (662)

Hart, F. R. Manuscripts of Wilkie Collins. Princeton Univ Lib Chron 18 1957.   (928)

(Can you explain how the compiler of this section came to make the last error?)

10. Morris Croll's *Style, Rhetoric, and Rhythm* (1966) is a collection of the author's essays that were earlier printed in journals. In his introduction the editor, J. Max Patrick, enumerates the sins of omission and commission that disfigured the essays in their original form and required wholesale checking and amendment when gathered for this volume. Select one of the essays and make a list of the scholarly lapses found in its original version.

11. The annotation of literary texts in modern classroom editions is sometimes defective. Here is a selection of errors (italicized) found in the notes to various modern editions of Carlyle's *Past and Present* (1843) and to anthologized excerpts from that book. What is the correct explanation in each case?

(a) "Yes, in the *Ugolino Hunger-tower* stern things happen; best-loved little Gaddo fallen dead on his Father's knees!" (I.i; the allusion is to Dante's *Inferno,* XXXIII.)

Annotator A: "Count Ugolino who with his two sons and two grandsons was starved in prison."

Annotator B: "He died, with four sons, in prison, starved to death."

Annotator C: "He was imprisoned with two sons and two nephews . . ."

Annotator D: ". . . the story of Ugolino and his two sons . . ."

(b) ". . . in killing Kings, in passing Reform Bills, in French Revolutions, *Manchester Insurrections,* is found no remedy." (III.i)

At least four annotators identify this as the Peterloo Massacre (1819).

(c) ". . . for him and his there is no continuance appointed, save only in Gehenna and *the Pool.*" (III.ii)

"The Thames River for several miles below London Bridge."

(d) ". . . *Owen's Labour-bank* . . ." (III.xii)

Annotator A: "Planned by Robert Owen . . . but not achieved."

Annotator B: "An enterprise proposed by the Chartists in 1847."

(e) "In the case of *the late Bribery Committee* . . ." (IV.ii)

One annotator identifies as a committee of Parliament appointed in 1835 to investigate charges of electoral corruption.

(f) ". . . mad Chartisms, *impracticable Sacred-Months,* and Manchester Insurrections . . ." (IV.iv)

"An allusion to the revolutionary calendar adopted in France in 1793."

12. What is the correct pronunciation of each of the following names? How do you know? (Do not depend on dictionaries; go to reliable biographies or similar sources.)

Thomas Carew
Sir John Vanbrugh
Abraham Cowley
William Cowper

Lewis Theobald
Lord Auchinleck
Robert Southey
Boz
V. S. Naipaul
Vladimir Nabokov
Jean Rhys
Anaïs Nin
· J. M. Coëtzee

13. (a) How many different birth dates can you find in contemporary sources such as obituaries, and in modern reference works, for the following figures? Which, if any, is the correct one in each case?

Eliza Cook
Bret Harte
Willa Cather
A. B. Grosart, editor of literary texts (in his case, fourteen sources cite five different years)

(b) How convincingly, and on what kind of evidence, did Albert E. Johnson (*Modern Drama* 2 [1968]: 157–63) solve the long-vexed question of when the famous actor and playwright Dion Boucicault was born?
(c) No record is known of the birth of the early American poet Edward Taylor. Upon what kinds of evidence have various scholars suggested dates between 1642 and 1646?
(d) The *NCBEL*, 3, col. 746, says that the Gothic novelist Charles Robert Maturin was born in 1782, as do other standard authorities such as the *Oxford Companion to English Literature* and the *DNB*. Benét's *Readers' Encyclopedia*, on the other hand, gives 1787. What is the evidence for the true date, and why was the compiler of the bibliography of Maturin in the *NCBEL* especially culpable in allowing the 1782 date to stand?

V. *The Critical Examination of Evidence*

1. What authority is there for each of the following stories? Which have been proved to be untrue or inaccurate?

(a) *Beowulf* as we know it was composed as a literary (i.e., written) rather than an oral poetic work.

(b) William Langland (born 1332 at Ledbury, Shropshire, educated at the priory of Great Malvern, the holder of minor orders, mendicant singer, died 1400) wrote all three versions of *Piers Plowman.*

(c) Shakespeare left Stratford because his poaching proclivities were getting him into constant trouble, especially with Sir Thomas Lucy.

(d) John Donne was a rake in his youth.

(e) Thomas Gray moved from Peterhouse to Pembroke College because a false alarm of fire, raised by prankish undergraduates, had forced him to use the rope ladder he had stored in his room.

(f) Boswell took stenographic notes of Dr. Johnson's conversation in the great man's very presence.

(g) Wordsworth made a secret trip to France in 1793.

(h) The Blakes had an amiable habit of sitting nude in their summerhouse.

(i) Thomas Hardy had an illegitimate child by Tryphena Sparks.

(j) The disabling disease from which George Meredith suffered in his last years was locomotor ataxia.

(k) When Arthur Conan Doyle (1859–1930), then an impecunious physician attempting to establish a practice in an English seaside town, filed his income tax return, Inland Revenue (the British equivalent of the American I.R.S.) rejected it with the notation "Most unsatisfactory." Doyle wrote back, "I quite agree." (If you can prove the veracity of this anecdote, try to relate it to the story Robert Southey told of the radical politician Horne Tooke [1736–1812]. See below, Exercise VII. 20 (a), page 314.)

(l) Nora Joyce refused to read her husband's books because

she found them "filthy" and their author a "dirty-minded" man.

(m) John O'Hara's practice was never to rewrite or revise; hence the manuscripts he sent to his publishers were, in effect, first drafts.

(n) Jack Kerouac composed at least one of his novels on rolls of toilet paper.

2. The following books contain psychological interpretations of various writers and literary works. How solid and extensive is the factual evidence upon which the argument rests, and how convincing is the argument itself?

> George L. Watson, *A. E. Housman: A Divided Life* (1957)
> Frederick C. Crews, *The Sins of the Fathers: Hawthorne's Psychological Themes* (1966)
> Richard J. Onorato, *The Character of the Poet: Wordsworth and "The Prelude"* (1971)
> Walter Jackson Bate, *The Achievement of Samuel Johnson* (1978)
> Frederick R. Karl, *Joseph Conrad: The Three Lives* (1983)
> Kenneth S. Lynn, *Hemingway: His Life and Work* (1987)
> Louise DeSalvo, *Virginia Woolf: The Impact of Childhood Sexual Abuse on Her Life and Work* (1989)

(Many articles suitable for this exercise can be found in the files of *American Imago,* the *American Journal of Psychiatry,* the *Psychoanalytic Review,* and *Literature and Psychology.* Authors like Stephen Crane have been repeatedly subjected to Freudian or Jungian interpretation; for such treatments, see the appropriate current "guides to research" and author bibliographies.)

3. What evidence would you require to be persuaded that the following statements are not exaggerated?

> (a) . . . the sale of books in general has increased prodigiously within the last twenty years. According to the best estimation I have been able to make, I suppose that more than four times the number of books are sold now than were sold twenty years since. The poorer sort of farmers, and even the poor

country people in general, who before that period spent their winter evenings in relating stories of witches, ghosts, hobgoblins, &c. now shorten the nights by hearing their sons and daughters read tales, romances, &c. and on entering their houses, you may see Tom Jones, Roderick Random, and other entertaining books stuck up on their bacon racks, &c. and if *John* goes to town with a load of hay, he is charged to be sure not to forget to bring home "Peregrine Pickle's adventures;" and when *Dolly* is sent to market to sell her eggs she is commissioned to purchase "The History of Pamela Andrews." In short all ranks and degrees now READ. (James Lackington, *Memoirs of the First Forty-Five Years of the Life of James Lackington* . . . [London, ca. 1791] 254–55)

(b) "Happy those who live and bear, and do and suffer and above all love him to the end"—were a less scrupulous revaluator to cite this April 1868 benediction from Annie's [Annie Adams Fields, wife of Dickens's American publisher] diary as a virtual declaration of love, nothing in the Fieldses' subsequent visit to Gad's Hill or in letters about it would indicate that she changed her opinion or underwent any revulsion of feeling during the remainder of Dickens's lifetime. She was convinced that, in knowing him, she had feasted on honeydew and was right to attempt to envision what drinking the milk of paradise as part of her daily regimen might be like. (Jerome Meckier, *Innocent Abroad: Charles Dickens's American Engagements* [Lexington, KY, 1990] 155–56)

4. Several books by A. L. Rowse, *William Shakespeare: A Biography* (1963), *Shakespeare the Man* (1973; rev. ed. 1988), and his modern-spelling Contemporary Shakespeare series begun in 1984, have stirred up fierce controversy. Read as many reviews as you can find, including those in such places as the intellectual weeklies and the Sunday book supplements, and then sum up what the chief issues are between Rowse and his critics.

5. (a) Robert G. Walker has argued that "the deaths of Rochester, Addison, Hume, and Paine . . . are all public deaths . . . in the sense that these men deliberately shaped the final days of their lives just as they would shape the conclusion of

a work of art to convey a particular polemical message, in full knowledge that their end would be reported not only to their peers but also to the public at large." ("Public Death in the Eighteenth Century," *Research Studies* [Washington State University] 48 [1980]: 1–24) Describe the arguments and the methods of investigation Walker uses to support the idea of a consciously manipulated death in the cases mentioned.

(b) Using the kind of evidence and reasoning employed by Walker, try to decide whether another classic instance, Lockhart's description of Sir Walter Scott's last moments, is believable. What considerations weigh in favor of its being more or less a myth?

6. Examine the following arguments to determine the nature and reliability of the evidence adduced, and the cogency of the reasoning by which the conclusion is reached.

(a) Olivia Clemens was not, as has been assumed, "a woman who wasted a fair portion of her married life dictating literal propriety to a recalcitrant husband and making his prose less salty than it might otherwise have been." (Sydney J. Krause, "Olivia Clemens's 'Editing' Reviewed," *AL* 39 [1967]: 325–51)

(b) The peculiarities of spelling in Milton's printed poems are attributable to his amanuenses or compositors; they do not reflect his own practice. (John T. Shawcross, "One Aspect of Milton's Spelling: Idle Final 'E,' " *PMLA* 78 [1963]: 501–10)

(c) There is no basis for the familiar story that Shakespeare and Ben Jonson had wit combats at the Mermaid Tavern. (S. Schoenbaum, *Shakespeare's Lives* [Oxford, 1970] 294–96)

(d) Pepys's diary as we have it is the result of his thorough re-writing and polishing of the original notes. (*The Diary of Samuel Pepys,* ed. Latham and Matthews, 1:97–106)

VI. Biographical Research

1. From the lists of "minor" writers in the various genres given in *NCBEL,* volumes 2 and 3, select one upon whom little if any recent biographical work has been done. (You will want

to check this further by referring to the appropriate serial bibliography covering scholarship published since the cut-off date of the *NCBEL* entry.) The existence of book-length lives or biographical articles dating from before, say, 1910 is no bar to the selection of a given figure, because these older treatments usually are more or less unreliable and require constant verification.

Having decided upon a promising figure, write as full a biographical account as the available materials permit, beginning with the *DNB* article (if he or she has merited one) but spreading a wide net to include articles and obituaries in newspapers and periodicals, contemporary memoirs and letters, official documents, and every other primary source of information. Present the results of your research in a thoroughly documented, tautly organized, and readable paper, such as you might offer to the editor of a learned journal.

The same exercise may involve a minor American author. There are ample lists in such reference works as Burke and Howe's *American Authors and Books* and Herzberg's *Reader's Encyclopedia of American Literature.*

2. The article on Thomas Powell in the *Dictionary of American Biography* is remarkable for what it does not say about its subject. What aspect of his character and career does the author discreetly omit?

3. Samuel Johnson paid Hester Mulso, later Hester Mulso Chapone, the "unusual compliment of quoting [her poem] 'To Stella' in his *Dictionary* in 1755 (under Quatrain)." Write a brief biographical sketch of this minor poet.

4. Narratives of Indian captivity, such as "A Narrative of the Sufferings and Surprizing Deliverance of William and Elizabeth Fleming" (1756), "developed from religious documents to anti-French and anti-Indian propaganda." Identify several authors and titles in this subgenre and develop a brief biographical sketch of one such writer.

5. Much important biographical data is now available on microfiche, as many biographical dictionaries have been repro-

duced in this format—e.g., *British Biographical Archive: 17th through 19th Centuries; British and Irish Biographies: 1840–1940; Biography and Genealogy Master Index*. Review one of these resources and discuss several uses for literary research of such a range of biographical data.

VII. Textual Criticism and Editing; Bibliographical Analysis; Publishing History

1. Scholars should never quote from popular reprint editions of literary works, however convenient they may be, if a more authoritative text can be had. Substantiate this axiom by comparing the text of, say, a Penguin, Riverside, or Signet edition of an older work with a scholarly one.

2. Summarize the particular problems (available manuscripts, printed editions, dubious ascriptions, etc.) involved in determining the text, and in some cases the canon, of Dekker, Ben Jonson, Donne, Tourneur, Crashaw, Herrick, Defoe, Matthew Arnold, Yeats, or Auden. (Be sure that you take into account the latest published information and discussion.)

3. What kind of textual scholarship remained to be performed on Thoreau's *Walden* after the publication of the Princeton critical edition of that work in 1971? Was it eventually accomplished?

4. William Faulkner revised his Nobel Prize acceptance speech for publication. What were the changes he made and how do you account for them?

5. During the nineteenth century, Harper and Brothers published in America such major British novelists as Dickens, the Brontës, Thackeray, and Hardy. What specific books of each author did the firm publish, and how much was paid to the author for each work?

6. John Barth's novel *The Floating Opera* was first published in the United States in 1956. In 1968 it was revised and published in England for the first time. Why was publication in England delayed and how extensive were the revisions?

7. To commemorate the 250th anniversary of the first edition of *Gulliver's Travels* an edition described as the "true 'original' " version was published. On what text was this later edition based? Where is that text to be found?

8. W. W. Greg's parallel-text edition of Marlowe's *Dr. Faustus* has been called "one of the major triumphs of modern literary scholarship." What is the apparent relationship between the two printed texts (1604 and 1616)? On the basis of what evidence, and by what reasoning, did Greg arrive at his conclusions? What is the value of this edition to literary students?

9. What is the relation of the so-called "old *Arcadia*" (first discovered in two manuscripts in 1907) to the printed texts of Sidney's romance (1590 and 1593)? Is there an edition that embodies the readings of all the manuscripts (several more have subsequently turned up) and of the dozen editions printed down to 1674?

10. Coleridge's *Biographia Literaria* in the Bollingen edition of his *Collected Works* (2 vols., Princeton, 1983) is generally considered an excellent edition. One area of criticism that has developed concerns sometimes "misleading information" in the footnote annotations of Wordsworth's post-*Biographia* revisions of poems Coleridge had discussed. Explain how the issues at the center of this criticism are part of a long-standing debate among scholars regarding the relationship between these two major literary figures.

11. Locate several articles considering textual apparatus for critical editions. Minimally, what specific categories of data should such apparatus include? Cite two or three editions exemplary for their apparatus presenting such textual information.

12. After consulting the introductions to modern scholarly editions of the following works or personal documents, or books and articles devoted to the topic, describe the special problems offered by the sources of the text of each work.

How have their latest editors dealt with these difficulties?
Which works are still in need of definitive editing?

Piers Plowman
Sir Gawain and the Green Knight
The Faerie Queene
Religio Medici
Hudibras
MacFlecknoe
Evelyn's diary
Pope's letters
A Sentimental Journey
Boswell's journals
Franklin's *Autobiography*
Don Juan
Dr. Grimshawe's Secret
Leaves of Grass
The Mysterious Stranger
The Education of Henry Adams
The Importance of Being Earnest
Winesburg, Ohio
The Red Badge of Courage

13. Select any one of the literary works listed in the preceding
question and summarize, with appropriate illustrations, the
light that a knowledge of its textual history throws upon its
meaning and art.

14. Describe the importance to literary study of each of the
following documents or collections of documents. Are they
all adequately edited? Where is each located?

Henslowe's diary
The Auchinleck Manuscript
Henry Silver's diary of the weekly meetings of the editors
    of *Punch* beginning in the 1850s
The Arundel Harington Manuscript of Tudor poetry
The Revels Accounts
The Term Catalogues
The Lovelace Papers

    Crabb Robinson's diary
    The Brontë juvenilia
    The Esdaile Notebook
    The Crewe MS of "Kubla Khan"
    The Mark Twain papers formerly owned by his daughter
    Woodhouse's interleaved and annotated copy of Keats's
        Poems (1817)
    Macaulay's diary
    The first draft of Yeats's *Autobiography*
    George Eliot's "quarry for *Middlemarch*"
    The corrected proofs of most of Dickens's novels
    The Civil War diary of Mary Chesnut

15. Describe the significance of the revisions Izaak Walton made in successive editions of his *Lives*.

16. Explain why the lifting, in the early 1970s, of the ban against quoting from Tennyson's manuscripts at Trinity College, Cambridge, rendered obsolete all previous histories of the composition of such poems as *In Memoriam* and *Idylls of the King*.

17. Most of the contents of the following collections were originally printed in periodicals. Select one or more essays, and determine whether or not they were revised for book publication. If they were, what was the extent and significance of the changes?

    William Butler Yeats, *Ideas of Good and Evil; Essays 1931 to 1936*
    Norman Douglas, *Old Calabria; Experiments*
    Aldous Huxley, *On the Margin; Essays New and Old; Do What You Will; Themes and Variations; Collected Essays*
    Virginia Woolf, *Collected Essays*
    Horace Gregory, *Spirit of Time and Place*
    Malcolm Cowley, *A Second Flowering: Works and Days of the Lost Generation*
    Benjamin De Mott, *Supergrow: Essays and Reports on Imagination in America*

> Kurt Vonnegut, Jr., *Wampeters Foma and Granfalloons*
> Tom Wolfe, *Mauve Gloves and Madmen, Cluter and Vine*
> John Updike, *Hugging the Shore; Odd Jobs*

18. The critic Francis Jeffrey made hundreds of significant changes in the text of his *Edinburgh Review* articles when preparing them for his four-volume *Contributions to the "Edinburgh Review"* (1844). For a sampling of these, see Ronald B. Hatch, " 'This Will Never Do,' " *RES* ns 21 (1970): 56–62. Try the same procedure with some other nineteenth-century critic who often wrote for periodicals, such as Macaulay, George Henry Lewes, Leslie Stephen, John Morley, Augustine Birrell, Edward Dowden, or George Saintsbury.

19. (a) Locate a copy of a first edition of a book by an American author who died after 1930, or who is not, in any event, represented in Jacob Blanck's *Bibliography of American Literature*. Examine it carefully, and describe it according to the formula used by Blanck.
    (b) Locate a copy of a first edition of any book listed in Blanck and compare it, detail by detail, with Blanck's description, identifying, if necessary, the printing, issue, or state to which it belongs.

20. Printed below are five extracts from the printed texts of documents written by or to prominent writers. Assuming that you are preparing a definitive edition of the private papers of one of these authors, annotate every allusion that you think a future user of your edition will need to have explained. Assume further that none of the allusions has been annotated in connection with previous letters in the edition.

    (a) Southey to his wife, Brixton, May 9, 1799 (Charles Cuthbert Southey, *Life and Correspondence of the Late Robert Southey* [London, 1850] 2: 16–17):

    > G. Dyer is foraging for my Almanac, and promises pieces from Mrs. Opie, Mr. Mott of Cambridge, and Miss Christall.

I then went to Arch's, a pleasant place for half an hour's book news: you know he purchased the edition of the Lyrical Ballads; he told me he believed he should lose by them, as they sold very heavily. . . . My books sell very well. Other book news have I none, except, indeed, that John Thelwall is writing an epic poem, and Samuel Rogers is also writing an epic poem; George Dyer, also, hath similar thoughts. . . . William Taylor has written to me from Norwich, and sent me Bodmer's Noah, the book that I wanted to poke through and learn German by. He tempts me to write upon the subject, and take my seat with Milton and Klopstock; and in my to-day's walk so many noble thoughts for such a poem presented themselves, that I am half tempted, and have the Deluge floating in my brain with the Dom Daniel and the rest of my unborn family. . . . Horne Tooke's letter to the Income Commissioners has amused me very much: he had stated his under sixty pounds a year; they said they were not satisfied; and his reply begins by saying he has much more reason to be dissatisfied with the smallness of his income than they have.

(b) Richard Harding Davis to his family, Managua, Nicaragua, February 13, 1895 (*Adventures and Letters of Richard Harding Davis,* ed. Charles Belmont Davis [New York, 1917] 152):

I had a great deal to tell you, but we have just received copies of the Panama *Star* and have read of the trolley riots in Brooklyn, a crisis in France, War in the Balkans, a revolution in Honolulu and another in Colombia. The result is that we feel we are not in it and we are all kicking and growling and abusing our luck. How Claiborne and Russell will delight over us and in telling how the militia fired on the strikers and how Troop A fought nobly. Never mind our turn will come someday and we may see something yet. We have had the deuce of a time since we left Tegucigalpa. Now we are in a land where there are bull hide beds and canvas cots instead of hammocks and ice and railroads and direct communication with steamship lines. Hereafter all will be merely a matter of waiting until the boat sails or the train starts and the uncertainties of mules and cat boats are at an end.

(c) F. Scott Fitzgerald to Maxwell Perkins, Paris, January 21, 1930 (*Dear Scott/Dear Max: The Fitzgerald-Perkins Correspondence,* ed. John Kuehl and Jackson R. Bryer [New York, 1971] 161):

> (3) Thank you for the documents in the Callaghan case. I'd rather not discuss it except to say that I don't like him and that I wrote him a formal letter of apology. I never thought he started the rumor & never said nor implied such a thing to Ernest.
>
> (4) Delighted with the success of Ernest's book. I took the responsibility of telling him that McAlmon was at his old dirty work around New York. McAlmon, by the way, didn't have anything to do with founding *Transition.* He published Ernest's first book over here & some books of his own & did found some little magazine but of no importance.
>
> (5) Thank you for getting *Gatsby* for me in foreign languages.
>
> (6) Sorry about John Biggs but it will probably do him good in the end. *The Stranger in Soul Country* had something & the *Seven Days Whipping* was respectable but colorless. *Demigods* was simply oratorical twirp. How is his play going?
>
> (7) Tom Boyd seems far away. I'll tell you one awful thing tho. Lawrence Stallings was in the West with King Vidor at a *huge* salary to write an equivalent of *What Price Glory.* King Vidor told me that Stallings in despair of showing Vidor what the war was about gave him a copy of *Through the Wheat.* And that's how Vidor so he told me made the big scenes of the *Big Parade.* Tom Boyd's profits were a few thousand—Stallings were a few hundred thousands. Please don't connect my name with this story but it is the truth and it seems to me rather horrible.

(d) Henry Miller to Lawrence Durrell, Paris, December 1936 (*Lawrence Durrell & Henry Miller: A Private Correspondence,* ed. George Wickes [New York, 1963] 35–36):

> Why not make the contributors to the review pay for the printing and mailing, etc.? Say about 250 francs apiece— about $12.50. No avant-garde magazine can hope to make money. Not today. . . . The first thing to do would be to write

the potential contributors and see if they were willing. I have a few people in mind who I would think would respond, with good contributions and with money. To wit: Fraenkel, Lowenfels, Saroyan, Laughlin, Anais Nin, James Stern, Van Heeckeren—possibly Hilaire Hiler and Mayo for drawings. Stern is a young Irish writer, who wrote a book of excellent short stories on Africa. Van Heeckeren might give us something about China—he is an adventurer. Mayo is a Greek painter whose drawings are almost made to illustrate my books. Hiler is a painter and a good friend of mine, now in Hollywood. There may be others—I think of these at random. The point is that the magazine, or anthology, or whatever you wish, should be fairly inexpensive. One could use both English and French, I imagine. Perlès could then come in with some of his marvellous passages from the *Quatuor.* You have your friends. Zarian sounds interesting. Make him write that letter, by all means! I would give you something from *Capricorn,* something beyond either *Tropic* or *Black Spring,* or something from *Hamlet,* or a long short story called "Max," which I am sure you would like. Or "The Universe of Death," from the Lawrence book. Anyway, there would be no dearth of material.

(e) Samuel Beckett to Barney Rosset, Paris, February 11, 1954 (*Review of Contemporary Fiction* 10 [1990]: 68–69):

Thanks for your friendly and understanding letter of Feb. 5th. You will have seen mine to Mr Turner thanking him for the jacket. The Dönitz photo makes a marvellous front to the book. If the little changes can't be made, no matter.

I don't make a cent of additional income out of the translations, except that of *Godot.* I'm compelled to do it by a foolish feeling of protectiveness towards the work. Am just finishing revision of German *Molloy,* well done I think, but with many mistakes and an irritating way of turning the unusual into the usual so that it won't read like a translation! Also beginning to work on *Malone* with German translator of *Godot,* a very nice man who lives here. Had the Spanish *Godot* too, that was awful.

I thought myself of trying again in English, but it's only evading the issue like everything else I try. If there was a head and a rock I'd rather beat that against this than start the old fake stravaguing again in another proxy. It's hard to go on with everything loathed and repudiated as soon as formulated, and in the act of formulation, and before formulation. I'll soon be assembling a queer little book for Lindon, three longish short stories, the very first writing in French and of which one at least seems to me all right, and the thirteen or fourteen very short abortive texts *(Textes pour Rien)* that express the failure to implement the last words of *L'Innommable:* "il faut continuer, je vais continuer." He also wanted to publish *Mercier et Camier,* the first "novel" in French and of which the less said the better, but I had to refuse. At the moment I have a "man" crawling along a corridor in the rock in the dark, but he's due to vanish any day now. Of course there's no reason why it should start again now or ever for that matter. I'm horribly tired and stupefied, but not yet tired and stupefied enough. To write is impossible but not yet impossible enough. That's how I cod myself these days.

VIII. Questions of Authorship

1. Three hitherto unknown literary documents of Henry Fielding—two autograph poems and a pseudonymous letter to the editor of *Common Sense* (dated April Fool's Day, 1738, and published May 13, 1738)—have been identified. Locate published discussions of these finds and summarize how their authorship was determined and what significance is claimed for them by their discoverers. Describe the pieces.

2. Some years ago a manuscript of an unknown play allegedly by Jane Austen was discovered. The play was called *Sir Charles Grandison, or the Happy Man, a Comedy* and was freely adapted from Richardson's novel. Give the details of this find. Has the authorship been firmly established?

3. Edward L. Saslow has written two articles raising questions about works generally attributed to Dryden: "Dryden's Authorship of the *Defense of the Royal Papers,*" *SEL* 17 (1977): 87–95, and "Dryden as Historiographer Royal, and the Authorship of *His Majesties Declaration Defended,*" *MP* 75

(1978): 261–72. Choose one or the other of these articles, summarize Saslow's argument, and present your assessment of his evidence and the effectiveness of his presentation.

4. In 1972 a hitherto unknown Renaissance play was discovered and attributed to Thomas Heywood. Where was the manuscript found and on what basis was the attribution made?

5. Select an author other than Shakespeare writing before 1660 for whom computer analysis of style has increased or decreased his canon. Describe the major differences established via computer analysis and summarize the effects of these findings.

6. The *DNB* incorrectly attributes *Poems and Essays* (1786) to Henrietta Maria Bowdler. What is the actual full title of this work, who was its author, and how many editions appeared between 1787 and 1800?

7. Who wrote the review of Coleridge's *Christabel* published in the London *Times,* May 20, 1816? What is the evidence for this ascription?

8. Following is a list of works whose authorship is, or until lately has been, in doubt. Summarize the arguments found in the existing discussions of each problem, and decide what the most acceptable answer is, so far as the available evidence permits one to judge.

   (a) The "anonymous" life of Milton
   (b) The play of *Sir Thomas More*
   (c) The glosses (by "E.K.") in Spenser's *Shepherd's Calendar*
   (d) The poems signed "Anomos" in Francis Davison's *Poetical Rhapsody* (1602)

9. In the *Knickerbocker Magazine* 12 (1838): 349–66, James Fenimore Cooper wrote a lengthy attack on Lockhart's life of Scott. In it he clearly implied—while stoutly denying any such suspicion—that Lockhart had been the author of a scathing review of Cooper's recent book on England ("so ill-

written—ill-informed—ill-bred—ill-tempered, and so ill-mannered a production it has never yet been our fortune to meet"). In what British periodical did that review appear, and was Lockhart actually the author?

10. In the appendix of his ground-breaking little book, *New Essays by Oliver Goldsmith* (1927), Ronald S. Crane listed a number of essays and other contributions to periodicals that he suspected to be by Goldsmith but in lack of sufficient evidence declined to attribute to him. Of these possible ascriptions, how many have subsequently been strengthened or rejected?

11. Did the *"Gawain* poet" write the saint's legend of St. Erkenwald?

12. On what grounds have the following poems been attributed to their respective "authors"? How sound is each attribution?

    (a) "A Fragment of an Epic Poem": Charles Churchill?
    (b) "Epilogue Intended to have been spoken by the Lady Henr. Mar. Wentworth when *Calisto* was acted at Court": Dryden?
    (c) "Jack Frenchman's Lamentation": Swift?
    (d) Metrical paraphrases of the first seven Psalms (the first beginning: "Blest is the man that never would/ in councels of th' ungodly share"): Herbert?
    (e) "The Sparke": Carew?
    (f) "Autumn. an Ode": Dr. Johnson?

13. Generously sample the pages of the *Wellesley Index to Victorian Periodicals, 1824–1900,* particularly volume 5. Make a list of the kinds of internal and external evidence used by the editors to establish authorship. Which kinds are usually the most reliable, and which result in only tentative attributions? Even beyond the new identifications of authors of anonymous and pseudonymous writing, how is the *Wellesley* a valuable extension of the kinds of materials contained in Halkett and Laing's *Dictionary of Anonymous and Pseudonymous English Literature?*

14. Identify and describe in a paragraph or two the Pseudonym Library. What well-known authors wrote for this series?

IX. Problems of Source and Influence

1. By an analysis of internal and (if possible) external evidence, estimate the debt of Thomas Love Peacock's *The Four Ages of Poetry* to Sidney's *Defense of Poesie*. Is it likely that Peacock consciously modeled his essay, at least in part, on Sidney's?

2. From such sources as the *MLA International Bibliography,* the annual *American Literary Scholarship,* and the quarterly bibliography in *American Literature,* select a half-dozen recent articles dealing with the purported use made of sources by Poe, Melville, Hawthorne, Longfellow, Stephen Crane, or Thomas Wolfe. After critically reading each article, decide how sound each argument is.

3. In what ways did Macaulay, in his essay on Sir William Temple, draw upon Monk's *Life of Bentley,* Boyle's *Dr. Bentley's Dissertation on the Epistles of Phalaris,* and Bentley's *Dissertation* itself?

4. How persuasive are the following books and articles on sources and influences?

   (a) Alfred S. Reid, "Hawthorne's Humanism: 'The Birthmark' and Sir Kenelm Digby," *AL* 38 (1966): 337–51
   (b) John Shroeder, "Miles Coverdale as Actaeon, as Faunus, and as October: With Some Consequences," *Papers on Language and Literature* 2 (1966): 126–39
   (c) John Hazel Smith, "The Genesis of the Strozza Subplot in George Chapman's *The Gentleman Usher,*" *PMLA* 83 (1968): 1448–53
   (d) Thomas B. Gilmore, Jr., "Swift's *Modest Proposal:* A Possible Source," *PQ* 47 (1968): 590–92
   (e) Harry Stone, "The Genesis of a Novel: *Great Expectations,*" *Charles Dickens 1812–1870,* ed. E. W. F. Tomlin (New York, 1969) 109–31

(f) Hershel Parker, "Dead Letters and Melville's Bartleby," *Resources for American Literary Study* 4 (1974): 90–99

(g) Sara DeSaussure Davis, "Feminist Sources in *The Bostonians,*" *AL* 50 (1979): 570–87

(h) James K. Chandler, *Wordsworth's Second Nature: A Study of the Poetry and Politics* (Chicago, 1984)

(i) Robert DeMaria, Jr., *Johnson's "Dictionary" and the Language of Learning* (Chapel Hill, NC, 1986)

5. Anne Bradstreet revealed a sophisticated seventeenth-century knowledge of medicine in "Of the Foure Humours in Mans Constitution" (*The Tenth Muse,* 1650). What was the probable source of this knowledge?

6. Scholars are generally agreed that Émile Zola strongly influenced Frank Norris's style and choice of subject matter. Most of the evidence for this conclusion comes from Norris's novels and journalism. What other evidence exists? How persuasive is it?

7. In his "Dorothea's Husbands: Some Biographical Speculations" (*TLS,* February 16, 1973: 165–68), Richard Ellmann suggested a number of men whose character traits may have served George Eliot in her delineation of the character of Edward Casaubon in *Middlemarch.* In doing so, Ellmann stirred a lively reaction in the correspondence columns of the *TLS* that lasted for some months. Summarize the major issues in these exchanges and determine which arguments seem most ably supported.

8. Examine several issues of the journal *Publishing History* and write a brief essay summarizing articles on the "influence of the publisher on literary trends" or "publishing as a reflection of the social and cultural influences of the time." Either write about a single historical era or compare two or more periods.

9. Discuss the influence of official Catholic church publications on the writings of Gerard Manley Hopkins.

10. Thomas Shadwell's *The Libertine* (1675) was the first version of the Don Juan legend in England. What details of the

Don Juan story and aspect of French libertinism and Hobbesian philosophy have scholars looked to in explicating the play and defining the spirit of Shadwell's age?

11. Summarize the negative criticism that has focused on Faulkner's *Pylon* for its alleged borrowing from Eliot's *The Waste Land*.

12. Recent scholarship, particularly focused upon *The Sun Also Rises*, has demonstrated Hemingway's unexpectedly wide reading and specifically the influence on this novel of the writings of Turgenev, Tolstoy, Flaubert, Stendhal, Conrad, Anderson, Ford, Stein, Arlen, Stewart, Fitzgerald, and others. Select one of these novelists and summarize the research documenting the use of his or her works in *The Sun Also Rises*.

X. *The Historical Background of Literature*

1. Collect authentic information sufficient for a substantial explanatory footnote (or, in some cases, an appendix for a paperback edition of a pertinent literary work) on one of the following topics:

   (a) Rules of conduct for cultivated young ladies in Jane Austen's time
   (b) Periodicals published by American utopian communities
   (c) The social makeup of the congregation who listened to Donne's sermons
   (d) Shipboard conditions in the American merchant marine at the time of *Two Years Before the Mast*
   (e) The interior arrangement and furniture of medieval inns
   (f) Means of household illumination in Dickens's England
   (g) The response of the people to the elimination of eleven days from the calendar in 1752
   (h) The nature of the medical training Smollett and Goldsmith received

(i) The attitude toward astronomical portents in the Elizabethan age

(j) The social status of actors in Shakespeare's time

(k) Dinner menus and table habits in Dr. Johnson's time

(l) The sources of fresh drinking water in London in 1660

(m) Copyright protection for authors at the time of the publication of *Robinson Crusoe*

(n) Lower-class games, sports, and popular amusements during the Regency period

(o) The introduction of movable scenery on the London stage

(p) The buying power of the dollar in 1850

(q) Patronage in Washington politics during the Reconstruction period 1865–77 *(The Gilded Age)*

(r) Russian expatriates in Berlin at the time of the Weimar Republic (for information clarifying action in one of Nabokov's works)

(s) The condition of the legitimate theater in New York City on the night in 1927 when the first "talking" film, Al Jolson in *The Jazz Singer,* opened

2. Find a contemporary source, preferably a first-hand account or personal reaction (such as a diary entry, passage in a letter, or a newspaper or magazine story) describing each of the following events that are mentioned in English and American literature:

    The bad weather in the summer of 1594 (*A Midsummer Night's Dream,* 2.1)

    The stage war involving the children's companies (*Hamlet,* 2.2)

    Fears of the end of the world (Dryden's *Annus Mirabilis*)

    The Great Plague (Defoe's *Journal of the Plague Year*)

    The execution of the Rev. Dr. William Dodd (Boswell's *Life of Johnson*)

    The Gordon riots (Dickens's *Barnaby Rudge*)

    "The Dark Day of New England" [May 19, 1780] (Whittier's "Abraham Davenport")

    The Convention of Cintra (Wordsworth's tract)

The Luddite riots (Charlotte Brontë's *Shirley*)

Sir Samuel Romilly's suicide (Byron's *Don Juan*, 1.15)

The Peterloo Massacre (Shelley's "The Mask of Anarchy")

The dedication of the Concord monument (Emerson's "Concord Hymn")

Layard's discovery of the great bulls at Nimrud (Rossetti's "The Burden of Nineveh")

Adulteration of food in the 1850s (Tennyson's *Maud*)

The laying of the transatlantic cable (Whitman's "Passage to India")

The funeral of the duke of Wellington (Tennyson's "Ode on the Death of the Duke of Wellington")

The burning of Atlanta in *Gone with the Wind*

The volcanic explosion on the island of Krakatoa in 1883 (Bridges's *Eros and Psyche*)

The wreck of the *Deutschland* (Hopkins's poem)

The "Easter Rising" in Ireland (Yeats's "Easter 1916")

The "Black Sox" baseball scandal (Fitzgerald's *The Great Gatsby*)

The murder of Stanford White by Harry K. Thaw (Doctorow's *Ragtime*)

Barnstorming (Faulkner's *Pylon*)

Marathon dancing (Horace McCoy's *They Shoot Horses, Don't They?*)

The murder of four members of the Clutter family in Holcomb, Kansas, on November 15, 1959 (Capote's *In Cold Blood*)

The march on the Pentagon (Mailer's *The Armies of the Night*)

3. Select a literary event that occurred in your locality (e.g., an important writer lived there briefly but vividly, Dickens toured through it, Emerson or Matthew Arnold lectured in the old Opera House), and using as many files as are accessible, report on contemporary newspaper coverage of this subject.

4. Using newspaper and magazine files as your primary source, write a comparative survey of the London and New York (or

Boston, Philadelphia, or Cincinnati) theater during a given season in the nineteenth century.

5. You are preparing an edition of H. L. Mencken's *Prejudices*. The abundance of topical allusions in Mencken requires much annotation. Select one or more of the following essays, and write an explanatory note for every allusion that you think will puzzle a future reader. Add the source of your information in the proper scholarly form.

> First series: "Professor Veblen," "The American Magazine"
> Second series: "The Sahara of the Bozart"
> Third series: "The Forward-Looker," "Education," "The Dismal Science"
> Fourth series: "The American Tradition," "Reflections on Human Monogamy," "Totentanz," "Meditations in the Methodist Desert," "The American Novel"
> Fifth series: "In Memoriam: W.J.B.," "The Father of Service," the individual parts of "The Fringes of Lovely Letters"
> Sixth series: "Journalism in America," "God Help the South!," the individual parts of "Souvenirs of a Book Reviewer," "Invitation to the Dance," "Appendix from Moronia"

If directed, write a short introduction to the essay you have annotated, explaining the background of social, cultural, or literary circumstance that occasioned it.

6. The following sentences come from Emerson's essay "The Poet" (1844):

> Readers of poetry see the factory-village and the railway, and fancy that the poetry of the landscape is broken up by these; for these works of art are not yet consecrated in their reading; but the poet sees them fall within the great Order not less than the beehive or the spider's geometrical web. Nature adopts them very fast into her vital circles, and the gliding train cars she loves like her own. (*The Complete Works of Ralph Waldo Emerson,* Centenary Edition [Cambridge, MA, 1903] 3:19)

In order to annotate these sentences, ascertain the extensiveness of the railway system in the United States in the early 1840s. What first-hand knowledge of the railroad could Emerson have had at that time?

7. For an essay, find out all you can about the "Wanton Wife," a favorite subject of printed broadsides in Renaissance England.

8. How many plays were produced at the Globe theater? How long did the theater survive?

9. Select an important work of English literature published between 1725 and 1925, or of American literature published between 1825 and 1925, for which the exact date of publication can be ascertained. (For instance, the first two cantos of *Childe Harold* were published on March 10, 1812.) By every means that occurs to you, assemble materials directly bearing on the English *or* American literary scene at that moment. You are allowed a leeway of one week in each direction; for example, if you should select *Childe Harold,* anything occurring between March 3 and 17, 1812, would be admissible.

  Write an essay entitled "The Day ——— Was Published." Your purpose is to give the reader, who may be assumed to be well educated but not a specialist, an authoritative, panoramic, and meaningful account of the whole immediate literary (and relevant historical) background. Primary emphasis should be upon the immediate topicality of the book—the various ways in which its subject-matter (ideas, social setting, etc.) is illuminated by the events and attitudes then in the news: the elements in the contemporary scene that made it "timely."

  The following are among the topics you might investigate:

  (a) The principal nonliterary events of the day (political, economic, military, social, etc.)—the sort of things newspapers were reporting and people were worrying over or rejoicing about, from governmental crises to new fashions in women's clothing.
  (b) What readers of various classes were reading and dis-

cussing (bestsellers, magazine articles, literary gossip, etc.): the "literary news" of the hour.

(c) What the author of the book was doing and saying, and what was the nature of his or her private life.

(d) What each of the important living authors was doing and saying. (Include prospectively important writers, even if at this moment they are still in diapers or in school, as well as writers whose eminence has by this time faded. Account for the whereabouts and activities of as many figures as you can. If no documentary evidence is available for the specific two-week period, cautious inference is permissible; e.g., if a certain poet of the next generation is known to have been in boarding school during the year in question, you are entitled, in the absence of contrary information, to place him there during the particular period with which you are concerned.)

Practice the technique of skillful condensation. Make every fact count; pack as much as you can into a limited space. Keep your survey continuously interesting. And *document* every statement you make.

XI. The Quality of Essays and Reviews

1. In "A Mirror for the Lamp" (*PMLA* 73 [1958]: no. 5, part 2, 45–71) Maynard Mack and other experts printed an interesting list of what they considered the most "outstanding and influential" articles published in *PMLA* over fifty years. Their reasons for their selections provide a good cross-section of opinion on what a successful scholarly paper should be like.

    (a) Bearing these criteria in mind, examine a selection of the following articles, published in *PMLA* and subsequently awarded the William Riley Parker Prize for articles of distinction appearing in that journal, to determine whether they did in fact deserve such recognition.

    David H. Miles, "Portrait of the Marxist as a Young Hegelian: Lukács' *Theory of the Novel*" (January 1979)

George T. Wright, "Hendiadys and *Hamlet*" (March 1981)

Honorable mention: Gerhard Joseph, "The *Antigone* as Cultural Touchstone: Matthew Arnold, Hegel, George Eliot, Virginia Woolf, and Margaret Drabble" (January 1981)

Hans Eichner, "The Rise of Modern Science and the Genesis of Romanticism" (January 1982)

Paul B. Armstrong, "The Conflict of Interpretations and the Limits of Pluralism" (May 1983)

A. Kent Hieatt, "The Genesis of Shakespeare's *Sonnets:* Spenser's *Ruines of Rome: by Bellay*" (October 1983)

Honorable mention: Marshall Brown, " 'Errours Endlesse Traine': On Turning Points and the Dialectical Imagination" (January 1984)

Terry Castle, "The Carnivalization of Eighteenth-Century English Narrative" (October 1984)

Donald W. Foster, "Master W. H., R.I.P." (January 1987)

Thomas C. Caramagno, "Manic-Depressive Psychosis and Critical Approaches to Virginia Woolf's Life and Work" (January 1988)

(b) Using the same standards, rate the articles appearing in the current issue of one of the leading scholarly journals. Are any of them of award-winning caliber? Should any of them not have been printed?

2. Select a major work, published since 1970, of bibliography, biography, or criticism, or an edition of correspondence, or an edition of a literary work. Acquaint yourself thoroughly with the book. Then locate, read, and take notes on at least six scholarly reviews of it, and write a paper entitled "————: A Review of Reviews," in which you describe and evaluate the various critics' estimates of the book. What various conceptions of the nature and purpose of a scholarly review are represented in the notices you read? What do *you* think constitutes an ideal scholarly review?

3. The following is a representative list of reviews that, because of their controversial subject-matter, made special demands upon their respective authors' fund of scholarly decorum.

How effectively, in each case, does the reviewer reconcile the sometimes conflicting duties of forthright criticism and professional courtesy? Does the tone of any of them strike you as being inadmissible in scholarly discourse?

Morse Peckham, "Recent Studies in Nineteenth-Century English Literature," *SEL* 3 (1963): 595–611. (Contrast Jonas Barish, "Recent Studies in the Elizabethan and Jacobean Drama," *ibid.*, 6 [1966]: 357–79.)

William E. Fredeman, review of Lona Mosk Packer's *Christina Rossetti, VS* 8 (1964): 71–77.

James Rieger, review of K. N. Cameron's edition of *The Esdaile Notebook, Essays in Criticism* 14 (1964): 401–9.

Douglas Bush, "Calculus Racked Him," *SEL* 6 (1966): 1–6.

Brewster Ghiselin, "The Burden of Proof," *Sewanee Review* 74 (1966): 527–40.

Robert W. Dent, " 'Quality of Insight' in Elizabethan and Jacobean Tragedy," *MP* 63 (1966): 252–56.

U. C. Knoepflmacher, "Mr. Haight's George Eliot: 'Wahrheit und Dichtung,' " *VS* 12 (1969): 422–30.

J. M. Osborn, review of Peter Quennell's *Alexander Pope, PQ* 48 (1969): 380–82.

Donald T. Torchiana, review of Denis Donoghue's *Jonathan Swift: A Critical Introduction, PQ* 49 (1970): 383–85.

George H. Ford, "Leavises, Levi's, and Some Dickensian Priorities," *Nineteenth-Century Fiction* 26 (1971): 95–113.

Fredson Bowers, "McKerrow Revisited," *PBSA* 67 (1973): 109–24.

Mark L. Reed, review of Richard E. Brantley, *Wordsworth's 'Natural Methodism'', MP* 75 (1977): 97–101.

Michael West, review of Philip Gura, *The Wisdom of Words, MP* 81 (1983): 81–85.

4. Each volume of the annual *Review* contains a variety of lengthy critical reviews. Examine two or three volumes and briefly describe the range of different types and techniques of scholarly criticism they exemplify.

5. Read Grant T. Webster, "A Potter's Field of Critical Rhetoric,"
   College English 27 (1966): 320–22; then examine a dozen or
   so reviews in current issues of scholarly periodicals. How
   many of Webster's "ploys" do you find there? How many can
   you add to Webster's list?

Index

333